Nellie L. Smith.
July 17, 1868.
A reward for perfect deportment during the whole of the Summer Term of the Comer High School at West Meriden, Conn.
From her teacher & friend
Homer B. Sprague

HISTORY

OF THE

13TH INFANTRY REGIMENT

OF

CONNECTICUT VOLUNTEERS,

DURING THE

GREAT REBELLION.

BY

HOMER B. SPRAGUE,

PRINCIPAL OF THE CONNECTICUT STATE NORMAL SCHOOL, NEW BRITAIN, CONNECTICUT.

HARTFORD, CONN.
CASE, LOCKWOOD & CO.
1867.

PREFACE.

The following history was undertaken near the close of the year 1865, at the request of a certain publishing house, while the author was still actively engaged in military duties in the State of Georgia. It was substantially completed and ready for publication on the return of the Veteran Battalion to New York, May 1, 1866, and was soon afterwards placed in the hands of the intended publishers. Various circumstances caused long delays, and it finally became necessary to entrust it to the enterprising firm which now issues it to the public.

The book never would have been commenced, but for the earnest and repeated solicitations of the officers and friends of the regiment. It was composed at intervals in the midst of pressing duties and in spite of serious discouragements; and, although the author had collected many materials, the work was found to be so laborious that it would often have been at the point of abandonment, had he not been deeply impressed with a conviction that some permanent record ought to be made of the remarkable services of this regiment. Some public tribute, too, was due to the memory of those brave men, our departed compatriots, who gave up their lives so freely in battle, in hospital, or in prison, and whose heroic deeds ought to be inwoven with the legible history of the republic which they died to save.

The regimental narrative is based mainly on the author's private diary — The "Life and Sufferings of Captain Sprague." So far as the events came under his personal observation he is quite confident of the essential correctness of the statements; but even here, he dares not hope he has escaped all errors. Jotted down at odd moments, in the midst of weary marches, on picket duty, on horseback, in the rain; sometimes by the light of blazing buildings, often in presence of hissing bullets, as during our six weeks at Port Hudson; undoubtedly mistaken impressions may have been recorded. Having been present, however, in every battle, skirmish, siege, and march, in which the regiment was engaged, until the nineteenth of September, 1864, when he had the misfortune to charge too far and hold his position too long, and so fell into the enemy's hands, the author fears more that his observations may lack breadth than that they may be wanting in distinctness.

For the history of the Thirteenth during the six months of the author's imprisonment, the statements of Messrs Blinn, Bradley, Perkins, Clary and Clark have been his main reliance; though others furnished important facts. It was contemplated at first to publish the story of that imprisonment, but it was found that it would swell the volume beyond the assigned limits.

This work has been its own reward. At every step it has brought vividly to remembrance the dark realities and the bright romance of war. As in a grand panorama the scenes and experiences of other days again passed successively through the mind,—the dreary barracks, the rolling ship, the luxurious city, the rapid, exhausting marches, the blistered and bleeding feet, the scorching sun, the rainy nights passed without shelter, the sickness that wasted or convulsed the stoutest frames ; the rush, the frenzy, the fascinating pomp, the terrible energy of battle ; the wheeling and plunging of cavalry, the thundering of batteries, the steady and resistless charge of infantry ; the thrilling shout of victory ; the unutterable magnificence of midnight bombardments ; the patient endurance, the triumphant faith, and the beautiful patriotism of those suffering in hospital ; the slow martyrdom in rebel prisons of those brave soldiers of the Thirteenth who would not turn traitor to save their lives, but deliberately chose rather to die by inches, of cold and hunger ; and then the thousand interchanges of kindly sympathies ; the warm friendships ; the story, the wit, the songs of love and home and country around blazing camp-fires ; and, to crown all, the satisfaction of having done what one could for God, for Freedom, and for the Great Republic !

To keep alive in the breasts of the survivors those feelings, to perpetuate those friendships, to rekindle those memories, to collect and preserve in permanent form the pictures of those scenes, and so to add one drop to the great current of liberty-loving and patriotic sentiment that is bearing our country on to her sublime destiny, this little book is respectfully dedicated to his former companions in arms, the surviving officers and soldiers of the glorious Thirteenth, by

THE AUTHOR.

New Britain, Conn., August 16, 1867.

CONTENTS.

CHAPTER I.

CHAPTER II.

CHAPTER III.

CHAPTER IV.

CHAPTER V.

CHAPTER VI.

APPENDIX.

History of the Thirteenth Connecticut.

CHAPTER I.

WHAT true American can ever forget those dark days that followed the first battle of Manassas! how the nation was bewildered, blinded, stunned for an hour, by that unexpected blow! what thrills of shame and rage tingled in every nerve of the body politic! with what frantic energy it then began to gird itself for a death grapple with the monster Rebellion! how beautiful the first flashes of a million bayonets in the northern sky!

Of all the regiments in that vast host, few, if any, were more patriotic or more brave than the Thirteenth Connecticut. Not with hot haste or mad excitement, not with noisy or glittering parade, nor yet with lavish outlay of money, did its officers collect a thoughtless or mercenary throng. But uniting ardent zeal with a cool estimate of the dangers and sacrifices, and holding up to view the great issues of Religion, Liberty, Civilization and Union, they made deliberate selection of their men. The day of bounties had not come. Conscription had not been thought of. The romance of a march "On to Richmond" had vanished. The holiday of McDowell's army had closed with fireworks that rained blood and death. The giant nation would play with rebellion no longer. War, grim-visaged, hideous, confronted the soldier.

No man has a right to engage in sanguinary combat, unless he feels that he fights for what is more precious than life. Liable at any moment to inflict and suffer death, executioner at once and martyr, his position is inconceivably solemn. With many exceptions, there was yet in the breasts of our officers and soldiers generally a deep sense of this responsibility. "I selected men," said Cromwell, "who made some *conscience* of what they did; and, after that, they never were beaten!" A like praise deserves this regiment, which, having volunteered from a sense of duty, in four years of active service never mutinied, never shrunk from danger, never retreated a step without orders from a general officer, never murmured at hardships—a regiment whose brilliant charges wrested victory from the enemy on more than one closely-contested field, and whose heroism at Labadieville, Irish Bend, Cane River, Marksville, Mansura and especially at that great "slaughter pen," Port Hudson, was the boast of the whole Army of the Gulf. If the life of every individual is full of interest to one who knows the inner as well as the outer acts, surely the narrative of a regiment intensely engaged in this terrific struggle may claim attention at least from the friends of those who fought in its ranks. And so, while master artists are picturing for all the world the history of this unparalleled rebellion, and wisest statesmen and profoundest philosophers are solving for all time its momentous problems, a brief hour may perhaps not unprofitably be given by many to the humbler yet not insignificant story of the Thirteenth Connecticut.

Colonel Henry W. Birge, of Norwich, was a merchant before the war. He had been Major in the Fourth Connecticut Infantry (afterwards the First Heavy Artillery) from May 23d, 1861, Nov. 2d, 1861, he received his commission as Colonel of the Thirteenth Connecticut. During this preparatory training he had displayed a decided taste and aptness for military pursuits. He was a rigid disciplinarian, a quick observer, well drilled, dignified, courteous, brave, fond of making a good show, and possessing in a remarkable degree the gift of silence. Every inch a soldier, he made his subalterns understand at the outset that the Thirteenth was to be the best regiment, best looking, best drilled, fastest marching and hardest fighting, and he spared no pains to accomplish that object.

Except in the summer of 1862, when he was in command of the forces in New Orleans, he was with us personally nearly all the time until January, 1863, when he assumed charge of our brigade at Baton Rouge, La. On the 19th of September, 1863, he received his appointment as Brigadier, which was confirmed by the Senate at its following session. He was afterwards brevetted Major-General for gallant and distinguished services in the Shenandoah Valley.

Since the war he has been a lumber merchant in Savannah, Ga.

Lieutenant-Colonel Alexander Warner of Woodstock, Conn., was a manufacturer of twine. He had served creditably as Major of the Third Connecticut in the summer of 1861. A severe attack of inflammatory rheumatism, brought on by the cold and dampness of the New Haven barracks, which he shared equally with the private soldiers, deprived us of his presence during most of the winter of 1861–2 and the whole of the following spring. He was mustered-in on the ninth of April. He rejoined us about the first of June, 1862.

Colonel Warner was an active, energetic officer, and the drills he gave the regiment were valuable in preparing it for the field. He was a clear-headed business man, attentive to the comfort of the soldiers and desirous of securing to them their rights. In June, 1863, while the regiment was at Port Hudson, being absent in New Orleans on "sick leave," he was assigned to the task of raising a battalion for the defence of that city. This service he performed with skill and energy. He resigned his commission and was honorably discharged on the twenty-ninth of July, 1863. He immediately accepted a position as special agent of the Treasury Department at New Orleans, which he held until recently. He is understood to be now cultivating a cotton plantation in Mississippi.

Major Richard E. Holcomb, of East Granby, Conn., had also served honorably in the three months' campaign of 1861 as Quartermaster of the Third Connecticut. Before the war he was a railroad contractor. He was a man of remarkable force of body and mind. Soon after we reached New Orleans he was selected by General Butler to raise a regiment of Louisiana men. This was the *First Louisiana* a white regiment, of which he was commissioned Colonel on the sixteenth of August, 1862. On the fatal fourteenth of June, 1863, at Port Hudson, he fell at the head of the assaulting column in a charge upon the rebel stronghold. The Thirteenth always loved his memory, and regarded him as one of their own number. There was a rugged grandeur in his stern yet generous nature, a rough strength, an unyielding determination, a heroic soul; and when his scattered brains besprinkled the van of our regiment on that day of horrors, a cruel pang tore our breasts, for we felt that the bravest of our brave had fallen.

Adjutant William M. Grosvenor, of New Haven, was local editor of the New Haven *Palladium* at the breaking out of hostilities. To the performance of the duties of adjutant he brought signal ability. He united untiring industry and an iron constitution with quickness of insight, clearness of comprehension, and an unwonted energy. On the 31st of December, 1862, he was promoted to be Captain of Co. D. On the 14th of June, 1863, he was shot through the arm at Port Hudson. On the 29th of October, 1863, he was mustered as Colonel of the Second Regiment Louisiana Native Guards (colored). After the war he was for a time one of the editors of the New Haven *Journal and Courier*. Recently he has assumed the editorial charge of the Missouri *Democrat* at St. Louis, where he is a decidedly rising man.

At mention of Quartermaster Joseph B. Bromley, of Norwich, a smile infallibly overspreads the countenance of every member of the Thirteenth. His inexhaustible wit and humor were irrepressible on all occasions, and many good jokes and amusing incidents are related of him. He was not less funny than his younger brother "Ike," editor of the Norwich *Bulletin*. Those who only knew of his mirth and facetiousness, however, only half knew him. He had a vein of serious thought, a keen conscience that never allowed him to do wrong with impunity, and an unwavering belief in the great doctrines of the Christian religion. His heart was as pure and warm as ever beat in human breast. Whatever conduct seemed questionable was the result of his desire to make his regiment comfortable, or to gratify the fun-loving propensities of his associates. His services ended with his resignation on the 29th of December, 1863. He was afterwards located at Thibodaux, La., as a special agent of the Treasury Department, or, as he termed it, "A snapper-up of unconsidered trifles." He was a valuable member of the Union Convention to form the new constitution for the reconstructed State of Louisiana, and was also a candidate for Congressional honors. He has since been engaged in planting near New Orleans in company with Colonel Charles L. Norton, of Farmington, Conn.*

Chaplain Charles C. Salter, of New Haven, was a graduate of Yale College, of the class of 1852, and afterwards a tutor in that institution. He had been settled as a minister in Minneapolis, Minnesota, but resigned his pastorate on account of ill health. He was distinguished for his thorough scholarship, and still more for his fervent piety and his zeal in every good cause. As a minister of religion, a kind, warm and affectionate friend, especially to the suffering and the distressed, he greatly endeared himself to many

*The generous and genial Bromley died of fever at New Orleans, Sept. 3d, 1866, at the age of 39.

of the soldiers. He realized the perfect picture which Goldsmith gives of the faithful preacher. Mr. Salter's health failed him. After a ministry of several months he was forced by bronchial disease to resign his commission on the 15th of June, 1862. He has since resided in Minneapolis.

Surgeon Benjamin N. Comings, of New Britain, Conn., had practiced medicine and surgery with success for many years. He compiled a popular school-book on Physiology, and was a lecturer on that science in the State Normal School. He had attained reputation as a temperance advocate, giving especial attention to the effect of alcohol on the brain. On the 6th of August, 1862, he nearly lost his life by the sinking of the steamer *Whiteman* on the Mississippi with a load of wounded of whom he was in charge, from the battle-field of Baton Rogue. An inflated rubber pillow, buttoned beneath his overcoat, kept him afloat. The doctor was a close student of natural history ; especially ornithology. Many a hapless wild fowl attested his accuracy as a marksman in the woods around Thibodaux, until our waggish quartermaster made the officers believe that guerillas infested the neighborhood. On all occasions he showed himself a skillful Surgeon. He resigned his commission in January, 1863, and has since resided in New Britain, where he is greatly esteemed.

First Assistant-Surgeon George Clary was a native of New Hampshire and a practising physician of Hartford, Conn. He entered the war from patriotic motives, and remained in the service until the final muster-out of the Veteran Battalion. In our first battle Dr. Clary accompanied the regiment into the hottest fire, and manifested that calm courage which proceeds from deep convictions of right and conscientious devotion to the cause of his country. His merits were recognized by his promotion, May 23d, 1863, to fill the vacancy caused Dr. Comings' resignation.

Second Assistant-Surgeon Nathan A. Fisher was sent as an additional medical officer by the State of Connecticut, which, in its parental care, left no means untried to promote the health and comfort of the soldiers. His extensive experience and his practice in the southern states previous to the war, were of much value to the regiment. He was held in high esteem by officers and men. Ill-health compelled his resignation June 16th, 1863. He has since resided in Norwich.

Sergeant-Major George W. Whittlesey, of Norwich, after serving with great fidelity in that capacity, succeeded Grosvenor as adjutant, Dec. 31st, 1862. He made a most excellent staff officer. He resigned on account of sickness, Oct. 9th, 1863 .He has since resided in Norwich, where he has been engaged in the coal trade.

Quartermaster-sergeant Andrew T. Johnson, of Montville, Conn., was one of the first non-commissioned officers promoted to a lieutenancy. He enlisted twenty or thirty men for "special service in the Quartermaster's Department," and was an officer of much promise. His commission as Lieutenant bore date June 30th, 1862. The high hopes of his friends were blasted by his sudden death, caused by the explosion of an ammunition car at the LaFourche Railroad Crossing, near Thibodaux, La., Nov. 7th, 1862.

Commissary-Sergeant Charles A. Tracy, of Montville, was promoted to a lieutenancy in Colonel Holcomb's regiment, the First Louisiana, on its organization, July 16th, 1862. His skill and economy in weighing out rations were valuable to the Quartermaster of the Thirteenth. He was afterwards made quartermaster of the First Louisiana, a position he filled with great credit.

Hospital Steward William Bishop, of Southington, Conn., was clerk in the apothecary establishment of Hale & Dickinson at New Britain before the war. He was conspicuous for the fearless discharge of his duty in the midst of the dangers of battle at Irish Bend. Though a non-combatant, he volunteered in the storming column at Port Hudson. On the 1st of May, 1864, he was promoted to be quartermaster, a position which he filled with honor to himself and advantage to the regiment. He is now travelling agent of the Union Paper Mills, Springfield, Mass.*

Principal-Musician, *alias* "Drum Major," Joseph Hadley, of New London, Conn., had been a musician more than twenty years before, in the Seminole War in Florida. He was one of the most accomplished of drummers, and would evoke a surprising amount of music from that most unmelodious of all instruments. Unfortunately he got into the habit of deserting in the summer of 1863, and finally disappeared altogether in August, 1864.

To fill the vacancy caused by the resignation of Chaplain Salter, Rev. Henry Upson, of Berlin, Conn., then a theological student at Yale, was commissioned on the 16th of June, 1862. He joined us about the

*Married Miss Ellen Lum, of Naugatuck, April 18, 1867.

first of the ensuing September and remained with us a year. In his care for the soul he did not forget the body. He was not only an eloquent and faithful preacher, but a good forager, as many a load of turkeys, pigs, sweet potatoes, and the like, brought into camp and distributed by him to the half-starved soldiers, bore abundant witness. At the battle of Irish Bend he displayed great courage, and rendered invaluable service by communicating orders, and by dispensing refreshments and consolation to the wounded. He is now settled in the ministry in New Preston.

Second Assistant-surgeon Samuel McClellan, of New Haven, cousin of Major-General McClellan, was commissioned March 14th, 1863. Having been detailed in charge of the University Hospital in New Orleans, he was absent from the regiment until their veteran furlough in July, 1864. As a physician he was successful, and the hospital under his charge was a model establishment. As a gentleman, he was cultivated, refined, and of steady habits. He had charge of the hospital boat "Laurel Hill," on Banks' Red River expedition, and not having the hospital flag, (a yellow flag, bearing a very large letter H), flying, his boat was hotly fired on by a party of guerillas, about the 1st of May, 1864. He gives an interesting account of his loading and discharging with his own hands one of the pieces of artillery during the fight. On the 9th of May, 1863, he was promoted to be First Assistant-surgeon.

Second Assistant-surgeon Lucius W. Clark, of Winsted, Conn., had been a Yankee schoolmaster. He was commissioned July 9th, 1863, and joined the regiment at Carrolton, La., next month. We were then, and for some months afterwards, suffering to an unusual extent from swamp fevers, and Dr. Clarke rendered invaluable assistance. Few surgeons ever took so much pains, or had so much success, in the treatment of the sick. The soldiers of the Thirteenth will ever retain a grateful recollection of his kindness and skill. He remained with the regiment and battalion until the final muster-out. He is now residing in Cambridge, Wisconsin; unmarried, but hopeful.

At least the nucleus of every company was in the New Haven barracks previous to December 1st, 1861. The building was the large carriage-factory of Messrs. Durham & Booth, corner of Chapel and Hamilton streets, since burned down. The regiment was not filled suddenly. Twelve regiments, comprising not less than eleven thousand men, had already been raised in Connecticut. The growth of each company was rapid or slow according to the popularity of the proposed officers, the influences of friends, the efforts made by advertising, by recruiting agents, by holding war meetings, and in some instances, by the offer of money. Every recruit was taken before Dr. S. G. Hubbard, or some other of the appointed physicians, and carefully examined as to his physical ability. If he passed the test, he was sworn into the United States service, made to sign enlistment papers in triplicate, furnished a suit of blue clothes, and sent to drill with a musket in the barracks. Once in two or three weeks the mustering officer, Lieut. W. W. Chamberlin of the Fourteenth United States Infantry, who afterwards fell at Fredericksburgh, visited and mustered them. The last company was accepted Jan. 7th, 1862.

Company A was commenced in August, 1861, in the town of New Britain by First Lieutenant John E. Woodruff and Second Lieutenant Charles H. Cornwell. It was at first intended for the Eleventh regiment, which left Connecticut on the sixteenth of December of that year. Mr. Henry L. Bidwell, of Brooklyn, N. Y., formerly of Hartford, was soon afterward associated with them as captain. The com pany was called after the popular governor of Connecticut, "The Buckingham Guards," and that distinguished official presented its captain with a beautiful sword. One autumn evening about twenty young men, members of some of the most respectable families of New Britain, joined the company in a body. Among them were First-sergeant Cowles, whose death on the 19th of February, 1862, was one of the first that filled the regiment with mourning; the two Frank Stanleys, whose life-blood moistened the sanguinary field of Irish Bend; Gladden and Carpenter, and other brave men whose names are forever enrolled among those of the martyrs of liberty. No town in Connecticut can point with more pride to its heroic dead.

On the 26th of November, 1861, the "Buckingham Guards" entered New Haven, and marched to the barracks. Here they occupied the corner room, second floor, at the intersection of Chapel and Hamilton streets. Being the right flank company they were armed with Sharps' Rifles.

B was begun in October of the same year as a company of sharp-shooters by Captain Apollos Comstock of New Canaan, Conn., assisted by First Lieutenant

William E. Bradley of the same town, and Second Lieutenant William C. Beecher, of Southbury, Conn. The test of most accurate shooting had to be abandoned after a few weeks' trial. This was about the middle of December, when the company entered the barracks. Captain Comstock was indefatigable in his efforts. His buggy was his recruiting office. He rode through the State holding war meetings, testing the skill of applicants, giving time and money freely to the cause. This patriotic and noble energy was well rewarded by the enlistment of one of the finest companies that served during the war.

Like A, they soon lost their first-sergeant, Hawley, by sickness. He was a man of character, ability, and integrity ; was discharged from service in June, 1862, and soon afterwards died of consumption. Being the left flank company, they were armed with Sharps' Rifles.

Co. C was raised by Captain Charles D. Blinn, of West Cornwall, assisted by his cousin, First Lieutenant Issac F. Nettleton, of Kent, and Second Lieutenant Charles E. Tibbets, of New Milford. They established a recruiting office in Cornwall and another in Kent. The company was raised almost wholly from the northwestern portion of the State especialy from the three towns which were the homes of the three officers, a fact which testifies to their personal worth and popularity. Another indication to the same effect is seen in the rapidity with which their ranks were filled. They marched into New Haven in November, eighty-three strong, under the designation of the "Lyon Guards," called after that distinguished son of Connecticut, who fell in Missouri early in the war.

Nettleton was the first of our officers to die. In September, 1862, he fell under the fatal stroke of disease in New Orleans. His death caused a deep gloom and heartfelt sorrow among his associates. His body was embalmed and sent north ; but the operation had been so unskillfully performed that it was necessary to throw it overboard in mid-ocean.

C was the color company, and right gallantly bore the beautiful flag of Connecticut and the ever-glorious Stars and Stripes through many a fight.

Co. D was raised by Captain Cyrus E. Prindle, of Roxbury, First Lieutenant Perry Averill, of Southbury, and Second Lieutenant Joseph H. Meredith, of New Haven. It lost its patriotic captain and second lieutenant by resignation the following August. In the same month its efficient first sergeant, George Mayne, one of the best drilled non-commissioned officers in the regiment, having served in the summer of 1861, was promoted to an office in the First Louisiana. This company, though small in numbers, contained many valuable men. Besides Mayne it gave sergeants Timothy Whittlesey and Eugene Ward in the summer of 1863 to officer other regiments. It was called " The Litchfield County Rifles," and that good old county, mother of so many distinguished sons, never had cause to be ashamed of the company that now bore her name.

Co. E was raised by Captain Eugene Tisdale, of New Britain, who had served in a Massachusetts regiment in the three months' campaign of 1861. He was ably assisted by First Lieutenant Eugene E. Graves, of Thompson, and Second Lieutenant William P. Miner, of Norwich. Captain Tisdale was afterwards promoted to the office of lieutenant colonel in a New Orleans regiment. Lieutenant Graves became successively captain and major on General Weitzel's staff, where he is said to have displayed much gallantry. Col. Tisdale still retains his military office, and resides in New Orleans.

Of the non-commissioned officers, First-sergeant Charles H. Beaton, who had served handsomely through the summer of 1861, and Sergeant George B. Deming, were afterwards promoted to be commissioned officers in the Thirteenth Connecticut. The latter afterwards accepted a captaincy in the Fifth Regiment, Corps d'Afrique. Beaton is now captain of a battery.

Co. E. was composed of good material and always showed real pluck. For its excellence it was detailed as Provost Guard at New Orleans in the summer of 1862, and afterwards at Washington, La., in the spring of 1863. It rejoiced at first in the appellation of "The New England Guards."

Co. F was raised by Captain James J. McCord, of Norwich, who had served honorably in the three summer months as Second Lieutenant of Company B, Second Connecticut Infantry. He was aided by First Lieutenant Charles J. Fuller, of Hartford, and Second Lieutenant John C. Abbott, of Norwich. Lieutenant Fuller had recruited about a dozen men under the name of "The Catlin Rifles" in honor of Lieut. Gov. Catlin, from whom he received a handsome sword and sash.

Captain McCord was one of our most exemplary and efficient officers. He now resides in Norwich.

His eminent military merit has recently caused his promotion to the colonelcy of the Third Connecticut. Lieutenant Abbott was soon detached as signal officer, in which capacity he distinguished himself by his skill, industry and courage. He was actively engaged on board the sloop-of-war *Richmond* at the great bombardment of Port Hudson, March 14th, 1863, when Farragut run the gauntlet of the rebel batteries.

Private David Black of this company was the first soldier of the Thirteenth Connecticut killed in battle. He fell at Georgia Landing, Oct. 27th, 1862. Sergeant James Torrance was the first offering of the Thirteenth at the investment of Port Hudson, May 24th, 1863. He was one of our bravest and best men. Among those discharged to accept commissions in other regiments were corporals George R. Case and Amos R. Ladd, and private George R. Sanders. Notwithstanding these losses the company never lacked for true manliness, nor failed to achieve an enviable reputation.

Co. G was raised by Captain Sylvester G. Gilbert, of Hebron, Conn., assisted by First Lieutenant Denison H. Finley, of Marlborough, Conn., and Second Lieutenant Joseph S. A. Baker, of New Haven. The Captain had been a successful professor of music. Lieutenant Baker had been Second Lieutenant of Company C, Third Connecticut, during the summer campaign of 1861. He was one of the most thoroughly drilled of our officers, having enjoyed the advantages of a semi-military education at Russell's Collegiate and Commercial Institute, New Haven.

The company lost its excellent Captain by resignation, July 16, 1862, and also soon lost all its Sergeants by discharge for physical disability. Yet, through the unwearied efforts of Lieut. Baker, it attained great excellence in drill, and was inferior to none in martial appearance or solid merit. It was always a fine company. It was recruited under the name of "The Hebron Rifles." Finley was promoted to a captaincy and was for a long time assigned to duty on the staff of General Grover. He was an energetic and clear-headed officer.

After his discharge Captain Gilbert was again connected with the army as sutler, and was afterwards captain in a colored regiment. Lieutenant Baker, having served till the close of the year 1864 was mustered-out of service. He was afterwards engaged in vine-growing in Ohio, but now resides in New Haven.

Co. H was raised by Captain Homer B. Sprague, First Lieutenant Jonah F. Clarke and Second Lieutenant Julius Tobias, all of New Haven. Captain Sprague had previously used his law office for recruiting and enlisted fifty men for the Seventh Connecticut. These unanimously elected him captain, which office he then declined. In Nov. 1863, he was commissioned Colonel of the Eleventh Regiment, C. D. A. In November, 1861, Lieutenant Clark commenced raising a company under the name of "The Winfield Scott Guards." Lieutenant Tobias, who had been severely wounded in the Austrian service, had collected about twenty men. These bore the name of "The Welch Rifles," in honor of the patriotic mayor of New Haven. These squads were consolidated, and the company raised under the latter name.

Lieutenant Clarke died of fever at Baton Rouge, January 27th, 1863. He was a brave, intelligent, upright and patriotic officer, and his loss was deeply felt. Sprague is now principal of the State Normal School at New Britain, Conn.

First Sergeant Merrill, who had seen service in South America, and been First Lieutenant in the Second Connecticut, afterwards declined a commission which was offered him as Captain in the First Louisiana. Sergeants James M. Gardner and Charles H. Grosvenor became respectively lieutenant and major of the First Louisiana. Private Louis Meissner was successively promoted to be corporal, sergeant, first-sergeant, second lieutenant and first lieutenant. He fell gallantly fighting, April 23d, 1864, in the bloody battle of Cane River, La.

Co. H was a good company. "The men are better *set up* than the rest," remarked Inspector-general Dudley of them at Thibodaux, in the fall of 1862.

Co. I was raised by Captain Henry L. Schleiter, of New London, assisted by First Lieutenant Frank Wells, of Litchfield, and Second Lieutenant Joseph Strickland, of New London.

The Captain had begun to collect a company under the name of "The New London Rifles," and in company with Lieutenant Strickland had procured thirty or forty recruits. Lieutenant Wells had also been very successful in Litchfield county, and by the patriotic aid of his brother-in-law, Hon. John H. Hubbard, and other distinguished men, had obtained fifty or sixty. When the two bodies were consolidated, there was no better-looking company in the service, and its deeds were of corresponding merit.

Lieutenant Strickland was the first officer of the Thirteenth killed in battle. It was at the head of the charging column on the 14th of June, 1863, at Port

Hudson; and of the many gallant officers that then fell, there was none more fearless or more deeply mourned.

Lieutenant Wells served on the staff of the celebrated General Phelps, also of Generals Birge and King. He repeatedly distinguished himself by gallantry in action. He, as well as Sergeant Louis Beckwith, and Corporal Abner N. Sterry, became captain in the Veteran Battalion, after the muster-out of the regiment.

Co. K was originally intended for the Twelfth Connecticut. It was commenced in August, 1861, by First Lieutenant Jared D. Thompson, Second Lieutenant William F. Norman and Sergeant John T. Wheeler; all of New Haven. It was the first company to enter the barracks, reaching them one day earlier than Co. A. It was raised under the name of "The Knowlton Rifles." It had been the understanding that Lieutenant Thompson should be captain, and Wheeler, second lieutenant. But unfortunate difficulties having arisen, Alfred Mitchell, Esq., of Norwich, an author by profession and a particular friend of Colonel Birge, was commissioned captain. Sergeant Wheeler's merits soon secured his promotion to a lieutenancy. Sergeant William C. Gardner, John C. Kinney and George G. Smith were afterwards commissioned the first two in the Thirteenth Connecticut, the latter, who had brought a squad of recruits into the company, in the First Louisiana. Kinney was detailed as acting signal officer on the flagship *Hartford*. During the severe naval action in Mobile harbor he was lashed to one mast and Farragut to the other.

Captain Mitchell was commissioned major, May

12th, 1863, but declined. He resigned his captaincy March 11th, 1864, having been on the staff of Colonel (afterwards of General) Birge nearly all the time. On the 7th of November, 1862, Lieutenant Wheeler was instantly killed by the explosion of an ammunition car on the New Orleans, Opelousas and Great Western Railroad. The regiment thus lost a valuable officer and a true man.

Co. K was a fighting company, rarely missing an opportunity to distinguish itself in that line. It is due to the members, however, to state that their belligerent propensities were displayed, for the most part, against the public enemies. They were clearly of the opinion that war could not be conducted on peace principles. In the battle of Cedar Creek and on other occasions the company rendered eminent service.

The winter of 1861–2 was very severe. The barracks, three stories high, were only partially warmed by steam pipes, which often got out of order; when the temperature would suddenly pass to the extreme of cold. It was difficult to ventilate the rooms properly. The beds of the soldiers were arranged one above the other, each company by itself. The officers generally had rooms in town, but some chose to remain in the barracks. The soldiers suffered, and the seeds of many a sickness and many a death were sown in these dreary and unwholesome quarters. Measles, the invariable concomitant of a crowd of soldiers, broke out among them and carried off some of our best men. Small-pox made its appearance, but was managed so skillfully that the soldiers and the community knew nothing of it till the danger was past. The infected were quietly removed to a pest-house. Report was spread that they had deserted, or were absent without leave. One of the nurses of these patients, private James Barry, Co. F, was supposed to have deserted; and so generally was this believed, that his afflicted wife, giving full credit to this report, left Norwich and returned to her native Scotland! First-sergeant Cowles of Company A, private Slover of C, Welch of D, Warner of G, Wm. F. Scribner of H, Ferris and Tyrell of I, Ryan and Goldsmith of K, were among those who died before the regiment left New Haven, of disease engendered within those unhealthy walls.

One large room in the east side of the building was set apart as a chapel. Here divine services were held every morning at 9 o'clock, with preaching every Sunday. Rev. J. M. Dudley, residing in Olive Street, New Haven, usually officiated. Occasionally Rev. James H. Bradford, at that time a student in the Yale Theological School, afterwards chaplain of the Twelfth Connecticut, conducted the services. Sergeant (afterwards Lieutenant) John C. Kinney, Co. K, then a theological student, could also be depended upon to lead the devotions. His Excellency, Gov. Buckingham, was present at one of these meetings and offered a fervent prayer. About the first of February, 1862, the field and company officers were called upon to choose a regimental chaplain. The two prominent candidates were Rev. Mr. Winslow, formerly of the New Britain Center Church, and Rev. Mr. Salter, of whom mention has already been made. Mr. Winslow's ready eloquence and social qualities made him a powerful competitor; but Mr. Salter's long acquaintance and companionship prevailed, and he was commissioned accordingly on the 5th of February, 1862.

At evening the chapel room often presented a scene of surpassing interest. Lectures were delivered by eloquent orators, speeches made by professional and other gentlemen, the fairest ladies of the city sung sweet and stirring songs. Especially was the subject of temperance urged upon the soldiers, and with good effect. A temperance society was formed, and large numbers signed the pledge of total abstinence. Rev. Mr. Dudley deserves the thanks of every soldier for his efforts to make us all better and happier.

The patriotic ladies of New Haven merit a more particular notice in this history. They sent innumerable comforts to the sick, and presented every soldier with what they called a "house-wife"—a nice little arrangement of pin cushion, needles, thread and the like, in compact form and sometimes with the name of the fair maker embroidered thereon. They hardly need the assurance of our thankfulness now; as many a marriage knot, tied during and since the war, will testify that these names, and the beautiful faces and forms that sometimes glided through our gloomy barracks and reappeared in dreams as we lay on the frosty ground or beneath pelting storms, were never forgotten. Especially is a sumptuous dinner, given by them to our soldiers on the anniversary of Washington's birthday, gratefully remembered; when the delicious viands were rendered doubly attractive by their charming presence.

When a sufficient number had enlisted in a company, an election of officers was held, and the successful candidates were immediately commissioned by Gov. Buckingham. A few Lieutenants had received appointments previously, to facilitate recruiting.

Daily drills by the officers and sergeants were had in the barracks or outside except sundays. In the chapel room the officers were thoroughly exercised in the manual of arms and the school of the company by John Arnold, Esq., formerly General of the State militia, and Colonel of the 3d Connecticut in the three months' campaign. Upon the suggestion of Captain Tisdale, the so-called Zouave stack-of-arms was adopted by the regiment. Aware of the great importance of pride of appearance and *esprit du corps*, Col. Birge early endeavored to induce the officers to pay extraordinary attention to neatness, cleanliness, and martial bearing. He secured dark blue trousers in place of the regulation sky-blue; every belt, shoe and box must be neatly polished; every gun-barrel and bayonet must shine like a mirror; every hand must wear a glove of spotless white; every form must be erect and manly; every soldier must feel himself a gentleman. A few months later, when we entered New Orleans and marched to the custom-house in all "the pride, pomp and circumstance of glorious war," we were greatly amused and edified by the frequent comment among the thousands of spectators, "This regiment is composed only of *rich* men's sons!" "They say they didn't receive any soldiers taxed for less than five thousand dollars!" Parton, in his "Butler in New Orleans," styles the Thirteenth Connecticut a "*dandy* regiment." Many prophesied that our men would prove parlor soldiers, fit only to

> "caper nimbly in a lady's chamber,
> To the lascivious pleasing of a lute,"

and that those fine clothes would never tarry to be riddled by bullets. A year or two afterwards, at the close of a hot battle, Captain Sprague reminded Colonel Birge of these predictions. "Well," he replied, "I noticed they did'nt run away, like some of those *dirty* regiments!"

Little occurred to break the monotony of the daily routine. Occasionally the Governor would visit us, when special pains would be taken to present a good appearance. Frequently we marched through the streets of New Haven, drilled in front of the Tontine Hotel or on Whitney Avenue, or attended church by companies. In the latter part of February the regiment turned out in funeral procession in honor of the lamented Colonel Russell, of the Tenth Connecticut, killed at Roanoke Island. During this winter Colonel Birge was disabled for some weeks by a severe injury to his knee, having been thrown from his horse. In February, a board of examiners, of which Brigadier General Daniel Tyler was chairman, examined the company officers in the Regulations and Tactics.

Of course we were not free from the usual bickerings of army life. At one time eighteen men were shut up in our guard house for refusing to do duty. They claimed that they had been enlisted under false pretences, "for special service in the Quartermaster's Department," and that they were unjustly put into the ranks. They employed counsel and refused to drill. Great was the excitement, for their complaints were not unfounded. At the request of the Colonel, who remarked, "If I had them in the field, I should know better how to deal with them; but I fear that severe measures now would retard the recruiting," the captain of Company H visited them in the guard room, listened to their complaints, explained to them their obligations, showed them that no one had authority to enlist them for "special service," but that by their voluntary enlistment they had bound themselves in writing and by a solemn oath to obey the orders of their superior officers, promised them their choice of companies, and appealed to their patriotism and manhood to show themselves true men and good soldiers. The appeal was successful. They were released from arrest and did their duty manfully ever after.

At another time, during our stay at the New Haven barracks, the soldiers grew clamorous for their pay, and many refused to drill until their demands were satisfied. Major Holcomb called some of the most obstinate, loaded his pistol in their presence, and read to them the ninth Article of War, which threatens death to those who "disobey the lawful order of their superior officer." It needed but a single look at the Major to satisfy them that he was not trifling. They yielded, and in a few days after received their pay.

Nor is the "undress parade" of company K forgotten. Lieutenant Thompson had somehow excited the ire of those of his men who were unpoetically styled "Head-of-the-wharf *Rats*." One midnight, on returning to the barracks, he found bottles, guns, valises,

4

chairs, tables and various trumpery piled to the ceiling on his bed. Thereupon he ordered every man out into line, where they shivered two mortal hours, almost as

"Naked as when from earth they came."

It was generally conceded that the Lieutenant had the best of it.

On the 18th of February most of the officers were mustered into the service of the United States by Lieutenant Chamberlin. Until that date they were in the pay of the State of Connecticut. Into the usual form of the oath, "to serve" the nation "faithfully against all enemies or opposers whomsoever," he inserted the words, "against England or any foreign power that may wage war against us."

We now awaited orders to depart. We hoped for any other destination rather than the Department of the Gulf. But Major General B. F. Butler was at the time engaged in organizing his great "New England Division" for service in the extreme south, and he so managed as to secure the ninth, twelfth and thirteenth Connecticut regiments. The ninth had left us in the preceding November; the twelfth, on the twenty-fourth of February.

Sunday, March 16, 1862, the long-expected orders came. Colonel Birge called the officers together: "You will hold your commands in readiness to move to-morrow. Our destination is undoubtedly Ship Island."

Monday, March 17, was a sad day to most of us, though the bustle and excitement of preparation kept the officers busy till the moment of embarkation. Parents, brothers, sisters, wives and other loved ones gathered around us for a parting grasp of the hand and a last good-bye. We were well assured that many of us would never return; that sickness would prostrate some, the sword others; sorrow and hardship and danger would encompass all. Yet high hopes and firm resolves mingled with these forebodings, as, proudly conscious that we were the representatives of the great republic, we filed with streaming banners down Chapel Street to the landing near Tomlinson's Bridge, and marched on board the steamer "Granite State."

CHAPTER II.

Arriving in New York Harbor on the morning of March 18th, 1862, we were transferred to the ship *City of New York*, a staunch vessel of eighteen hundred tons. The ship had been fitted up for our reception under the superintendence of Captain Mitchell, who had been sent to New York for the purpose by Colonel Birge, and whose extensive experience in traveling by sea had thoroughly qualified him for the task. The " bunks " for the officers had each the sliding tin dish fastened alongside suggestive of the effects of sea-sickness. We laughed at the idea at first, but most of us came to regard the contrivance with a friendly and solemn interest. In one particular the arrangements were defective. No proper and sufficient room had been allowed for a hospital. Col. Birge and staff and Captain Mitchell occupied the cabin rooms on the quarter deck with Mr. Salter, the captain of the ship. The rest of the officers were in the ward-room below. The nominal aggregate of the regiment was one thousand and seventeen, of whom thirty-nine were commissioned officers. Many of the enlisted men were left behind, sick or deserters; so that the number on board, all told, was about nine hundred and fifty, besides the crew.

We remained in New York Harbor and Sandy Hook Bay five days, taking in stores and waiting for favorable winds. Sunday, March 23d, we weighed anchor about noon, and in a few hours saw the heights of Neversink vanishing beyond the distant waves.

For twenty days we were afloat. We stood far out into the Atlantic, passing around the eastern coast of Great Abaco, one of the Bahamas, and in full view of the famous "Hole in the Wall," through which the billows are forever tumbling. A barren group appeared these islands, windy, rocky, sandy; the peaks and ridges of submerged mountains scorched by every sun and swept by every blast. We thought if Guanahani, the San Salvador of Columbus, and the first land discovered by him looked like the rest, a melancholy satisfaction must have rewarded the great navigator after his seventy days' sail; but the books say that to his vivid imagination the island seemed "covered with forests and decked with all the flowers of the tropics!"

Soon after passing Cape Hatteras we had the usual "Storm at Sea." We were in the Gulf Stream. It came on at night with much lightning and heavy wind, rain and thunder. Some of the soldiers, who had never been on salt water before, were afflicted with anxiety and sea-sickness; a combination amusing enough to all but the sufferers. It was a night of horrors to poor Underwood, our fife-major, the beginning of whose fatal sickness dates from this storm.

An officer of the day was regularly detailed to look after the order and cleanliness of the ship and men. The work of scrubbing was renewed every morning by fatigue parties. Messrs. Wait and Champion, sutlers, accompanied us. Either the soldiers or the sailors committed extensive larcenies of their goods. Tobacco, cigars and raisins strangely disappeared. Poor Wait was reduced to the point of death by rheumatic fever. This was but a prelude to their woes; for soon after arriving in New Orleans, they were robbed of a large sum; in the following autumn Champion had both legs broken, and his stock of merchandise was smashed by a railroad explosion.

Daily, when the weather permitted, the Colonel assembled the officers on the quarter deck at three P. M., and heard them recite carefully-prepared lessons from Hardee's Tactics or the Army Regulations. These lessons and the discussion of disputed points were of great utility.

Occasionally for some misdemeanor it was found necessary to punish a soldier by tying him to the mast, gunwale, or rigging, or thrusting him into the stifling air of the "dark hole." Many of us recollect how Captain Salter pursued one of the seamen with cocked pistol, endeavoring to shoot him for mutinous language, and how emphatically he swore on the occasion; which drew out from Captain M., the remarkable statement, "I should never dare to cross the ocean in a ship with a captain who did *not* swear."

Every morning at nine o'clock the soldiers were called together for prayers by our faithful chaplain Salter, when a chapter of the bible was read, a hymn sung, and prayer offered. At evening, religious meetings of great interest was held in the quarters of the enlisted men. Cases of undoubted reformation and conversion gladdened the chaplain and those seriously disposed. The experience of after years often showed us what indeed must be evident to a thoughtful observer, that, of all persons, the soldier has most need to be a religious man. Napoleon's maxim (if he ever uttered it), "The worse the man, the better the soldier," may be true in a clearly unrighteous cause; but not otherwise.

Sometimes dramatic representations were given at evening, with recitations and songs. In fact, quite a theatre was started. Sergeants Gardner, of K, and Gardner, of H, corporal Devereaux Jones, of A, afterwards lieutenant in the First Louisiana, and private Charles Raffile, of K, all actors of experience, gave scenes from Hamlet and other plays. Between the scenes songs were sung by private Jeremiah Keefe, of H, musician James McAllister, of I, private William B. Bragg, of D, afterwards captain in the First Louisiana Cavalry, and by others. These performances afforded entertainment to hundreds of delighted listeners until near midnight.

Often at evening in fair weather Co. A's accomplished Glee Club, comprising Lieutenant Woodruff, sergeant Gladden, corporals Warren, Jones and Carpenter, and private Gladden, assembled on the quarter deck at twilight, and charmed all with such songs as *The Star Spangled Banner*, *The Sword of Bunker Hill*, *Hurrah for Old New England*, *Home Again*, and the more modern music of patriotism and the fireside.

On the 27th of March occurred the first death on ship-board. It was that of private Michael Dobson, of Co. H. The disease had long been undermining his constitution, and the close, crowded, unhealthy quarters had quickly destroyed his remaining vitality. The funeral services made a deep impression, as they always do on those who behold for the first time a burial at sea. Chaplain Salter officiated, reading the Episcopal service from the Book of Common Prayer. The body had been sewed up in the blanket of the deceased, with a cannon ball at the feet to sink it.

The pall-bearers laid it on a plank and lifted it on the gunwale. The tender pathos of the chaplain's voice touched every heart. *Earth to earth, ashes to ashes, dust to dust!* The corpse splashed heavily in the dark green waves and vanished forever. Three times was this solemn scene repeated before we arrived at Ship Island.

With the usual curiosity we gazed upon the gulf-weed drifting on its aimless journey; saw the dark-blue forms of sharks gliding like attendant demons beneath us; saw the dolphins flash past us, the porpoises rolling, the flying fish leaping, the sea-gulls perpetually hovering in our wake. On the distant line where sky and water seem to meet, we loved to watch with our glasses the projecting masts of invisible hulls, proving so plainly the convexity of the ocean. Sleeping on deck as we advanced further south and the air grew warmer, we nightly witnessed the stupendous march of the moon and stars across the sky; and at the great miracle of sunrise and sunset, we could almost imagine we heard the hiss of the burning wheels.

The unpoetic side of sleeping there was this: that precisely at earliest dawn the deck was flooded with water by the sailors, who took a malicious delight in wetting us as we lay unconscious in the arms of Morpheus!

About daylight, Sunday morning, April 6th, we were suddenly aroused by noise on deck, the loud voice of the first mate, Mr. Craig, shouting, "Belay, there! Belay!" the stopping of the ship, the heavy rumbling of the great anchor-chain down the side. We were wedged in among the most dangerous of the

Florida keys, having been drifted several miles out of our true course by unsuspected currents. Two or three old wrecks lay in sight. The white breakers and coral reefs all around us betokened our peril. A couple of miles distant in the direction of the mainland lay a beautiful circular island, shaded with cocoanut trees. Half hid among these were buildings that so far off looked like well-built mansions. An old man came from the island in a boat. He told us the place was Indian Key; he lived by wrecking; did not know much about war; the war did not disturb him; the last he had heard was that the Yankees were rather getting worsted, but that was several months before. He gave us valuable information about the "lay" of the land, or rather, of the rocks. As it was likely to take several hours to extricate the ship, Col. Birge went ashore in a row boat, accompanied by Adjt. Grosvenor, Captains Bidwell, Mitchell, Sprague, Lieut. Tibbets and one or two others. The sun's rays were intensely hot, but with sergeant (afterwards major) Grosvenor, and several other picked oarsmen, we quickly reached the little island, that looked up so pretty in the distance. We found it two or three acres in extent. The romance vanished, for the most part, on reaching the place. It was low, sandy, almost destitute of vegetation except a few clusters of cocoa-nut tree. It had three or four small families, as many cows, and a dozen pigs. The buildings shrunk into poor, dilapidated houses without glass windows and almost without furniture. For drink, the inhabitants depended on reservoirs of rain-water beneath the houses. They gained a rather precarious and miserable subsistence by wrecking and fishing, selling cocoa-nuts, shells and sponges. On every side the sea-water broke monotonously over the worn, porous, coral rocks. The margin was fringed with sand which was bespangled with shells. These, with some enormous sponges and a few cocoa-nuts, were all we brought away as curiosities.

After two or three hours' strolling about the island, during which some of the party went in bathing and got the prickles of the sea-urchin or some equally sharp acquaintance introduced to their feet, we commenced returning. On our way back we were startled by the sight of a large ocean steamer, which seemed to rise like an apparition from the waves. It made swiftly for our ship, on board of which we observed considerable commotion. The troops took post for fighting, hoisted the Star Spangled Banner, and run out the two cannon. The strange craft showed no colors, nor was any one to be seen on her. She steered straight for the ship, but when about half a mile distant she suddenly shifted her course and passed away like a phantom.

We had heard before leaving New York that the rebel privateer *Alabama* was on the Atlantic coast, and after some sort we had made arrangements to show fight if attacked. We had taken on board two old twenty-four pounders from the Brooklyn navy yard, with a supply of ball cartridge. Every morning at sunrise, First Sergeant Merrill, with private Thomas Harrison and the rest of his squad of cannoniers, fired a shotted gun, and went through an artillery drill.

On reaching the ship, Colonel Birge was greatly annoyed to find that nearly all the officers had taken the liberty to go off in one of the ship's boats, and had not returned. This breach of discipline he rebuked in terms so emphatic that no officer of the Thirteenth cared to repeat the offence.

Passing Key West we stood in a northerly and afterwards in a westerly direction, keeping not far from the Florida coast. As we passed Pensacola the wind freshened, and by and by it blew almost a gale. Next morning, off the mouth of Mobile Bay, a violent thunder storm overtook us. Its effects on Ship Island were quite serious, prostrating tents and destroying property. Several soldiers on guard were killed by lightning. The view of our anchored squadron lying opposite Forts Morgan and Gaines, and tossing in dreary solitude on the wild waste of waters, gave us a repulsive idea of the monotony of life on a blockader.

Saturday, April 12th, towards evening, we first came in sight of Ship Island. The lower end was thronged by shipping. It is a long bank of the finest sand. The greater portion is utterly destitute of trees and verdure. A few blades of coarse grass and weeds straggled here and there. We gained a more just appreciation of the simile in Coleridge's Ancient Mariner,

> "Thou art long and lank and brown
> As is the ribbed sea-sand."

The water at high tide covers most of the island, and a storm sometimes rolls the billows quite across, sweeping everything before them. A few summers ago it was thus submerged, and quite a number of lives were lost of persons visiting it from New Orleans for pleasure. The unfinished fort and the lighthouse, half destroyed by the rebels soon after the commencement of the war, were the only evidence of prior occupation. A sergeant of Co. H informed the writer that he had hunted wild hogs on the upper end of the island while engaged in smuggling!

As we drew near, the island seemed almost covered with tents. Sixteen regiments of Butler's command were already there, besides artillery and cavalry. As we came to anchor, several batteries were practising on the level beach, and in the deepening twilight their flash and roar made the scene quite sublime.

We disembarked next morning, Sunday, April 13th, 1862. For the first time we pitched tents as a regiment. We were much straitened for want of room. The camp ground was an irregular sand-heap. While the rest of us were leveling it, marking out company limits, and quarreling about the possession of shovels, the cooks were busy boiling coffee. Colonel Birge coming along took a cup, and for want of a spoon stirred in the sugar with his forefinger, remarking, "This is what we've got to come to."

On the 15th of April, musician Underwood, of Co. E, died; a man of pure character, and simple unpretending piety. He had enlisted from patriotic motives, and won the sympathy of all by his sufferings on the ship. His comrades buried him in the sands; the first of our regiment to mingle his dust with southern soil.

We remained three weeks on Ship Island, having daily battalion and company drills and dress parades. Colonel Birge pursued his design of perfecting the personal appearance of the men, by selecting at every guard-mounting the neatest and handsomest for his orderly, and bestowing special honor upon all such. His maxim was, *Good officers make good men.* Slovenliness was the unpardonable sin. Those were days of crocus, emery paper, paste blacking, and white gloves. A spirit of emulation prevailed among the officers, and they contributed from ten to a hundred dollars each to purchase the means of display for their commands. Our first dress parade at Ship Island is well remembered. The long line of eight hundred men in dark blue clothing with white gloves and burnished arms showed like a beautiful painting in the yellow rays of the setting sun. "Look at them!" said the Colonel, pointing to the soldiers with enthusiastic pride as the officers marched up on the dismissal of parade.

We soon found the island an uncomfortable place. A small fly abounds here, that bites as vigorously as the African *tsetse*, though not poisonous. The fine white sand would not soil the cleanest linen, but it drifts like snow in the perpetual breeze, unerringly insinuating itself into every crevice. No pains nor skill could keep it out of our food. Months afterwards on unpacking clothing from the inmost recesses of our trunks, we found the omnipresent sand even there. It has one admirable quality: it holds rain water like a sponge. Dig down two or three feet, and you find fresh, sweet water in abundance. It is said, however, to be impregnated with sulphur, and it had a very laxative effect. In a week or ten days, too, the water of each well became vitiated, and it was necessary to dig in another spot. Beneath the sand lies a beautiful, compact, blue clay, which seems to form the bottom of this sort of rain-water reservoir.

Above it the sun glares like a white-hot furnace; so that we found it necessary to use green goggles.

It was exceedingly difficult to get wood for cooking. We were obliged to send parties to cut and haul it through the surf from the upper end of the island several miles distant.

On Ship Island we first saw General Phelps, of Brattleboro, Vermont. He had preceded Butler in arriving on the ground, and had published the celebrated Ship Island Proclamation, in which he declared the death of slavery, and invited the Louisiana planters to adopt free labor. It required two years for the nation to come up to that high standpoint, and the country could not even bear to hear the truth at that time. They thought him insane, and he was soon forced to resign his commission rather than submit to what he deemed the tyrannical requirements of a political general in the interest of slavery. Like so many of the illustrious advocates of progress in every age, he may have been too much in advance of his times; yet this is his imperishable glory, that he alone of all our generals at this early day had the intellect to perceive the truth, the courage to proclaim it and the hand to execute it; and that, in the summer of 1862, he dared, first of all our generals, to arm the blacks in defence of liberty, as the rebel governor of Louisiana had already done in defence of slavery.

The General used to amuse his soldiers by his dry wit and shrewd criticisms. He had a cool incisive way of taking out conceit, that was refreshing to the beholder. One day a red-legged Zouave officer in the fantastic dress of his regiment swaggered past a group among whom was General Phelps. The general asked, "What are you?" "Me! I'm a Zouave." "A Zouave!" said the general, "Why, what on earth is that?" "A Zouave, sir, is a soldier," replied the "Zou Zou." "Ah! a *soldier*! I thought you was a *circus rider!*"

Another day on Ship Island the general was attentively watching an officer who was pompously displaying his ignorance of the very rudiments of tactics at a battalion drill. The general called him aside, and said, "I have been observing for a long time your remarkable performances in the way of drill." Here the officer's eyes brightened, expecting some high compliment. "I noticed," continued the general, "that you seem acquainted, I might say, perfectly acquainted, with everything," (here the officer's face wore the blandest of smiles)—"perfectly acquainted with everything; *except your duty!* Now, you go to your tent. Study tactics a few weeks; and when you have learned something about war, I'll come and see you drill your company!"

Near the end of April we heard the distant booming of cannon, and at night some thought they could distinguished the occasional flash of exploding shells. It was the bombardment of Fort Jackson, about sixty miles in a direct line from Ship Island. We had hoped to share in the first grand attack in Louisiana, but never doubted we should see fighting enough in the expected battles around New Orleans. It seemed incredible that they should give up their chief city without one tremendous conflict by land as well as by water. The naval fight was indeed terrible; hardly paralleled in the annals of war, either for the fierceness with which the combatants fought, the destructiveness of the contest, or the completeness of the victory. To the surprise of all of us, the chivalry that had flamed so brightly seemed to have been suddenly extinguished in the river. The great city tamely surrendered at sight of the first gunboat; her thirty-thousand soldiers vanishing before Farragut came near. The forts surrendered on the twenty-eighth; the city, on the twenty-ninth of April, 1862.

On the 3d of May we received orders to be in readiness for re-embarkation on the ship *City of New York*. Sunday, May 4th, we struck tents in the morning, and after waiting all day in the hot sand and sunshine, we commenced going on board at night. On the fifth we set sail for the southwest pass of the Mississippi. As we approached this great outlet, Captain Salter insisted that it was impossible to cross the bar without first lightening the ship of its enormous ballast. Accordingly several scores of soldiers were kept at hard work a day or two, shoveling the dirt overboard. It was strongly suspected and loudly complained by many of the laborers, who "had been there before," that all this statement about the difficulty of crossing the bar at that stage of the water was a mere pretence of Captain Salter's, who thus anticipated, they said, the labor which would have been necessary at New Orleans, and saved a few hundred dollars by the operation. "Sugar," they argued, "makes as good ballast as pure gravel."

A small steam-tug slowly towed our ship up the majestic river. It was the second week in May. The breath of orange groves and millions of flowers, the broad level fields, bounded by the green woods in the distance, and rich in all the waving glories of that lovely climate and unequaled soil, the beautiful pillared mansions of lordly planters, whose taste, culture, luxury and pride had been amply ministered to by the unpaid toil of hundreds of slaves—all contrasted strongly with the white burning sand of Ship Island, or the limitless expanse of the " harvestless sea."

The Mississippi had not been so high for many years. It filled its channel to the top of the levees. Like the Po, as it nears the ocean it becomes more and more, and increasingly from year to year, an enormous aqueduct between artificial banks; and the day may arrive when the deposit of sediment and the necessary rising of the levees will have lifted the very bottom of the river above the surface of the surrounding country. On a level with the house roofs we glided along as if by enchantment. Hoeing in the green fields, or thronging the banks of the Father of Waters, were swarms of many-colored slaves, from the delicately-tinted white of the octaroon with the soft, lustrous eyes, to a darkness before which night grows pale. These, with indubitable demonstrations of joy, waved their handkerchiefs, shouting, " Welcome! Welcome! Glory to God!" while their white masters and mistresses scowled defiance, or turned their backs in impotent scorn and rage.

We anchored a day at Fort Jackson, and had opportunity to examine the effect of the iron hail which Farragut had poured upon it. All the ground within a quarter of a mile of the fort on every side was thickly dotted with great holes scooped out by the explosion of the thirteen-inch mortar shells. The river face of the fort was considerably battered. A few guns had been dismounted. Two casemates had been nearly knocked into one. But though somewhat disfigured, covered with debris, and blackened by the fire that had consumed the wood-work of the interior, the fort was pronounced by Chief Engineer Weitzel "as strong as before the bombardment." Evidently it might have made a much more protracted resistance. Fort St. Philip, lying diagonally opposite, on the other side and a little higher up, was entirely unharmed. In the river we saw the ugly hulk of the iron-clad Manasses and other rebel wrecks. The deep stream, now swollen by the spring floods, covered nearly all; an occasional mast or smoke stack, like a grave stone, marking the spot where a buried vessel lay. Quite a number of fire-rafts loaded with pitch pine, tar, rosin, and other combustibles, were seen here and there along the banks.

At last on the twelfth of May we came in sight of the city. How changed from the New Orleans of other days! A dozen government vessels were all the shipping that could be seen, where, a year before, hundreds of sea-going vessels and river craft crowded upon one another along the whole front of the city. Many of these had gone up the Red River for safety; some had been sunk; some burned at the wharves; many concealed in the numerous bayous that connect with the Mississippi. A charred and blackened mass of burnt cotton lined the wide empty levee for miles, where, a few months before, bales, barrels, boxes, bags, and every kind of merchandise, were piled high as the roofs. A hundred or so of jubilant negroes of both sexes, and a score or two of white men and boys immediately gathered at the pier. The second mate threw ashore the looped end of a stout cable. "Boy," said he to a youth of a dozen years, who wore a confederate artillery cap, "Boy, won't you just put that 'ere rope over that log?" "No, I'll be damned if I will!" was the instant reply.

Towards evening Colonel Birge buckled on sword and pistol and went unattended from the ship up through the streets to report to General Butler. Apprehensive for his safety, we were gratified to see him return safe, after an hour's absence.

May 13th, we landed on the levee and marched a short distance to the yard of the Orleans cotton press, where the regiment went into temporary quarters. We immediately proceeded to make ourselves comfortable, and had just got nicely settled when orders came to move again. General Butler's eye had rested on the regiment, and he assigned us the post of honor, the Custom House. So, on the morning of May 15th, every man put on his best attire, and we marched through the streets with great pomp, going a little further than was absolutely necessary, in order to give the rebels a full view of a live Yankee regiment. Many old citizens of New Orleans told us afterwards they had never seen so fine-looking troops, either in the Union or Confederate service.

We found the building filthy beyond expression. Never completed nor even roofed, though millions of dollars had been spent upon it by the United States, under the superintendence of Beauregard and other engineers, it had been tenanted a year by the Confederate troops; cannon had been mounted on the topmost story and peered through the upper windows; the walls were disfigured by disloyal and obscene inscriptions; and a confused mass of rubbish had been piled up in the numerous rooms. In front and rear were many half-burnt gun-carriages. Here, too, were scores of church bells, which the frenzied inhabitants had contributed from all parts of Louisiana, to be melted into cannon—fit illustration of the demon power of war, which substitutes the horrible clangor of arms and the din of hell itself for the melodious chimes that call to prayer and praise.

> "Is it, O man, with such discordant noises,
> With such accursed instruments as these,
> Thou drownest Nature's sweet and kindly voices,
> And jarrest the celestial harmonies?"

The Custom House was now the military center of the Department of the Gulf. From this point Butler fulminated his famous orders. Here was the Post Office. Here the Provost Court, the Courts Martial, and the Military Commissions sat. Here, in case of insurrection in the city—no improbable contingency at that time—was the strongest, most defensible position; a fortress in itself.

General Butler's office was in the second story, northeast (rear) angle. The Provost Court, of which Major Bell, of the old firm of Choate & Bell, was Judge, was held in the second story looking out on Magazine Street. The officers of the Treasury Department occupied rooms in the same story, on the river side. Hon. Reverdy Johnson, during his inquisitorial visit, occupied the front center room, same story, on Canal Street. The Post Office was on the first or ground floor, on the corner of Canal and Magazine streets. Prison rooms, blacksmith shops, kitchens, sutler's rooms, guard-houses, stables, boat-builders' shops, Quartermaster's and Commissary's rooms were on the same floor. The companies of the Thirteenth Connecticut were scattered through the large building. Company A took the rear room, top of the building, fourth story, near the center; Company C, directly under Company A; Company H, directly under Company C, and therefore in the second story; Company D, alongside Company H; Company G, third story, back corner room, on Magazine Street; Company B, the same side and story, front corner room; Company F, front room, third story, next to Company B; Company D, front corner room, third story, on the river side; Company E, a large room, second story, on Magazine Street; Company K, the front corner room, next to Company E.

Battalion drills were commenced, but soon discontinued on account of the other laborious duties and the oppressive heat. Returning in *route step* one May morning from our second battalion drill, the regiment at suggestion of Colonel Birge struck up as one man the song, never before heard in New Orleans,

> "John Brown's body lies a mouldering in the grave,
> His soul is marching on."

We immediately began to put the Custom House in order. Overwhelmed by the influx of contrabands, who came from every part of the country as well as the city, making their way by stealth or force past the Confederate pickets, and past the city police who used every effort to exclude them, we set about a hundred of them at work cleaning the floors, ceilings, stairways, walls, drains, casement, and kept them so employed week after week, until the Augean Stables presented an appearance worthy of the "finest-looking regiment that ever entered New Orleans." Among other permanent improvements, Major Holcomb built a broad, handsome and substantial flight of stairs in the center of the front on Canal Street, leading from the sidewalk to the second story. On the summit of the Custom House we flung to the breeze, amid the enthusiastic shouts of the soldiers and the peals of artillery, a large United States flag. It floated from a beautiful flag-staff which had been mysteriously "conveyed" from a ship lying at anchor at Ship Island when the Thirteenth took its departure for New Orleans.

In addition to the heavy guard about the Custom House, we sent out every night an officer with a company to patrol the streets till morning. At nine every evening we also sent a company to serve as the special body-guard of the hated prince of policemen.

Prince of policemen! for General Butler had, perhaps, the most villainous set of rascals to deal with that ever disgraced and endangered a city. Deserters from the Confederate army, deserters from the Union army, foreign rogues from the four quarters of the world, gamblers, "fancy men," thieves, cut-throats—all to some extent banded together, and forming a sort of "Devil's regiment of the line," under the significant appellation of *Thugs!* A vigilance committee had to be organized a few years ago to protect decent people from the assaults of these *Thugs!* The city to a man, yea, to a woman, was hostile to Federal rule. "Every union man is drunk, and every union woman a ——," remarked Colonel Birge to the writer, one evening—an assertion too sweeping, but yet conveying some idea of the truth, though exaggerated. Add to this moral Gehenna the material filth that had accumulated for a year, and that made the most pious of the confederates believe that God would mercifully sweep away the Yankees by yellow fever, when the set time to favor the rebel Zion should have fully come; and some idea may be gained of the need that existed in this city for the prince of policemen. They needed a master and they found one. He governed the city with "an iron hand" *without* "a velvet glove," and he governed it well. He made it safe for any man or woman to pass alone, on any street at any hour, from one end of New Orleans to the other. The streets, the drains, the canals, were cleaned as they never had been before. The sanitary condition of the city was perfect. Yellow fever did not come. "Order reigned in Warsaw;" Thugdom was tranquil.

Before we had been a week in the Custom House we began to discharge the disabled and to receive recruits. We took in about two hundred and twenty in all, filling the regiment to the maximum. Nearly all were of foreign birth, and most of them had lived in the northern states. For illustration: Company H received twenty four recruits in May. Of these twelve were born in Ireland, ten in Germany, one in NewYork, and one in Massachusetts. All but five had lived in the North. All but six had been in the Confederate service. These New Orleans men were a valuable accession to our ranks, many of them being brave men, experienced in war. They were credited to the quota of Connecticut, and few of them ever dishonored her name. They were well aware of the risk they incurred of being executed as deserters if recaptured by the rebels. At the Bayo Des Allemands, on the New Orleans, Opelousas and Great Western Rail-Road, during that very summer, several companies of the Eighth Vermont, stationed at Algiers, were ambushed and captured, and seven of their number were recognized as having served in the Confederate ranks. They asserted that it was by compulsion; but the plea did not avail. They were taken about five rods from the rail-road, a single shallow pit was dug, they were placed on the brink, and without respite were shot down; their bodies tumbled into the ditch, and a few shovelfuls of earth were thrown over them. The desolate spot has a mournful interest, and we often visited it. Overgrown with weeds, it is yet easily recognized, beside some trees, nearly abreast with the earthworks, on the right side as you go from Algiers. The traveller who has either sentiment or patriotism will hardly restrain his tears, when he stands there and listens to the story of a father's anguish as he shoveled the dirt away to find the mouldering remains of his handsome and manly boy. Will not the great republic some day rear a monument to mark the last resting place of the seven martyrs who died for her at the Bayou Des Allemands in the summer of '62?

About two weeks after our arrival in the Custom House, we concluded to have a brass band. We accordingly engaged the services of Mr. Charles Bother, one of the best band leaders in the United States. He selected sixteen other musicians, all of them distinguished for their skill. They were enlisted into the regiment, and mustered into the United States service. The same band, with two or three exceptions, had been in the Confederate army, and had played on the bloody field of Shiloh. All being professional musicians, the band of the Thirteenth soon became famous in the Department of the Gulf. Active and long-continued operations in the field finally forced us to the conclusion that it was impracticable to retain them, and they were accordingly mustered out after a year and a half with the Thirteenth.

We were more than four months in the Custom House, during which the regiment by its general good conduct gained the esteem of the citizens. Of course there were exceptional cases. About the first of June a band of burglars was organized, including one member of Company F, Thirteenth Connecticut, and Mr. Craig, First Mate of the ship *City of New York*. They represented themselves as officers of our army, and empowered to search houses for arms and contraband papers. With forged orders and in disguised uniforms they forced their way at dead of night into the dwellings of peaceable citizens, searched trunks, drawers, wardrobes, seized whatever money or plate they could lay hands on, and made off with their booty. The villainy was quickly laid before General Butler. A Military Commission tried them on Friday, sentenced them on Saturday, and four of them, including the two above named, were hanged the following Monday, June 16, at the Parish Prison.

Butler executed only one other person during our stay in New Orleans. It was the gambler, Mumford. He was hung at the Mint. His offence was endeavoring to excite insurrection by tearing down the United States flag from the top of the Mint after the surrender of the city. After his conviction he was confined in the Custom House under a guard from our regiment. Here Chaplain Salter repeatedly visited him, and with tears offered him the consolations of religion, and begged him to accept a Saviour's mercy. Mumford's reply to the exhortation to prepare for eternity was singular enough. He said in substance as follows: "I have no fear of death, because I have lived a blameless life. Having never done anything wrong, I am prepared for a future world, if there is any future world. I only hate to leave my friends." Well might our kind chaplain be perplexed and amazed. In this stoical indifference, without a prayer on his lips, Mumford met death as coolly as did old John Brown on the Virginia scaffold. But Brown was a man of different mould; of austere morals, trained to piety, accustomed to spend much of his time in reading his bible or on his knees in prayer. Mumford was conceded to have no religious convictions, was dissolute, intemperate, and a noted gambler—poor material to exalt into a martyr, even in the cause of slavery, for which he died.

Six other men were doomed to be shot by sentence of a Military Commission, for the offence of recruiting for the Confederate army within our military lines. The appointed day came. A detachment of the Thirteenth Connecticut was detailed to do the shooting. At early morning the prisoners, with a strong military escort from our regiment, proceeded a couple of miles towards the lake, with a vast concourse of spectators thronging around. Passing out of Canal Street, they halted in an open field on the left. The troops were drawn up on three sides of a square. The soldiers charged with the execution stood in line about ten paces from the victims, who were seated on their coffins. Perfect silence reigned. The order for trial, the charge, specifications, findings and sentence, were read by the Provost Marshal in a clear voice. The muskets were loaded. The fatal word "*Fire*," was just on the point of being uttered, when an orderly rode up with a reprieve! Two of them listened to the merciful tidings in silence. Two thanked God aloud and manifested ardent gratitude. But one of them damned General Butler with horrible oaths for having "fooled" him and the others by this mock show!

The irrepressible conflict met us constantly. Whatever a Federal bullet struck, wherever a Federal bayonet pierced, the demon of Slavery started up into visible and gigantic proportions, like Satan at the touch of Ithuriel's spear. Butler at first tried hard to pacify the people, and avoid wounding their feelings. On the subject of slavery he was especially anxious to win their favor. For about three weeks he used all his influence, and in at least one instance* his authority, to cause fugitives to be restored to their masters. Vain and foolish attempt. To serve liberty by propping slavery! To soothe Niagara by pouring on a little sweet oil! Yet he tried it. The police as of old were allowed to seize and deliver up fugitive slaves. The punishment of whipping them in jail was still inflicted with the full sanction of the military authorities.

When the Thirteenth Connecticut had established itself in the Custom House, most of the companies employed, as laundresses, colored women, who had run

* Case of the slave girl Caroline. See Appendix.

away or been driven off to the Yankees. Besides these slaves, about a hundred negro men had been set at work by Bromley in the Quartermaster's Department, as black-smiths, carpenters, shoemakers, wagoners, and laborers. Somehow we got the reputation of being an anti-slavery regiment; or as a certain high officer on Butler's staff expressed it, "a d——d abolition regiment!" Butler issued stringent orders to keep the negroes out of the Custom House. On the 26th of May he caused the names of all to be taken, and ordered all unemployed negroes to be driven out. On the 27th he commanded that all laundresses should be put out. On the 28th he directed that the pay for servants be deducted from the pay for officers, in order to prevent officers from harboring runaways.

The night after the promulgation of the order to admit no more slaves into the Custom House, several able-bodied negro men from the plantation of Alexander Grant, twenty miles down the river, made their way with much difficulty and danger to our quarters. They had been shot at, hunted with dogs, and some of them bore the marks of recent whipping. With tears they begged to be protected from the police, who would pounce upon them at daybreak and lodge them in jail to be again whipped and returned to their rebel master. Here was a quandary. It was past midnight; the Custom House was full; there was no work for any more blacks. Butler's order was still ringing in our ears. The Officer of the Day (Captain of Company H) went to Bromley, in whom as in Daniel of old, "were found an excellent spirit, and knowledge, and understanding, * * * and showing of hard sentences, and dissolving of doubts." "I have no use for them," said Bromley; "I have more now than I can well employ. I can take them up on my papers, however, and will do so, if you'll find work for them. Will you agree to find labor for them?" "Yes. But I'm curious to know how you'll enter their names on your papers so as to evade the General's order." "Oh! that's easy enough," replied the Quartermaster. "I'll give them a pass dated a week back in red ink. There's great magic in red ink!" So the Quartermaster received them. Next morning the Officer of the Day set them at work washing floors; and week after week they scrubbed with unwearied industry, and endless repetition. They proved to be most valuable hands, and we never regretted our kindness to them. In due time they enlisted in the military service and fought well for freedom.

The idea of a Southern slave was associated with that of a black skin. In this we were quickly undeceived. On the 19th of May, a handsomely dressed young man, having found his way into our quarters, asked the captain of Company H if he could not furnish him employment. The officer surveyed the well-behaved applicant, and noticed a certain diffidence and respectful air mingled with his otherwise aristocratic bearing, remarked his polished manners, faultless broadcloth, and soft white hands, and with real compassion said:

"I regret, sir, that I have no such position at my command as you would probably desire."

"I would accept a'most any situation, sir."

"Excuse me, sir, but I presume you are in the same condition as scores of others in this city—temporarily reduced to straitened circumstances by the fortune of war—and that you would prefer a clerkship, or some writing in the Custom House or Post Office."

"O no, sir, I can't *write!* My Massa never learnt me to write! But I should be glad to do most anything. I can take care of your clothes, black your boots, wait on table, and do a right smart heap o' things."

"What! Are you a slave?"

"Yes."

"Why, I had'nt noticed any African features."

"My father was a white man—Mr. Barnes, my former master."

"What's your name?"

"Charley Barnes."

"Whom do you belong to now?"

"Mr. Oviatt, on —— street. He's from Connecticut."

"You'd easily pass for white."

"Yes. But if you notice my hair carefully, you'll see it a little kinky about the roots. There's many slaves a heap whiter'n me."

Lieutenant Julius Tobias employed him as his servant, gave him the name of Julius Cæsar Thompson, and in a few weeks got him enlisted as a white soldier in the First Louisiana regiment. There he served faithfully and gallantly, to the great grief of Mr. Oviatt, who was afraid some harm would befall his valuable chattel, and often called to enquire after his welfare.

In spite of Butler's stringent and repeated orders, the negroes would get inside the building, which was besieged daily by owners hunting for their slippery property. Some of these chattels had their backs shockingly lacerated by whipping; others had huge freshly-burned marks of the branding iron. Many had chains on their wrists, ankles and necks. A few wore great iron collars with long projecting prongs, like the spokes of a wheel. More than once did the writer of this history work till past midnight filing off these collars. "I used to think," said Captain McCord, "that the stories about cruel treatment of slaves were exaggerated; but the reality is fully equal to the worst description." It was hard to resist the piteous appeals of these slaves for protection. And even when received within our quarters, they were not safe. Repeatedly slaves were seized in the Custom House, sometimes by the connivance of United States officers; repeatedly were they knocked down, and brutally dragged away from under the folds of the "Flag of the Free." Colonel Warner rescued one of these victims at considerable personal risk. The captain of Company H was Officer of the Day, on the 6th of June. That day, one of the Quartermaster's employees was violently torn away by armed policemen, and was dragged across Canal Street, in spite of his vigorous resistance, in the midst of a great crowd. The captain was notified of the high-handed outrage in time to interpose. Drawing his sword and seizing a revolver, he rushed to the scene, forced his way to the center of the mob, released the negro, brought the two men-stealers back in custody, and lodged them in the guard house.

Another time, the same captain, as Officer of the Day, stood at the door on Magazine Street, through which Butler usually entered. A venerable looking gentleman with white neck-tie approached, and the following conversation ensued:

"Captain, I would like to come into the Custom House and look round a little."

"What for?"

"I want to look for a boy of mine that has run away, and I think he's inside."

"Oh! You want to come in and hunt for a nigger?"

"Yes. He's a boy I've always been kind to—always treated him as one of the family. He's always had every thing he wanted. It's very strange he should treat me so. But they're an ungrateful race."

"I dont think I can admit you without a pass from General Butler to come in and hunt your nigger."

"Cant I go in and see the General?"

"Not about the nigger. The General has more important business. Besides, you are probably aware that the United States Government forbids its officers to return fugitive slaves to their masters."

"But the boy is my *property*—my own nigger."

"We can't investigate questions of that sort. The military law don't acknowledge the right of one man to own another."

"You come here pretending to respect our rights; our constitutional rights, our bible rights; and yet you wont let me get back my nigger, my nigger that's my lawful property. I say it's unconstitutional, it's inconsistent, it's unchristian."

"I dont know whether you own the nigger, or the nigger owns you. I would as soon deliver you to him, as him to you. I tell you we can't investigate such questions."

"This is strange language—strange language!"

"Very common language where I came from. I guess it'll be common here before long. Look here, sir. You appear to be a minister. What do you make of that passage which says, 'Thou shalt not deliver unto his master the servant which is escaped from his master unto thee'?"

"I dont choose to argue that question, sir. Do you say I can't come in to look for my nigger?"

"That's what I said."

"Can't I come in to see General Butler?"

"Good morning, sir."

"Good morning."

Such cases were of daily occurrence. Some officers were disposed to allow indiscriminate slave-hunting. Large bribes were offered.

To protect our servants still more from the man-stealers we gave our blacks new names. Among them were John C. Calhoun, Horace Greeley, Tiglath Pileser, Henry Ward Beecher, Julius Cæsar Thompson, Solomon, Wendell Phillips, Prince of Darkness, King Richard, Polyphemus (a one-eyed man), Sardanapalus (a "slow coach").

The change of views at Head Quarters in regard to slavery, was announced by deeds rather than words. One night twenty or thirty slaves fled from a plantation, and attempted to enter New Orleans. But a body of policemen sent out to patrol by the slaveholders, who still tenaciously clung to the reeling institution, undertook to arrest them as they entered the city limits. The negroes were armed with cane-knives; the police, with pistols; and a hard fight ensued. Some negroes were shot dead, others were severely wounded; but eleven of them reached the

Custom House just as morning tinted the east. The Officer of the Day, making his nocturnal visits to the sentinels, came to the contrabands, heard their story, and determined to secure fair play, if possible, to men who had shown by their courage that they deserved liberty. That day, on complaint of their overseers, the slaves were arraigned before Judge Bell for violating the peace, riotous conduct, assault with dangerous weapons, and the like. The case was pretty clearly proved. Captain Sprague acted as counsel, and insisted on the failure of the prosecution to identify. Judge Bell cut him short in the midst of his argument, and much to his chagrin said, "I think there can be no doubt about their guilt." "But, your Honor," said the captain, "there surely is no evidence to inculpate more than two, or three, and are these eleven to be delivered to their masters on such a pretence as that?" A roguish twinkle and a knowing smile from Judge Bell, re-assured the captain as he proceeded with his decision: "I find them all guilty, and sentence them to six months at Fort Jackson!" This was precisely what the owners did not want. One of them went to General Butler. Lieutenant Tibbets was present and heard the master ask the General, "What assurance have I that I can get my niggers back after their six months at Fort Jackson?" "None at all," replied the General. "Then I'm afraid I shall never get 'em again," sadly exclaimed the proprietor of the sable merchandize. "Very likely," responded the General. They found their way subsequently to the Corps d' Afrique.

Surgeon ——— of our army, an associate of Dr. Fisher in hospital, had employed a fugitive slave as hospital nurse. The former master, finding the girl in the street near the hospital, forcibly seized her and hurried her off to his home. The surgeon brought the matter to the attention of General Butler. The General opened the law books and found that, by the Code of Louisiana, the least penalty for abducting a slave was a term of two years in the Parish Prison. He took the position that the slave being rightfully in the surgeon's possession, had been abducted by her own master! Consequently, he sentenced the patrician owner to two years in the Parish Prison; a decision which made the New Orleans aristocrats open their eyes very wide. The prince of policemen was progressing fast.

The rebel Governor, Moore, having raised, armed, drilled, and reviewed a regiment of negroes, and called them into service in behalf of the Confederate cause, Butler took the very same appeal in which the Governor had summoned these colored men to the side of treason and slavery, and, changing only a few words, the General bade them fight for union and liberty. Three regiments were quickly raised, and officered by colored men, whereat all the confederates sent up a howl! How atrocious the man who had first dared to follow their own example!

Some of the city magnates having threatened Butler with French or English intervention, he silenced them by declaring with tremendous emphasis, "Gentlemen, *I warn you that if England or France intervenes, I shall call on Africa to intervene, and the men that cut your bread to-day will cut your throats to-morrow!*"

These anecdotes are recorded as illustrations of life in the New Orleans Custom House in the summer of

1862. There was no escaping the omnipresent negro. It did not require much discernment to see the signs of the times. Butler did not have a very tender conscience, but he had a great deal of tough common sense. And even a little common sense will sometimes wonderfully light up one's path. He was a rather rough specimen of civilization, but not a savage; severe, but not cruel; summary, but not a Jeffries; as far removed from Polyphemus as from Abdiel. He had a Napoleonic vigor, but a kind heart. He sometimes stooped to blackguard, but oftener rose to generous deeds. He never was marked as a perfect man, and he never was the slave of low vice. If some of his subalterns stole books, furniture and plate, he was not therefore a Verres. If he kicked a fashionable courtezan down stairs, who had been put up by the waggish secession lords to call on Mrs. Butler, that did not make him a Haynan. If he unceremoniously bade the rich leaders of rebellion "stand and deliver," he bounteously fed the poor victims of rebellion from the proceeds. If he told the high-born ladies who spit on Federal officers that such conduct would make them "liable to the treatment of common women plying their avocation," there was none more prompt than he to punish any officer or soldier who should interpret that order as licensing to insult any woman.

During the summer several of our companies were temporarily detached from the rest of the regiment. Company A, Lieutenant Cornwall commanding, was stationed at Hickox's Landing on the lake; Company E, Captain Tisdale commanding, was detailed as Provost Guard, (with Captain, afterward Colonel, Stafford Provost Marshal); Company I, Captain Schleiter commanding, was stationed as body-guard for General Butler at General Twiggs' house; Company K, Captain Mitchell commanding, as guard at Colonel Birge's head-quarters, in St. Charles Street. Squads were stationed as guards at other points in the city; as at Lieutenant Colonel Warner's house, Carondelet Street; Adjutant Grosvenor's house, Burgundy Street; and other places.

Occasionally an expedition was sent up the Mississippi or across Lake Pontchartrain to procure sugar, corn, cattle, cotton, and other supplies, or to chastise parties of guerillas. Companies B and C, under command of Captains Comstock and Blinn, respectively, embarked as part of a force under Major (afterwards General) Strong, to cross the lake, surprise and capture the rebel force at Pass Manchac and Pontchatoula, the head-quarters of the eccentric general, Jeff. Thompson. The steamers grounded as they approached their destination, and only a portion of the troops disembarked. They were but partially successful. The rebels rallied, drove them back, and inflicted a loss of a considerable number killed, wounded, and prisoners. Among the latter was Dr. Avery, surgeon of the Ninth Connecticut, a pretty good specimen of a smart Yankee. While a prisoner, he beat Jeff. at cards, got him drunk, and challenged him to a horse-race, in which he managed to run Jeff. off among some trees. Jeff. fell from his horse and nearly broke his neck. Altogether, the rebel general gained some new views of Yankee character.

On the return of this expedition, Major Strong represented it as a brilliant success, inasmuch as he captured a sword and a pair of spurs. He was soon promoted to be General, and afterwards fell, gallantly fighting, at Fort Wagner.

In August, Companies A and K, under command of Captain Mitchell, made a foraging expedition up the Mississippi, and returned, partly by steam-boat and partly by land, down the left bank to New Orleans. They had some skirmishing with guerillas, but without loss returned, bringing a few prisoners, and an immense number of horses, cattle, mules, sheep, swine and poultry. While up the river, Captain Fuller, with a detachment of Company D, went up on a steamer, and by some misunderstanding, they were smartly shelled by one of our own gunboats.

On Monday, September 22, Captain Sprague, with fifty men of Company H, proceeded up the Mississippi as a guard to the Steamboat *Iberville.* On the 23d they reached a point six miles from Bayou Goula. Here they found a Frenchman with four hundred cattle, trying to cross the river to the same side as the rebel rendezvous, not many miles distant. Captain Sprague demanded his papers; whereupon he produced a pass dated a few days earlier from the United States Provost Marshal at Jefferson City. The captain, not satisfied, searched him, and found another similar pass in his pocket signed by the rebel colonel commanding in that vicinity; also a permit from the rebel general Dick Taylor. It was decided to take him and his cattle to New Orleans. If he proved to be honest, he could have his cattle on paying twenty dollars a head for transportation; if dishonest, his cattle would go to the United States Commissariat. In any case it was thought unsafe for his cattle to be so near Camp Moore. We commenced taking them on board. They were the wildest, fiercest of Texas oxen. The fifty soldiers formed a circle around them, taking the position of "Guard against Infantry!" Crowding in a compact mass, which moved like a rolled wheel circularly round the center, the desperate beasts manifested a most passionate hostility to man. Often two or three would dart off in a tangent, trampling down, as if all flesh were grass, the soldiers that stood in their way. Bayonets had no terrors for them; nearly twenty were bent double on the foreheads of the brutes. Others of the infuriated animals would rush along the plank, cross the steamer and plunge into the stream. Gunboat No. 8 "headed them off" by steaming up and down the river, and drove them back to the same bank. Occasionally a few would be secured on our boat. This exciting affair lasted from noon till night; when the frantic beasts made one grand charge, broke *en masse* through the line, and dashed away into the darkness. The region being infested with guerillas, and the captain of the steamboat being very drunk, we steamed rapidly down with one hundred and seventy-six cattle, and eight hundred hogsheads of sugar. Reaching New Orleans September 25th, Captain S. repaired immediately to General Butler, stated the facts of the seizure, submitted the papers, and said he had felt some hesitation about taking the cattle by force. After about five minutes examination and study, the general fixed his half-shut eye on the captain and with a smile said, "Captain, you did right. You followed the old rule in Hoyle, '*When you're in doubt, take the trick*'!"

In July, 1862, Major Holcomb, of the Thirteenth Connecticut, was empowered to raise a regiment of white Louisiana volunteers. His recruiting station was the old United States barracks, a few miles below the Custom House and on the same bank. Company G, Thirteenth Connecticut, under Captain Finley (successor of Captain Gilbert) and Lieutenant Baker, was stationed there as a guard. The Thirteenth contributed quite a number to the offices in the First Louisiana. Besides Major Holcomb, the following among others were commissioned: Commissary Sergeant Charles A. Tracy; First Sergeants Oscar F. Merrill, Company H, and George A. Mayne, Company D; Sergeants James T. Smith, James M. Gardner, Charles H. Grosvenor, George G. Smith; Corporal Deveraux Jones; Private Leonidas R. Hall. We lost also scores of other valuable men, who were detached from the regiment to officer colored troops, and to act as clerks, orderlies, telegraph operators, messengers, recruiting agents, signal-corps men, and the like. No regiment was so constantly culled from, and yet the supply of good men seemed inexhaustible.

Parton, in his *Butler in New Orleans*, relates what he considers a pretty good joke perpetrated at the expense of the Thirteenth. It appears that two very handsome girls, the Misses C——e, of New Orleans, who had made deep inroads into the affections of certain officers, and who professed a great love for the *Union*, had made a beautiful embroidered silk flag for the Thirteenth Connecticut. Arrangements were perfected to have it presented in fine style on the coming Fourth of July. The day came. General Butler, with his brilliant Staff, reviewed the regiment on the levee. The troops looked as beautiful as extraordinary efforts could make even the Thirteenth; resplendent in brass and steel, neat clothing, and polished accoutrements. The review closing and the distinguished officers taking proper stations, the fair donors of the flag rode up to the front of the regiment in a magnificent carriage, under the escort of our most stylish officer, the handsome Lieutenant T——, of Company K. The banner was brought out, unrolled, and presented to Colonel Birge in a neat and tasteful speech by one of these dark-eyed beauties. Colonel Birge received it in a dignified and graceful manner, amid thunders of applause. Everybody was happy that day! But how horrified were certain fine gentlemen on the morrow, when it began to be whispered around that those seraphic patriots had African blood under that celestial skin! In fact they were perfect specimens of the effects of that miscegenation which the Chivalry of the South condemn so loudly and practice so freely!

The halcyon days of the summer of 1862 quickly passed. Colonel Birge longed for active service in the field, and the regiment shared his desire. They thirsted for adventures, marching, fighting, and "glory." "Fortunati, si sua bona norint!"

CHAPTER III.

On Monday, September 29, 1862, orders came to hold the regiment in readiness to move at ten o'clock next morning. On the 30th we accordingly left the Custom House, and went into camp close by Greenville Station Carrollton, some five miles above New Orleans. It was near the residence of Honorable Christian Roselius, who often visited us. The ground had been a Confederate rendezvous, called by the name of Camp Lewis. We christened it Camp Kearney, in honor of that valiant and lamented General.

Here we formed a portion of what was known as the Reserve Brigade, under the command of General Godfrey Weitzel, who had just received his commission as Brigadier. The other regiments were the Twelfth Connecticut, Colonel Colburn, the First Louisiana, Colonel Holcomb, the Seventy Fifth New York, Lieutenant Colonel Merrit, the Eighth New Hampshire, Colonel Fearing; with Perkins' Massachusetts Cavalry, Barret's, Godfrey's, and Williams' Louisiana Cavalry, Carruth's Sixth Massachusetts Battery, and Thompson's First Maine Battery. We spent twenty four days here. Colonel Birge being sick at his house in New Orleans, Lieutenant Colonel Warner drilled the regiment. Captain Comstock undertook the same task, but the regiment was not yet quite well enough drilled to form at this time an oblique square! General Weitzel personally gave the officers instruction and practice in skirmishing, and showed himself an accomplished drill-master. The men were exercised in target shooting, as well as the usual tactics. On the fourth of October the General carefully inspected his brigade, and complimented us, especially the Thirteenth, in very high terms. On the eighteenth of October there was a grand review of the Reserve Brigade by General Butler. We marched down to New Orleans and were paraded in Canal Street, where the review was held. We returned to Camp Kearney the same evening, where rations of water, slightly tinged with whiskey, were distributed to the tired soldiers by the Quartermaster, who said he was "fearful of the effects of 'whiskey straight' upon the empty stomach!"

At Camp Kearney we had Sibley tents, and were very comfortably situated. The regiment was a thousand strong. Company A, however, was absent until the middle of October, at "Dan Hickox's" on the lake.

The principal difficuty at this time was in getting wood. Our Quartermaster, never long at a loss for expedients, finally proceeded to the depot of the Carrollton Rail Road, and commenced loading his teams. The Superintendent is said to have come up, and to have held the following dialogue with Bromley:

"What are you going to do with that wood?"

"Cook rations. (Go on with your loading, corporal.)"

"Who are you?"

"Bromley, Q. M. Thirteenth C. V. Allow me, sir, in turn to inquire whom I have the distinguished honor to address?"

"I'm Superintendent of this railroad."

"All right. (Go on with your loading, corporal.)"

"That wood belongs to the railroad."

"So I supposed."

"But I forbid you to take it."

"Put your protest in writing in red ink. Tie it up with a piece of red tape. I 'll approve it and forward it. You see, we 've got to have wood to cook with. Cant eat beans and pork raw. *I'd* prefer 'em raw, but the men are so unreasonable they want 'em cooked."

"But that wood 's necessary for the use of the railroad."

"It 's necessary for the use of the Thirteenth Connecticut."

"I should like to know how a locomotive is going to run without wood."

"I 've often wondered how a regiment could be run without wood."

"General Butler orders me to run this railroad."

"Colonel Birge orders me to run the Thirteenth Connecticut."

"Who 's Colonel Birge?"

"'Who 's Colonel Birge?' Why—the d—deuce! dont you know Colonel Birge? If there 's one man above another that everybody knows it 's Colonel Birge."

"Will Colonel Birge pay for the wood?"

"Colonel Birge pay for the wood! why, no. It 's a reflection on your sagacity to ask such a question."

"Who *will* pay for it?"

"The Quartermaster's Department. If there 's one thing above another that I admire in the Quartermaster's Department, it's because they 'll always pay for wood. Now, my friend, of the railroad persuasion, if you 'll come and see me, I 'll give you receipts, and help you fix up the proper papers to present to the Quartermaster's Department."

"How long will it be before I get pay?"

"It will be at some future day—the futurest kind of a day, I 'm afraid."

The superintendent posted off to see Colonel Birge. Bromley preceded him, however, and cautioned the sentinels to observe the rule to admit no citizen without a pass. "Halt!" said the sentry; and the superintendent gave up the pursuit in despair.

The instructions which Bromley gave to Corporal Strange, a member of his Staff, as he termed him, were quite significant. "Strange, we 're going on an expedition. I want my Staff to be on the look-out for turkeys, geese, pigs, and sheep. Dont be the aggressor in any contest. Stand strictly on the defensive. But if you 're attacked by any of these animals, show fight, and *dont forget to bring off the enemy's dead!*"

On the twenty-first of October orders came to embark on steamers. Next day the Thirteenth moved on board with the remainder of the infantry. Immediately, however, the orders were countermanded, and we returned to camp, and were held in readiness to move at a moment's notice.

The plan of the La Fourche campaign, on which we were about entering, as I learned a few days previously from a discussion between General Butler and some of his subordinate officers, and from subsequent developments, was substantially as follows:

Weitzel's brigade was to drive the enemy down the Bayou La Fourche; the Eighth Vermont, Colonel Thomas, and the First Louisiana, Native Guards, (colored), Colonel Stafford, were to intercept them in the neighborhood of the La Fourche Rail-Road crossing, three miles below Thibodaux, which is thirty-six miles from Donaldsonville; a naval force co-operating with the Twenty-first Indiana, under Colonel (afterwards General) McMillan, was to pass around the coast, ascend the Atchafalaya river as far as Brashear City, and so cut off the enemy from their only available line of retreat, which would be across Berwicks Bay. It was essential to its success that the arrival of our troops by rail at the crossing below Thibodaux, and of the gunboats at Brashear City, should be nearly simultaneous with the successful advance of Weitzel on Thibodaux.

On the twenty-fourth of October we again embarked. Under convoy of three gunboats we proceeded about ninety miles up the river to Donaldsonville, La., where we arrived next morning, it being Sunday. We disembarked. For that latitude the day was very cold. The troops were quartered in the Market-House, Court-House, Theatre, abandoned hotels and dwelling-houses. The Twelfth Connecticut occupied a large church. Many excesses were committed by the soldiers; for which General Weitzel took the blame partly on himself. "I have violated," said he, "one of the first principles of campaigning, never to encamp in a village, when one can just as well remain outside."

Donaldsonville was a neat and thriving place before the war, but had now suffered from a shelling by our gunboats in retaliation for guerilla firing on Farragut's fleet at that point. It was destined to suffer still more severely during its investment by the rebels the following summer. The enemy made no opposition to our landing, but retired along the Bayou La Fourche, which flows from the Mississippi at this point in a south-east course to the Gulf of Mexico.

Sunday night, October 25, was very cold, windy and uncomfortable. Next morning overcoats were in demand. Leaving the First Louisiana to hold Donaldsonville, and throwing out skirmishers and flankers the brigade moved along the Bayou in pursuit of the enemy. These, to the number of about five hundred cavalry, received us as we advanced. Their intention was to avoid battle until the troops at Thibodaux, about two thousand in number, should concentrate at some strong position. The Thirteenth, with the greater portion of the brigade, moved down the left bank. The enemy, like ourselves, were on both sides, their rear occasionally skirmishing with our van, and their numbers constantly increasing. They were commanded by General Mouton. We passed several villages, and saw two camps, just vacated, the fires still blazing. One of these was well built, with comfortable cane-roofed huts. These quickly disappeared in smoke, the burning stalks bursting with loud explosions, which rattled like pistol firing. At several points we saw hastily-constructed breastworks and rifle-pits, which the enemy abandoned without a contest. The soldiers straggled a great deal on this, their first march, but committed few depredations. Great numbers of negroes left their owners' plantations and joined us, bringing with them mules, turkeys, furniture, and bundles of clothing. It was the first time they had ever seen the Yankees, and their ivory teeth and shining eyes glistened behind every fence, as they shouted, "Glory to God!" "God bless you 'uns!" They were only too happy to carry our soldiers' knapsacks, and this satisfaction was quite mutual.

We passed that Monday night on the bare ground without tents or other shelter. It was our first night, as a regiment, in the open air. Happy the man who was able to procure a few cornstalks for a pillow. Suffering from the cold we nevertheless slept pretty well, and were in good spirits for the battle which occurred next morning.

We were ignorant of the real position and strength of the enemy, and knew not on which side of the bayou to expect the principal resistance. So the Thirteenth marched on gaily for an hour or two with banners flying and music from our magnificent band. A scout named Miller was our guide. About nine o'clock, Company A., being deployed as skirmishers under the command of Cornwell, who had just been promoted to a captaincy (*vice* Bidwell, dismissed, Lieutenant Woodruff having resigned), met the enemy's pickets and skirmishing commenced on the left bank. At the same time, very nearly, the scouts of Perkins' cavalry on the other side met the enemy's skirmishers.

The rebel position was well chosen. It was at a bend in the Bayou La Fourche, a mile above Labadieville, at a point known as Georgia Landing. Here they dug extensive rifle-pits and made embrasures in the levee, which admirably answered the purpose of a parapet. Their right wing consisted of Sims's battery, quite celebrated in Louisiana, a regiment of militia, and two or three hundred irregular cavalry. Their center consisted of a battery of field pieces, the splendid Crescent City regiment, and another veteran regiment from Bragg's army, then at home recruiting; and a few hundred cavalry. Their left wing contained a section of a battery and about five hundred cavalry. Their principal rifle pit was behind and almost directly under a stout cypress-post fence, which extended nearly a quarter of a mile perpendicular to the course of the bayou on its right bank. Here their two veteran regiments lay. Immediately in rear of this was a thick wood which concealed their operations, while the open ground in front would leave the federal troops in full view. Most important of all was the fine bridge across the bayou and only a mile in their rear, by means of which they could rapidly concentrate their whole force upon whichever wing of our little army they might select. A narrow road was along the levee on each side of the bayou.

Our main force being on the left bank, we had only the Eighth New Hampshire and Perkins' cavalry on the right bank. Weitzel's plan was to advance cautiously, feel the enemy sufficiently to ascertain his position; concentrate rapidly by means of a floating bridge, if matters wore a favorable aspect; fight the enemy and drive him into the trap at Berwick's bay, where the gunboats were supposed to have already arrived. The floating bridge has not been mentioned before. It proved to be of most vital importance. It consisted of two huge Mississippi flat-boats, which had been towed along from Donaldsonville by mules and negroes keeping pace with the rear guard. During Monday night it had occurred to Weitzel that it might be necessary to cut down the levee, to allow the passage of artillery over the bridge. Pioneers and negroes were immediately detailed with shovels and pickaxes to be in readiness for that work.

The plan of the enemy was similar: to concentrate the whole of their force upon a portion of ours by means of the Labadieville bridge. They attempted the capture of our right wing, not knowing our ability to make a sort of pontoon bridge; or, if they knew of it, yet hoping to strike the Eighth New Hampshire and Perkins' cavalry so quickly that our main body could not bring relief in season.

Skirmishing having commenced in front and on the left of the Thirteenth Connecticut, Cornwell's company being at work, and the artillery on both sides being engaged, and an unknown force of cavalry, infantry and artillery before us, we filed from the levee road into an open field. Here one of our batteries was at work. We threw off knapsacks and overcoats, leaving a few half-sick men to guard them who were soon afterwards frightened away by the enemy's shells! The Thirteenth Connecticut and the Seventy-fifth New York now formed line of battle, the Thirteenth being on the right. It was the first time we had formed line on the field of battle. The Twelfth Connecticut was still acting as rear guard. In front of us was a vast field covered with green, full-grown cane, standing eight or ten feet high. In this field on its further side the enemy were likely to be concealed. As we entered it everything was hid from view, and there was little noise beyond the breaking of the stalks as we vainly endeavored to keep in line, forcing our way through the well-nigh impenetrable growth. Nothing but the regimental colors was visible above it. Momentarily we expected the flash of hostile rifles in our faces; yet it was simply impossible to keep a regimental line. Without orders to that effect the companies gradually fell into a flank movement, and then into one rank, advancing irregularly by the right of companies to the front. Several of the deep draining ditches which cross these fields at right angles were a momentary obstacle. Had the enemy indeed been posted in the field, we must have retired worsted; for we were broken completely into long single files, and it was impossible to see half-a-dozen rods ahead. Emerging at last, breathless with the extraordinary fatigue of that rapid march, were Col. Birge, one captain, and one private, William Keating, Co. H. "Well, captain, where's the Thirteenth?" said Birge. "There's one of them," he replied, pointing to Keating; "the rest of them will be here as soon as they can squeeze through." They were already arriving in squads, and soon nearly all had come up. "Where's your horse?" said Colonel Birge to Lieutenant-colonel Warner. "I couldn't get him through, sir," was the reply. "I got mine through," said Birge, patting with pride the splendid animal he rode, a perfect Bucephalus.

While we were struggling with infinite difficulty through the cane, the enemy had hastily withdrawn from that side, had crossed the bridge in the rear, and were pouring down to their strong position on the right bank. Weitzel divined their plans. "We are on the wrong track," said he. "The fighting will be on the other side." He immediately ordered us back to the bridge, to cross it and support the Eighth New Hampshire. Having already re-formed line we filed by a flank movement in quick time into the road alongside the levee, which was here about eight feet high and was a perfect protection against everything but exploding shells. These the enemy sent after us profusely, though little besides our colors could have been visible above the levee. Several wounded men, covered with blood, were borne past us. The first man wounded in the Thirteenth Connecticut! Private Coffce, company D, a large fragment of shell mangling his back. Dr. Clary put him in a one-horse cart and sent him to the rear. We passed on rapidly, and soon forgot his sufferings in the excitement and danger.

To make sure work, the rebel commander, at the time he withdrew his right wing, had sent a section of battery and a strong force of cavalry by a circuitous route through the woods to get in the rear of the Eighth New Hampshire and cut off its retreat. His arrangements were admirable. Had there been no flat-boats, nothing could have saved our right wing. But while his cavalry was pressing ours slowly back, not too slowly, and their flanking party was making its long circuit in a swampy road, the two best regiments of Weitzel were in process of rapid transfer across the bayou. The pioneers cut the levee in a trice. The flat-boats swung end to end. The bridge was made. To the astonished eyes of the rebels, it must have appeared the work of magic. They instantly opened a fierce cannonade upon the frail structure; two twelve-pound howitzers responding. Amidst the shrieking of shells and round shot which splashed the water over them but did no harm, the Twelfth Connecticut, which was already on the spot and fresh, dashed over the bridge, and debouched into the open field, a distance of about a quarter of a mile at right angles to the bayou; then halted, faced the front and advanced.

The Seventy-fifth remained on the left bank, and now moved to the rear to guard the baggage trains and the approaches to the bridge.

For the first time the Thirteenth was now fairly in battle. The big solid shot were pounding upon us, and the rifled shells were whistling demoniacally over our heads. We had great confidence in General Weitzel and in Colonel Birge, but not yet in ourselves. Would our men stand fire? Would they resist a cavalry charge? for the enemy were superior in cavalry. Would our men march straight against a bristling fence of bayonets? Would they stand firm and cross bayonets to resist a bayonet charge? Would they see their comrades falling, and still press on in the teeth of batteries vomiting death? Such questions agitated our breasts as the enemy's shot came, ripping up the ground, smashing the trees, or screaming and exploding over-head.

We neared the opening in the levee. Our step changed to the double-quick. The enemy were pressing the Eighth hard, which had just formed square to resist a cavalry charge. It seems they had mistaken the horses of the rebel battery for squadrons of troopers! "File left!" commanded Colonel Birge, and the regiment at a double-quick glided down the bank and upon the bridge, with muskets at a right-shoulder shift. Our pace quickened almost to a run, while the cannon balls were flying over us or ploughing up the water under our feet. Up the steep bank on the other side, and straight out among the brambles and trees! We glanced to the left as we passed them and saw the Eighth retreating slowly, crouching, broken, somewhat disordered, but still fighting, the men blazing away here and there without orders, those in the rear shooting over the heads of those in front or between them! It is said they attempted to form line *by inversion;* an arrangement which brings the right companies on the left, and is very likely to confuse the men and entangle the companies. We reached the middle of the field. "Battalion, halt! front! On the centre, dress!" rang out the voice of Colonel Birge. A shell exploded over his head at this moment, and a large fragment dropped under his horse's feet. "A piece of shell for you, boys," said he smiling. They soon came thicker than was amusing.

The three regiments were now in *echelon* descending from the right, at about ten rods lateral and perpendicular distance between the steps; the Eighth resting on the bayou, the Thirteenth in the center, the Twelfth on the right. The Twelfth were already in motion to the front, when our colonel commanded, "Battalion! Forward! Guide Centre! March!" Through the thick thorn-bushes and among scattering trees, over stumps and ditches, we pressed forward, our greatest immediate anxiety being to keep a straight line. Victory seemed hardly worth gaining, unless the regiment presented an even and regular front: such was the effect of habit in drilling! It gave us real pain to see the line become wavy! There was an astonishing and somewhat shocking quantity of swearing expended, to keep the ranks closed and the companies even with the colors. There was, however, no lagging, except when an exhausted, sick or wounded man fell behind. The Twelfth and Thirteenth were moving steady forward, the Eighth still peppering away in our rear, the enemy's artillery for the most part firing as if we were thirty feet high, when we came to a straight rail-fence, extending parallel to our battalion. "Break it down!" shouted Birge, and the front rank rushed against it striking it with their breasts, and laying it flat on the ground nearly its entire length. The writer of this history, being on the top of the fence when the front rank of his company struck it, was precipitated about twelve feet forward into a ditch, breaking his scabbard but singularly sparing his neck! Hastily re-forming the broken line without halting, we penetrated a very thin woodland, or rather bramble-land, interspersed with trees. Weitzel rode a little distance behind us and on our left, dressed in sky-blue overcoat, smoking a cigar, looking like a common soldier and keeping amusingly cool while so many officers and soldiers were bowing and dodging at every sound of an iron projectile. We were a little more than a quarter of a mile from the rebel line, and had not yet fired a bullet, when the enemy's infantry opened upon us with a rattle like the discharge of an endless string of fire-crackers. The invisible messengers came humming and singing in our ears, and striking a man here and there with a quick *chuck!* that sounded far uglier than the rush of the larger missiles, which can often be seen and frequently give a little warning before they strike. Here we passed the band of the Thirteenth Connecticut, and some of the drum-corps, not standing up or, marching to the front blowing and drumming as if their life depended upon it, as one sees them represented in pictures ; but lying flat on the ground behind stumps, and clinging fondly to mother earth. We passed a few rods further, halted, dressed accurately on the center, and stood a few minutes in line, while the hail flew over us. David Black, private of company F, dropped dead, a bullet passing through his heart : others fell wounded. A large tree stood in touching distance of the line. A quick rush was made by a dozen soldiers and two or three officers to get behind it. " Come out from behind that tree, and go back to your places in the ranks, or I'll blow your brains out !" exclaimed our colonel, with a succession of oaths that sounded at the time emphatic rather than profane. Weitzel came close up. " It's getting pretty warm," said he ; " you'd better lie down." " Lie down !" commanded the colonel. This order did not need to be repeated ; nor did any other. We had passed through the severest test of discipline ; that which requires a soldier simply to stand straight up and be shot at, without flinching and without returning the compliment. It is very easy to press forward in a charge with flying banners and the belief that a moment of heroism will be crowned with everlasting laurels. It is even not difficult to endure a heavy fire at a stand-still, provided one can defiantly hurl back the blows. But to stand immoveable at shoulder-arms and let the iron and lead smash through the ranks, to be a target for a thousand muskets and never deliver a shot in reply,—this is indeed trying.

As Weitzel sat on his horse at our left intently watching the enemy, he suddenly said, " Rise up !" A moment after he remarked quietly, " Their cavalry are coming." Bayonets were fixed, but there appeared not to be time to form square. We stood breathlessly awaiting the onset. "You may lie down. They're not coming," said the General; "We must charge them." "Rise up! Battalion, Forward! Guide Center! March!" Colonel Birge again commanded. The Twelfth were in motion the same instant, and the final grand charge began. The enemy's fire redoubled its fierceness. From their cover in the edge of the wood, and down in their rifle pits behind the stout fence, they had a full view of the four hundred men of the Twelfth, and the long line of six hundred bayonets of the Thirteenth, that came steadily forward with unbroken ranks; while we could see very few of our antagonists, though the innumerable puffs of white smoke and the terrible roll of their musketry and cannon fully revealed their position. With difficulty, by savage threats, we restrained our men from shooting, while the tempest of missiles was hissing past us, tearing through our colors, our clothing, and our persons. Two captains of the Eighth were shot dead. How we longed to return the fire! But our leader seemed determined to rely on the bayonet alone. The flanking force which the enemy had sent round, might fall upon our rear at any moment. Not a second was to be lost by stopping to fire even a single volley. Forward, still forward we pressed, shoulder to shoulder, and still we were the targets of their two batteries and three infantry regiments. Our impatience to be shooting grew extreme, and I think the sweetest sound that smote upon our ears during the war was the sudden crash of the four hundred rifles of the Twelfth Connecticut on our right. Heavens! What a volley! Unable to hold back longer, the Thirteenth instantly answered with a tremendous roll of musketry. Both regiments poured in an unceasing fire, all the while marching steadily forward. The fence beneath which the first line of rebels lay, was splintered, riddled, honeycombed. The excitement grew intense. Will they stand a bayonet charge? See, the rebel line wavers! Their officers frantically brandish their swords and in vain try to hold their men! Many are leaping out of the rifle pits! Many more are fluttering their white handkerchiefs in token of surrender!

How wildly some of our men aimed! "What the devil are you shooting at up in the sky?" exclaimed the pious Lieutenant Clark to private George Hazen, Company H, whose musket ball must have gone that instant a quarter of a mile high!

Both regiments now rushed up to and over the rebel position, carrying it in the twinkling of an eye, and driving cavalry, infantry and artillery pell-mell through the swampy woods. Their cavalry column gained our rear at this moment, but too late, and only discharged a few straggling shots at our rear guard across the Bayou.

The commander of the rebel center, Colonel McPheeters, was killed directly in front of the colors of the Thirteenth Connecticut. He was a brave man, and we could not look upon his manly face without sorrow. A bullet had passed through his head. The famous Crescent-City Regiment lay opposite us, and many of its bravest men were gasping in the agonies of death. We were destined to meet that regiment again face to face at Irish Bend six months later.

The Thirteenth, having crossed the rifle-pit, halted. General Weitzel addressed them a few words expressing the highest satisfaction at their conduct. The regiment answered with enthusiastic cheers.

Captain Tisdale volunteered to go with his company into the woods to pick up the enemy's stragglers, a work which they performed well. Tired and faint from the hard work in the morning, we were yet pushed on several miles in pursuit, but were ordered back near to the battle-ground the same evening.

In the battle of Labadieville or Georgia Landing, we captured one piece of artillery, a brass twelve-pounder, many arms and accoutrements, and two hundred and eight prisoners. The whole of the rich La Fourche country immediately fell into our hands. The retreating enemy, however, were not caught at Brashear City, as we had hoped ; the vessels of the naval force having been detained two or three days off the mouth of the Atchafalaya, unable to cross the bar in consequence of adverse northerly winds, and the rebel General, abandoning much of his stores, having effected his escape with those of his men who did not improve the opportunity to desert. This was effected the more easily, as a very large proportion of his men were mounted.

The Thirteenth lost but few men in this conflict: one killed and thirteen wounded. Private Thomas Reilly, Company A, was taken prisoner while skirmishing, and the whole company narrowly escaped capture, but were extricated by the forethought and skill of Captain Cornwell. The Twelfth Connecticut lost three killed, fifteen wounded, and one, Lieutenant Francis, a prisoner. The whole loss of the brigade was about ninety, of whom the Eighth New Hampshire lost half. The knapsacks and their contents, overcoats, and the like, which our men had thrown off at the commencement of the battle, were inextricably mixed up with those of other companies and regiments, and for the most part, lost to the men. This loss came heavily on them, as the Government, though importuned, never replaced the articles.

This experience of the Thirteenth was invaluable. Our first battle was a victory; and it had been gained with just enough of difficulty and danger to give the soldiers confidence and thirst for military glory.

Next day we marched nine miles further along from Labadieville to Thibodaux, the capital of the La Fourche parish. It was with inexpressible pride that we bore the blue flag of Connecticut and the hated Stars and Stripes through the half-deserted streets, keeping step to the music of our re-enspirited and splendid band. No welcome greeted us from the white race. They closed their doors and window-shutters, or scowled with eyes askance from verandas and balconies. The negroes from far and near swarmed to us. "Every soldier had a negro, and every negro a mule. Many of the blacks also brought with them horses, wagons, house-furniture, provisions, bundles of clothing, bedding, with their wives and infants, till the bayou was thronged with them for miles. The question became exceedingly perplexing, "What to do with them?" Many of the able-bodied men soon enlisted in Butler's three regiments of Native Guards, and more were afterwards enrolled in Banks's Corps d'Afrique.

The second day after the battle the regiment marched to Raceland, a small hostile force being reported there. On the way a rebel wagon, loaded with flour, sugar and whiskey, and driven by a negro who was making off with it, came into the hands of Lieutenant-colonel Warner, then in command of the regiment in the absence of Colonel Birge. The whiskey was issued to the men at noon. At Raceland we found some military stores, and a few cannon on the cars ready to be whirled away; but no enemy.

On the thirtieth we returned to Thibodaux, and went into camp a mile below the town, on the same side of the bayou. Weitzel named the place Camp Stevens. The weather was delightful and the town pleasant. Many of the houses had been abandoned by their owners at the approach of our forces, and some of them were broken open and shamefully pillaged before Weitzel had an opportunity to establish guards. These disorders and abuses, though inseparable from a hostile military occupation, filled the officers generally with the deepest shame. A military Commission for the trial of such offences was convened in the Court House in Thibodaux, consisting of Lieutenant-colonel Merrit, Major Peck, Captains Thompson, Barret, Sprague, Mitchell and DeForest; but beyond the hanging of one negro they accomplished little towards the administration of justice.

General Weitzel occupied the house of a rebel officer on the plantation where our camp was. Colonel Birge remained in his tent. Colonel Warner and Quartermaster Bromley, whose respective wives had arrived from the North, occupied a house in town.

Three or four miles above us on the bayou was the

beautiful residence of the Reverend General, Leonidas Polk, who had laid aside the Bishop's robes for the sash and epauletts, and whose remains now rest in St. Paul's churchyard in Augusta, Ga.; a mournful illustration of the truth, "They that take the sword shall perish with the sword." Nearly opposite Bishop Polk's plantation, across the bayou, is the large plantation of General Braxton Bragg. For a week or two after our arrival at Camp Stevens, we suffered for want of sufficient food, and our new chaplain, Rev. Henry Upson, conciliated the good-will of the soldiers by foraging extensively on these plantations for the benefit of the hungry. There was a vein of fun in his composition, the solemnity of his look and demeanor adding greatly to its effect. One morning he and Adjutant Grosvenor were ploughing up sweet potatoes for the half-starved soldiers; Grosvenor held the plough, a negro drove the mule, and the chaplain walked along side picking up the vegetables and moralizing. The course of the plough was anything but straight, and the adjutant finally becoming impatient at the awkwardness of the driver, ejaculated, "Where in h—— are you going?" The chaplain discontinued his religious discussion for a moment, looked up gravely through his spectacles, eyed the African and the crooked furrow, and said slowly, "Perhaps, under the circumstances, that is a very proper question."

Colonel Warner and others one day visited Mrs. Bragg at her house, and politely expressed the wish that he might at some time meet her husband at his residence. Mrs. Bragg drew herself up to her full height, and with great dignity and dramatic effect, replied, "The place for you to meet General Bragg, sir, is on the battle-field!"

On the seventh of November, 1862, a startling event brought mourning into our midst. Lieutenants Wheeler and Johnson of the Thirteenth, had been left behind sick at Camp Kearney, with other invalids, on the departure of the regiment. On Saturday, the day referred to, they took the cars for Thibodaux. Colonel Birge was drilling the Thirteenth about four o'clock, P. M., when a loud explosion was heard, apparently several miles off, and a vast column of smoke was seen to ascend in the direction of the rail-road crossing. In an hour news came of the blowing up of a car loaded with ammunition, and the instant death of the two officers and ten or a dozen others, men and women. Rumor was rife that General Butler, who was expected to visit Thibodaux at that time, and who actually came next day, was supposed to be on the train, and hence the attempt to blow it up with an infernal machine: but the truth seemed otherwise. Those in the passenger cars heard the deafening explosion, saw the shells bursting in every direction, and the mangled remains of the victims scattered everywhere. Heads were torn from bodies, and limb from limb; the headless trunk of a female being found many rods off, blackened by powder. Many were wounded, and their groans filled the air. The car was totally destroyed, the track torn up, and the engine precipitated down the embankment. The dry grass and cane were immediately kindled by exploding shells, and this fire in turn exploded other shells that lay scattered over the fields. Hastening to the spot with other officers, the writer of this history found the bodies of the recently promoted Lieutenants Wheeler and Johnson, of privates Assant, Company F, and Richmond, Company I, among the rest. The disaster occurred some thirty rods from the bayou. The surgeons were busy with their amputations, and the whole scene was horrible as a battle-field. Champion, our sutler, lay with both legs broken among the other sufferers. The corpses of the officers were taken next day to New Orleans, where they were embalmed, and shortly afterwards were sent to their friends in the North.

Wednesday, November 26, at eleven and a half o'clock, P. M., the "long roll" was beaten, the pickets having suddenly commenced firing. The brigade instantly turned out under arms. The Thirteenth was one of the first regiments in line. By command of Weitzel we were ployed into column, deployed, and made to execute various manoeuvers with the greatest celerity. After a half-hour's evolutions, Colonel N. A. M. Dudley, Inspector General, Department of the Gulf, (familiarly known at that time as "The great North American Dudley"), for whose gratification Weitzel had ordered the alarm to be made, came in front of the Thirteenth Connecticut, as we stood shivering in the intense cold, and there delivered a spirited speech complimentary to us and to the gallant Weitzel, under whom he said he "should be proud to be a brigadier general!" He had been cordially treated on his visit to Thibodaux, and appeared to be in a very happy frame of mind.

On the last Thursday in November, 1862, the anniversary of our Connecticut Thanksgiving, we had a grand celebration. The day was set apart to hilarity and enjoyment. There were horse-races, mule-races, and foot-races, games of ball, and numberless other amusing exercises. Colonel Birge temporarily abdicated his position, and allowed the regiment to choose a colonel for the holiday. They accordingly selected Sergeant Ezra M. Hull, company D, who immediately arrayed himself in the garb of an Indian chief, and issued a series of amusing orders, one of which was, that whosoever should do anything right during the day should be put in the guard-house! He appointed a suitable officer-of-the-day, who arrested all that were orderly and punished all that committed no offence. A great dinner was eaten. The whole of the festivities concluded with a sham dress-parade, in which the line officers in disguise personated the band of music, and the whole regiment, attired in a style that would have broken even Falstaff's heart, obeyed the standing order to do nothing right. Such a Thanksgiving was never celebrated elsewhere.

On the tenth of December were held a review and inspection of the regiment, on half an hour's notice, by Colonel Dudley, who showed himself an energetic and able inspector. Like every other that examined us at any time, he bestowed special praise upon the perfection of our muskets and accoutrements. "Never," said he, "have I seen better belts and boxes in the volunteer service; nor better muskets among either volunteers or regulars."

December 17th, news came of the arrival of General Banks at New Orleans the preceding day, with orders to relieve General Butler. The same day a portion of Banks' force arrived at Baton Rouge.

December 27th, we received orders to proceed to Baton Rouge by way of Donaldsonville. Monday morning, December 29th, we left Thibodaux and marched through rain and deep mud twenty miles on the left bank of the bayou towards Donaldsonville. The roads were in a most wretched condition. The soldiers, being almost wholly unused to marching and far too heavily laden with knapsacks, found the labor fatiguing to the last degree. Like Stonewall Jackson, Colonel Birge marched his men faster and farther than was agreeable to themselves or the enemy. Hardly a foot, the sole of which was not one huge blister. Many sunk down exhausted. A year later, they would have thrown away their knapsacks at the end of the first half hour. A little after dark we marched eighty rods from the levee road to a sugar mill, where we lay on the ground until morning. At midnight companies E and H were alarmed at a herd of goats trampling over them in the darkness, which some dreaming soldiers mistook for a charge of rebel cavalry!

Next day we marched more leisurely to Donaldsonville. The captain of company B crossed to the other side of the La Fourche and preceded us in a buggy, without permission from Colonel Birge. The latter, arriving himself in advance of the troops, was indignant to find the captain already at Colonel Holcomb's head-quarters indulging in social refreshment.

The same day we embarked for Baton Rouge, which is some sixty miles further up the river. We reached our destination next morning, December 31. There we went into camp near a cemetery on the battle ground where Breckenridge had been repulsed in his assault the fifth of the preceding August. By what mysterious influence is it that cemeteries are fated to become battle-fields, as many a one from Baton Rouge to Gettysburgh testifies? This had its fences perforated like a sieve, its trees cut off, and its tombs torn open by cannon shot. In one case the body of an infant was still exposed to view in a half demolished tomb. The demon of war! From the day when the Roman Conqueror strode into the Jewish Holy of Holies, no place has been sacred or secure. Our camp-ground itself was evidently a place of burial after the battle. Digging a few inches under his tent, the writer struck the shoes on a soldier's corpse! But whose?

We remained in that field one night. Next morning we moved to the old United States Arsenal grounds, and pitched tents alongside the barracks. We had hardly established ourselves here when we were moved next day to still another portion of the same grounds, just inside the strong breastworks that were still in process of erection. We immediately resumed battalion and company drills. The captains successively drilled the regiment in presence of Col. Birge or Lieutenant-colonel Warner, and under their supervision.

January 9, Colonel Birge ordered a board of officers, consisting of Captains Sprague and Cornwell and Lieutenant Baker, to examine the sergeants with a view to their promotion to be commissioned officers.

January 26, the regiment moved into camp a mile from town near the Port Hudson road. About this time Colonel Birge assumed command of the Third Brigade, Fourth (Grover's) Division. His brigade comprised the Thirteenth Connecticut, One Hundred and Fifty-ninth New York, Twenty-fifth Conn. and Twenty-sixth Maine. Brigade drills immediately followed. Colonel Warner and Quartermaster Bromley, with their families, occupied a house in town. Colonel

Birge's headquarters and the camps of the whole brigade were on the upper or north side of the town, near the creek that flows past the Arsenal grounds.

On the twenty-seventh of January, Lieutenant Jonah F. Clark, company H, died of fever in hospital at Baton Rouge after two weeks sickness. On the twenty-ninth his funeral was attended by many of the officers and soldiers, and the body was interred with military honors. The sudden bereavement was deplored by all his brother officers, and his memory was sacredly cherished by his company, who knew his gallantry, his patriotism, and his integrity.

Difficulties and disputes having arisen in February relative to the support of the Thirteenth's fine band, and the amount appropriated by the quartermaster from the savings of rations and from the savings at the regimental bakery in New Orleans for the payment of the musicians, several excited meetings were held, and a committee of officers was appointed to investigate and report. Captain Cornwell at one of these meetings made in behalf of the committee a very lucid exposition of the result of his examinations; and the result of the whole was that the officers found it necessary to make liberal contributions and subscriptions to pay off the indebtedness. The enlisted men also contributed nobly to that object. The burden was heavy, but the music was sweet.

Bromley having been appointed acting brigade quartermaster, Captain Cornwell was detailed as acting regimental quartermaster. This office he filled satisfactorily for many months, the command of company A meanwhile devolving on Lieutenant Tibbets, than whom a more faithful officer could not be found.

Great interest was felt by the Connecticut soldiers at Baton Rouge in the approaching gubernatorial election. At a meeting called for the purpose of considering the subject, they appointed Colonel Bissell, Twenty-fifth Connecticut, and Captain Sprague, Thirteenth Connecticut, a committee to prepare an address expressive of their views. The latter accordingly, while on picket duty on the seventh of March, wrote an *Appeal to the People of Connecticut.* This document, after its adoption by the meeting, was extensively signed by the soldiers, then under marching orders. It was published with a portion of the signatures in the Connecticut papers shortly afterwards, and is said to have had some influence in the election of Gov. Buckingham.

For a week we were under marching orders. Two grand reviews had been held ; one by General Augur, one by General Banks. It was known that we were to march against Port Hudson. Indeed that intention was openly avowed. On the ninth of March we struck tents. Farewell to comfort thenceforward. Until the following August, with the exception of three days at Bayou Boeuf in April, we slept no more under tents or roofs of any kind. For five months we were without bed or shelter. Louisiana mud, snakes, musquitos, lice—they soon ceased to have any terrors for us. We acquired what Carlyle would term, "*Toughness plus Astucity.*"

A great struggle of some kind was evidently impending. Grover's and Augur's divisions had long been concentrating. The fleet of mortar schooners, gunboats, sloops-of-war, and iron-clads, was assembling above Baton Rouge. Banks was there and Farragut was there. Banks' record showed that he was at least brave, and no one supposed that Farragut ever knew fear. It is related of the Admiral that, at a dinner in New Orleans given by General Banks to the officers of the army and navy, amidst a number of speeches and toasts the brave old hero was called upon to respond. He made a speech, in which he strongly urged an immediate attack upon Port Hudson and the great duty of self-sacrifice. "Very likely," said he, "it would be very destructive of life. Many a brave man will fall. You, General Banks, may fall. I may fall. Every officer here may perish. But there will be others to continue the battle. There will always be a *last* man, and he will carry the flag on to victory and glory, and will save the country! Gentlemen, HERE'S TO THE HEALTH OF THAT LAST MAN!"

On the thirteenth of March the regiment left in the afternoon with streaming colors and the music of our unequaled band, and joined the grand column moving on Port Hudson. We marched eight or nine miles and then bivouaced. Next day we advanced slowly about the same distance, preceded by skirmishers, cavalry and infantry, till we nearly reached the outer works of the fortress. Colonel Clark of General Banks' staff, while reconnoitering, was seriously wounded. The enemy were reported eighteen thousand strong. Our regiments moved to the places assigned them, and the stronghold seemed to be invested. Companies E and H of the Thirteenth were stationed in an open field separately from the remainder of the regiment, which was in a wood; and these two companies were favored with a view of the bombardment.

The river at Port Hudson is very swift and narrow, shallow on the opposite side, but very deep where the channel curves a mile or more round the foot of the perpendicular bluff, seventy feet high, on which the village and fortifications stand. Eighteen or twenty huge columbiads and innumerable smaller pieces of artillery frowned from the continuous line of works, and were able to throw plunging shot right down upon our decks.

At eleven o'clock, the night of March fourteenth, the steamships attempted to run up past the batteries, and the bombardment commenced all around the works. It was a spectacle the like of which is not often seen. The night was intensely dark. Sometimes half-a-dozen shells from the thirteen-inch mortars would be visible in the air at once; each, like a spark of fire, at first swiftly rising and gradually slower, creeping on its vast semi-circumference up the sky; hesitating a moment at the zenith; then slowly descending, but with ever-increasing speed, till it plunged into darkness, or, with a lightning flash, burst in a tremendous roar. The smaller shells incessantly darted athwart the firmament like shooting stars. All the river front, for more than a mile, was ablaze with the fire of artillery from the land and from the ships, while the countless explosions kept up a continuous roll like heaviest thunder. Near one o'clock our attention was attracted to a bright light in the midst of the hottest battle. For a while it seemed stationary, but increased in vividness, and then seemed to be moving down the river. We were stationed two or three miles back, and intervening woods concealed the blazing mass itself. The fierce cannonade seemed fiercer than ever around it. What could it be? In our suspense and anxiety, the imagination conjured up the image of rebel iron-clads engaging our wooden fleet, setting one of them on fire and driving them helpless down the river, our heroic Admiral fighting to the last. For two hours this strange exhibition continued; the blazing object, whatever it might be, slowly drifting far down the current; the sound of its cannonade growing less frequent. On a sudden, the whole heavens were lit from horizon to horizon with a fiery splendor. The stars sank in an ocean of flame. For ten seconds the lurid glare filled the sky; then came a moment of dense blackness; and then, a crash so loud and deep that the earth shook for a hundred miles, and it seemed as if all the thunder of the past five hours had been concentrated in one terrific peal. The vessel had run aground, had been defended with frantic courage, had been set on fire and abandoned, had floated with the stream, its guns going off and its shells exploding as the flames successively reached them; until the conflagration touched the magazine, and in a blaze of glory the grand old steam frigate Mississippi vanished forever!

An orderly soon rode up and communicated the brief instructions: "The object of the expedition having been accomplished, the troops will immediately set out for Baton Rouge." Much wondering at this Delphic announcement, not yet knowing that Farragut had successfully passed the batteries with the flag-ship *Hartford* and the *Albatross*, we marched at daybreak. A heavy rain commenced falling, and the roads were soon flooded. We waded on mile after mile in the semi-fluid mud, our shoes and boots being filled by the torrents of water that seemed to leap from the open windows of heaven. All day and for an hour after nightfall we toiled slowly on, till we reached a point about eight miles above Baton Rouge, when we were marched by the flank out of the road and into a pond of water, and told to pass the night there! It was an old canefield. The water was from an inch to a foot in depth, with occasional mud islands, stumps, logs, and clusters of bushes. Egyptian darkness was upon us, and the rain was yet falling. Such nights are more destructive than battles. How we envied the horses of the general and his staff, in their warm, dry stables on the other side of the road!

The Twenty-fifth Connecticut were close beside us. They alone, of all the regiments, managed to get a little coffee, a part of which they generously distributed to other sufferers, though some of their men drove some of the Thirteenth from their fires. A few of our soldiers, going about forty rods and groping in the darkness, contrived to get a poor supply of wood, and after a time we had two fires blazing; but there was not room to sleep around them. Colonel Warner, with the surgeon and chaplain and several other officers, gathered around one burning stump, and, after a brief discussion, decided that Bromley's proposition was a wise one: "The only way to keep the water out is to keep the whiskey in." The chaplain hailed every passer by, with, "Halt! Who goes there? Advance, friend, and give the Countersign!" and then imparted spirituous comfort. Doctor C., usually so abstemious, distinguished himself on this occasion equally by his wit, his sound strategic views, and his medical skill. His advice, loudly proclaimed, and enforced by his own example, was: "If you cant take Port Hudson take Baton Rouge; and if you cant take Baton Rouge, take whiskey!"

Many were the uncomfortable nights we passed, but none worse than this. We named the spot, "Camp Misery," and by that appellation we shall always remember it. The generals called it "Camp Alden," but *they* did not sleep in the mud and rain.

Next day we moved three-quarters of a mile to the Mississippi bank, and bivouaced there. We remained till March twentieth, when we returned to our old camp ground at Baton Rouge. On the twenty-second, orders came to hold ourselves in readiness to move at fifteen minutes' notice.

On the twenty-fourth of March the position of Lieutenant-colonel in the Fifth Regiment Engineers, colored, was offered to Captain Sprague. The commission was sent him some days afterwards, but found a lodgment in some "pigeon hole" at intermediate head-quarters and never reached its destination.

The morning of March 28, 1863, we were notified that we should start for Donaldsonville that noon. We actually left at dark that evening, in the midst of a thunder storm. Thoroughly drenched, we embarked on the steamer *Empire Parish*. Several companies slept on the hurricane deck in the rain. Before light the next morning (Sunday) we reached Donaldsonville and disembarked, cold, wet and exhausted. Orders were issued that the soldiers should take no wood from fences and should cut no trees. The most stringent orders against straggling and marauding were issued, authorizing the killing of an offender found pillaging. It was currently related that some three weeks later General Dwight ordered the summary shooting, without even a drum-head court-martial, of a soldier whom he found with a stolen pair of citizen's pantaloons.

Tuesday, March 31, we moved at early morning along the right bank of the La Fourche twelve miles. Next day we advanced about the same distance, and bivouaced just below our old battle-ground of Georgia Landing. The rules against pillaging were rigidly enforced. Not a fence rail could be taken to make fire or bed for officer or soldier. It being the first day of April, Lieutenants Bradley, Kinney and Tibbets were put under arrest by the Provost Marshal, by General Grover's order, for crossing the bayou to purchase eggs!

Thursday, April 2, we marched through Thibodaux to the Terrebonne railroad station, where we took the cars. The same evening at half-past ten we arrived at Bayou Boeuf, where we remained just a week.

Sunday evening, April 5, an order was issued by General Grover, requiring all negroes who had joined the expedition since it left Baton Rouge, to be turned over to the Provost Marshal; an order which many supposed to be tantamount to delivering up the fugitives to their masters. Chaplain Upson that evening preached a sermon, in which he took occasion to say he should disobey the order.

Next day, General Order No. 68, Head-Quarters, Grover's Division, was issued, which restricted officers' baggage on the intended expedition to "a small valise or carpet bag, a small roll of blankets, and what messing utensils are absolutely necessary." We were ordered to store all other baggage in a large sugar-mill a few rods from camp. Accordingly we left trunks, our best clothing, records, papers, and every article we could possibly dispense with on a march. Few of us ever saw any of these things again, as the sugar-house was burned to the ground with all its contents the following June upon the capture of the place by the enemy.

At half-past two o'clock, A. M., Thursday, April 9, we were awakened, ordered to have reveille at four o'clock, cook a day's rations, strike tents, and be ready to march at eight o'clock, A. M. At the appointed time we marched out promptly, and at three o'clock, P. M., we reached Brashear City. We went into a field adjoining the camp-ground vacated the same day by the Twelfth Connecticut, whose tents were still standing. Here our soldiers stored knapsacks and every superfluous article, and we held ourselves in readiness to march at any moment.

Saturday night, April 11, we embarked on the steamboat *Laurel Hill.* Sunday morning, Grover's division, on board the seven steamers *Laurel Hill*, *St. Mary's*, *Estrella*, *Quinnebaug*, *Clifton*, *Arizona*, and *Calhoun*, all crowded with troops, moved slowly up the Atchafalaya river, which widens into Lake Paludre, Lake Chestimache and Grand Lake.

Simultaneously with the departure of Grover's division, that of Weitzel moved towards the rebel works just below Franklin on the Bayou Teche, where the enemy lay in heavy force and strongly fortified. The region is perhaps the richest sugar-producing country in the United States, and as beautiful as a level country can be. On this charming bayou the rebels had at this time the excellent gunboat *Diana*, which, after a gallant fight two weeks before, had been captured from us with company A, Twelfth Connecticut, on board. The plan of General Banks, who was present in person at Brashear City, was to land Grover's division on the shore of Grand Lake at a point where one of the bends of the Teche approaches the lake within one or two miles, and hold the bayou and the narrow strip of land on each side and so cut off the enemy's retreat if Weitzel drove them; or march down on Franklin and co-operate with Weitzel in the investment, if they made an obstinate stand. Having captured this force the road would be clear for an immediate march to the siege of Port Hudson.

The morning of April 13, the anniversary of our landing at Ship Island, we disembarked at a place called Sand Beach, near Irish Bend. The enemy with several pieces of artillery and with some small arms threw shell, solid shot, grape and lead among us while we were effecting our landing. The First Louisiana led the way. The Thirteenth Connecticut came next. We landed by companies, in flat boats, and formed line of battle on the beach. Pressing forward against the enemy, preceded a short distance by the First Louisiana, we drove the enemy before us into the woods a hundred rods distant from the shore. The First Louisiana had its Lieutenant Colonel (Fisk) and five men wounded. This affair is sometimes spoken of as the battle of Sand Beach.

In perfect silence we passed a mile through the dense woods in pursuit of the enemy, who retreated to Madam Porter's plantation. Emerging from the woods, we saw a few of their cavalry a mile distant, their mounted officers riding rapidly to and fro, or watching us with glasses, among a few scattered plantation houses. While the other regiments and batteries were coming up, we improved the opportunity to take a lunch. Late in the afternoon we moved towards them in force, they receding as we advanced. Crossing the bayou bridge, which the rebels attempted to burn, near the beautiful mansion of Madam Porter, proprietress of one of the richest plantations in the South, the soldiers helped themselves liberally to sugar from the large mill that stood by the roadside next the bridge. We marched a short distance further and then bivouaced, our regiment being thrown out as an advance guard. At intervals during the day we had heard Weitzel thundering at the gates of Franklin. We supped on hard-tack and sugar, sent Company A out to the picket line, and forty men of Company H under Lieutenant Deming to hold one of the bridges near us, and then lay down in a lane between two fences.

Showers occurred at intervals during the night, and the regiment got very little sleep on the wet ground. It appears that the enemy, on learning of the appearance of our fleet in the lake near Irish Bend, determined not to be caught between the two fires, and commenced moving stores, trains, and troops up the Teche roads. During this night they noiselessly evacuated their forts below Franklin, completely giving Weitzel the slip. Grover of course ought to have been in position to intercept them, but was a little too late. It was currently reported that the landing near Irish Bend was a mistake; that the understood plan was for Grover to land some miles further up, near Indian Bend, where the belt of ground practicable for military operations is narrower, and where he could have seized and held the only available route of retreat before the enemy could have arrived. All night, it is said, they were passing. If this was so, their object in fighting us the next day was only designed to check our pursuit, or overwhelm a detached portion of our force by superior tactics. But conjectures are useless. It was ours to fight battles; not to plan them.

Tuesday, April 14, 1863, the regiment fell into line at day-break. Some five hundred rods distant was a forest fringed with low cane on the right as we faced it. In this wood the enemy were posted, covering the Franklin road, to secure their line of retreat. General Grover remarked that he thought there was nothing more than a picket there. Mounting the fences we watched the woods for some time, while the Twenty-fifth Connecticut were deploying and advancing as skirmishers to the edge of the wood. We were fully exposed to the view of the rebels, but could see hardly any thing of them. The right wing of the Twenty-fifth first deployed under the immediate charge of their gallant commander, Colonel Bissell, and as these feelers neared the edge of the cane, we watched them with intense interest. Suddenly a sputtering fire opened upon them from the woods in front, which they warmly returned, and they were greeted with discharges from a battery posted a considerable distance to the left in the woods. The other companies of the Twenty-fifth now deployed and advanced to the support of the skirmish line, which had become warmly engaged along two-thirds of the whole front of the forest. An unexpected force of the enemy having been thus developed, General Grover ordered up the rest of Birge's brigade. Rogers' battery was also brought up to reply to the rebel artillery and to the gunboat Diana, whose guns now swept the field. She had come up the Teche that morning. Birge's brigade moved gaily to the battle-ground under the eyes of the whole division. The scene is described as having been exceedingly beautiful; the thundering of the artillery and the scattering musketry giving little indication as yet of the fierceness of the approaching storm. The regiments were all large, the Thirteenth having five hundred men in line.

The wood in which the enemy were posted extended with irregular front about half a mile. Two thirds of the distance from the right of the edge, as we stood facing it, a plantation road leads perpendicularly into the forest. The One Hundred and Fifty-ninth New York and the Twenty-sixth Maine moved in line of battle towards the front, while the Thirteenth Connecticut, having a much farther distance to traverse before advancing directly forward, moved by the flank to the left. Crossing the plantation road, the regiment came "on the right by file into line;" Company B having first been detached under command of Lieutenant Bradley to support a section of Rogers' battery.

The right of our regiment now rested on this road. Directly in front of us was a narrow skirt of thin woodland parallel to the main forest, and thirty or forty rods distant from it. Penetrating this strip of ground, Company A was deployed at a double-quick to skirmish and cover our advance.

A terrific fire on our right on the other side of the road told us that the three regiments, which were separated from our view by trees, had met with a stout resistance; but we did not dream how sanguinary was the contest there.

With a brisk and steady step the Thirteenth moved up in solid line close on the heels of our skirmishers, who were tired out, having been on duty all the preceding night. The instant we began to emerge from the narrow belt of trees and entered the freshly-ploughed field that now intervened between us and the enemy, a rapid fire greeted us from the battery, "St. Mary's Cannoniers," the Crescent City regiment directly in front, and from the gunboat Diana, a single shot of which killed two of our men. The Sharps' rifles of Company A's skirmishers now opened a brisk fire upon the enemy. The Thirteenth, though startled, did not retreat, but continued advancing with as much precision as if at a review, when Colonel Warner gave the order to commence firing. This mode of firing—firing while advancing in line of battle—is not laid down in the tactics. We had used it at Labadieville. It seemed the spontaneous action of the regiment, and it wonderfully supports the courage of the men. Nothing, however, is more difficult than to load and fire advancing without breaking into hopeless confusion. Here the rigid drilling we had received, and the perfect confidence we had in our success, sustained us, notwithstanding the shower of missiles that drove in our faces, and the hellish noise of battle where the rest of the brigade was engaged out of our view. Had we been able to survey that part of the field, we should indeed have been disheartened. The enemy had silently massed several regiments on the right of our brigade, and had suddenly opened such a front and flank fire upon the unionists there as mowed them down by scores. A few moments of stubborn fighting, and they retreated in disorder to the middle of the large field whence they came. Two officers of the Twenty-fifth were killed, and five wounded. The Lieutenant-colonel (Draper), Adjutant, and several other officers of the One Hundred and Fifty-ninth New York were killed, and the Colonel severely wounded. Draper was riding the magnificent horse of Colonel Baker, who fell at Ball's Bluff. All the horses of Birge's staff officers, except one, were killed or wounded. The rebels with their peculiar wild-cat yell rushed upon them and made many prisoners. The moment was an anxious one to the thousands of Grover's Division who were looking on at the distance of a mile or more. They saw Birge's brigade borne down by the weight of irresistible numbers, and the rebels forming line of battle in the open field. The Thirteenth had disappeared from view in the first strip of wood-land, and had passed beyond the new rebel line. The spectators in vain strained their eyes to catch some glimpse of our retiring colors, or looked to see us running in confusion. Our five hundred men were in the midst of three thousand rebels. All seemed lost. Suddenly, however, from the gleaming rifles of our advancing line, there poured a steady stream of lead, every man loading and firing three times a minute, and the twenty or thirty shots per second making with the answering fire of the rebel line a prolonged and tremendous roar. It had no cessation. The white smoke revealed the position of the regiment to our friends, and although they saw that we were in the very lair of the lion, the terrible and unceasing din of our arms assured them we had no intention of backing out. "When the Thirteenth commenced firing," said an officer who was among the lookers-on, "it didn't sound like the other regiments, but there was a steady roll without any break in the sound for near ten minutes." "That rebel battery ceased firing mighty quick!" said Lieutenant Leonidas Hall, of the First Louisiana: "I never heard such firing. It seemed like a never-ending peal of rolling thunder. I knew something had got to give way in front of the Thirteenth, for no troops that ever breathed could stand such a fire as that." Said another officer who wrote a history of the battle for the press, "It was the most heavy, rapid rolling fire to which I ever listened, whether in battle or on drill." Said our Lieutenant Bradley, who was supporting Rogers' Battery at a distance, "I felt a good deal alarmed for you, till I heard that stunning steady roar, and then I knew that the old Thirteenth was all right!" We certainly felt that we were all right, though fifty of our number fell in the first two or three minutes. A little extravagance was natural; and as the writer of this history was swinging his sword over his forehead a rebel bullet splintered on the hilt, and the fragments were buried in his hand and arm. The blood pattering in his face, and a numbness in the disabled hand, first apprised him that he was wounded. All the while we moved slowly forward in line, and just before we reached our antagonists their pet regiment followed the example of their pet battery, and disappeared. The latter did not even stop to carry off its banner which stood leaning there against one of their wagons.

It is impossible to describe the enthusiasm of the men at this moment. A few Parthian shots were still dropping among us, and the gunboat was still sending its iron missiles through our midst. Our men were firing irregularly, wherever they caught sight of a retreating rebel. "Battalion, halt! Cease firing!" now commanded Colonel Warner. The two or three companies on the right, however, continued to fire obliquely in that direction. "What does this mean?" said our commander; "I ordered you to cease firing." "Colonel, do you see those men in gray?" replied Lieutenant Averill, commanding Company D, in the absence of Captain Fuller, who being ill, had fallen out of the column in its advance that morning. At this moment the bullets commenced coming thicker from that quarter, and some even came from a direction obliquely in rear of the right of our regiment. This sprinkling of shot was fast increasing to a shower, and again the rallying rebels began to annoy us in front. The alarming truth flashed upon Warner's mind that the confederates had turned our right, as we had turned theirs, and had actually got in our rear! "What shall I do?" said he in the greatest perplexity; "they have given me no orders. Why don't they send me orders?" "Colonel," said one captain, "if you ask me, I say wheel round to the right and charge bayonets on their flank; or charge straight ahead, and then swing round and take them in the rear." This hazardous advice was not followed, for at that moment Colonel Birge rode up and communicated orders to fall back to the grove, or till we met the supports which General Grover had ordered up. We retired slowly and sullenly across the ploughed field, many of the soldiers refusing to turn from the enemy and marching in the backward step, as dreading to be wounded in the back. Reaching the thin grove, word came that the enemy's cavalry were about charging on the Thirteenth. We halted, fixed bayonets, and awaited their onset; but they did not come. We unfixed bayonets and re-opened fire on the rallying rebels.

The regiments on the right having reformed line, and Dwight's brigade of our division having made its appearance in the rear, the command "Forward!" was again given. This time the charge of our united brigade swept everything before it along the whole front.

In this battle the enemy fought handsomely. They had, it is true, the advantage of position, and were comparatively hid from us, while every movement of ours was distinctly visible to them. This enabled them to concentrate on the right of our brigade, and at first defeat us in that quarter. But at this critical moment the splendidly audacious charge of the Thirteenth broke the rebel lines, threw them into disorder, made them believe a heavy force was getting in their own rear, and wrested victory from their grasp.

But though we had driven the enemy's cavalry, infantry and artillery, the gunboat was still dropping its shells with remarkable precision among us. Lieutenant Wells, with thirty sharpshooters of the Thirteenth and Lieutenant Beaton of Co. E were sent to pick off its pilot and gunners. This contest was ended by the approach of Weitzel's artillery from Franklin, when the rebels set the *Diana* on fire, and it soon blew up with a deafening explosion.

Great numbers of dead and wounded men and horses strewed the ground in front of the Thirteenth, and attested the terrible destructiveness of our firing. Besides the property we were obliged to abandon when we received orders to fall back, the Thirteenth captured two caissons, one limber, four artillery horses; one particularly fine horse, evidently an officers', splendidly caparisoned, and long afterwards known as "Irish Bend;" many swords; muskets; a great quantity of ammunition; sixty prisoners; also the large and elegantly embroided silk flag, bearing the inscription, "THE LADIES OF FRANKLIN TO THE ST. MARY'S CANNONIERS." This trophy has found its way at last to the archives of the State of Connecticut.

Marching away from the field that evening we passed the Ninety-first New York under the command of Colonel Van Zandt. "Good evening, Colonel," said our commander; "Was your regiment engaged to-day?" "Was my regiment engaged?" he answered with astonishment; "I rather think my regiment *was* engaged. The heaviest part of the fighting was done by my regiment. I lost six men." It seems that after Birge's brigade had dislodged the enemy and they were in full retreat, Dwight's brigade arrived on the spot in time to receive a few parting shots from the gunboat. What was our surprise a few weeks later to see in one of the illustrated New York papers a glowing account of the battle, ascribing all the honor to General Dwight and adding in substance, as follows: "Thus did Dwight's brigade, with a loss of six men accomplish in a quarter of an hour, what Birge's brigade had failed to accomplish in three hours with a loss of several hundred men!"

In this battle we had seven men killed outright. Forty-six were wounded. Among the latter were three officers, Captain Sprague, and Lieutenants Strickland and Kinney, neither of whom, however, left the field. Captain Fuller, though not actively engaged in the fight, was struck on the leg by a spent ball.

As we moved away at sunset with martial music, bearing our battle-torn flags and the rebel trophy, our pride was tinged with inexpressible sorrow and many eyes filled with tears as we passed the new graves where First-sergeant Frank E. Stanley, one of our manliest and most promising soldiers, and his brave compatriots lay. While a member of the Thirteenth shall live, the memory of the two Stanleys and the rest of our noble dead fallen on the bloody field of Irish Bend, shall never cease to be cherished.

Chaplain Upson and Hospital-steward William Bishop deserve special praise. They fearlessly exposed themselves, and rendered most valuable aid in ministering to the wounded and removing them to the sugar-house a mile or more in the rear, which had been suddenly converted into a hospital. One of the officers of the Thirteenth thus describes the place: "After my wound had been dressed I visited the sugar-mill which had been turned into a hospital for both union and rebel wounded. Twelve of my company had been hurt—some of them severely, and I wished to find them and supply their wants if possible.

The night was very dark and cold. Several hundred lay there. But one or two candles could be obtained, and the surgeons were busy with these. There should have been at least twenty surgeons, but only three or four were present. Some of those worst wounded did not have any attention for several days. Quite a number of dead lay at one door, and a pile of legs, feet, arms, hands, beside the bloody table where the surgeons were still amputating. Nothing was to be heard but cries, groans, entreaties. It really seemed as if nobody cared for the sufferers, so few were there to assist them. Groping a few minutes among the wounded, for the building was pitchy dark, and the ground was covered with victims, I started for a light. It was nearly an hour before I was able to procure the use of one for a few minutes. I soon found my first-sergeant. He had been shot through the neck; yet as if by a miracle, the wound was not fatal. He was suffering from cold and thirst, and was faint from loss of blood. Throwing my blanket over the poor fellow, I returned to camp and brought him a canteen of hot-coffee, and some food for him and for my other wounded. Detailing William Patterson, one of our most faithful men, with strict orders to remain with them and nurse them, I left, being completely exhausted, sick at heart of war and all its surroundings."

Glorious, yet mournful at best, is death on the battle-field. Happy he, whose brain is instantly darkened by the missile crashing through it, or whose life gushes away in a crimson torrent! But sadder than words can tell is the fate of him who lingers hour after hour in agony, and then dies. The usual consolations of the last hour are wanting: the soft hand; the last kiss; the cooling draught that quenches the mortal thirst; the whisper that bids the soul look heavenward when the earthly eye is growing dim. Alas! no angel graces or heavenly charities there! But yells, curses, groans, the rattle of musketry, the shrieks of shot and shell, the earth ploughed by iron projectiles, the air rent by explosions, the roll of ponderous wheels crushing all beneath them,—a hell on earth!

CHAPTER IV.

Next morning we were marched away in pursuit of the flying foe. Our road lay along the Bayou Teche through a charming sugar region. Madame Porter's plantation, already mentioned, seemed a tropical paradise. The elegant mansion, the delightful grounds, the wilderness of flowers, orange groves with fruit like the golden apples of the Hesperides, Madame Porter herself, a splendidly beautiful woman,—all looked lovely as peace itself in contrast with the ugliness of war. Her young son was taken prisoner, but soon released. We passed the residence of a wealthy negro, himself an extensive slave-owner, who had raised and equipped at his own expense a company of white soldiers for the Confederate service. His wife, it was said, was a white woman, who had come South to teach. How often the sublime topples over into the ridiculous.

That morning a rebel planter requested Col. Birge to furnish a guard to protect his property. "Certainly," said the Colonel, "if you are a loyal citizen of the United States." "I'm a loyal citizen of the Confederate States," he answered with an oath. "Then I can't furnish a guard," was the rejoinder. In a few minutes we saw, on looking back, a dense mass of smoke ascending from his dwelling; a sight far too common in Louisiana.

We marched fifteen miles that day, the enemy occasionally attempting to retard our progress.

Many of them were taken prisoners. April 16, we continued the pursuit. At night we bivouacked in New Iberia. April 17, we passed, as we left town, the carcasses of fourteen horses that marked yesterday's cavalry fight. At evening, after a twenty miles march they made a stand at Vermilion Bayou. Here they set the bridge on fire after a sharp resistance to our van. The Thirteenth marched rapidly in line of battle to the scene of action. The shells fell harmless around us. At night the regiment moved cautiously and silently in the darkness to the river side. No lights were allowed. We lay on our arms in line all night; one of the first instances of a nocturnal experience that became very common. Instructions were carefully communicated in reference to our duty in case of a night attack.

Next morning, Captain Grosvenor was sent with Company I to reconnoitre. No enemy in sight. During the day a large number of soldiers in bathing were frightened by what they took for the advance guard of the rebels, and rushed back to camp in precipitate flight, "naked as when from earth they came!" Companies A and B, having been deployed and advanced as skirmishers, found only a squad of deserters coming in.

The march had begun to be severely felt, and many of our men fell behind exhausted. Scanty rations, nights without cover, no change of clothing, the heat of noon, the cold of midnight, heavy dews, fast marching with the regiment always compact and ready for action, some of us suffering from wounds—all combined to render the intelligence most welcome, that we must rest a day to rebuild the burnt bridge.

The enemy, too, were mostly mounted, and our efforts to catch them would have been amusing, had they not been so hopeless and fatiguing. The battle of Vermilion Bayou was inscribed on the colors of some regiments, and might have been with equal propriety on ours.

At night, a cold, heavy rain flooded the ground, and nearly drowned us. Next morning, Sunday, April 19, we marched fifteen miles in pursuit towards Opelousas. April 20, we marched an equal distance, halting a mile from town. Companies H and D went out on picket. The rest of the regiment, having just got sound asleep, were waked at ten and a half o'clock, and pushed eight miles further to Washington, La. Here the two companies rejoined them next day at sunset.

Much dissatisfaction prevailed at being so hurried along in pursuit of a foe who appeared to have outgeneraled us and rendered nugatory our victories of Franklin, Irish Bend and Vermilion Bayou. One day General Banks rode past our regiment as we lay sweltering in the sun. Not a cheer greeted him. As he passed in silence, our chaplain, Rev. Henry Upson, remarked to several who sat exhausted in the dust beside the fence, "What abominable mismanagement on the part of Banks! I think he'd better declare again, 'The object of the expedition being accomplished, the troops will return to Baton Rouge!'" "Why, Chaplain," inquired the writer, "who, after all, could have done better than Banks?" "Who could have done better!" he replied; "Grover could have done better; Birge could have done better; Warner could have done better; you could have done better ; I could have done better. What's your name, boy ?" he said to a little soldier. "McDonough, yer Riverance." "Well, *McDonough* could have done better ! Seriously, I'd rather be under McDonough than Banks !"

April 22, Dwight's brigade passed us on the road to Alexandria. We moved this day through Washington to a beautiful grassy knoll, half a mile from the village and close to the residence of a Captain Prescott of the rebel army. Colonel Warner was appointed Military Commander of the town. Mrs. Warner having arrived, the Colonel occupied Prescott's house as head-quarters. It was well furnished and contained many fine pictures and valuable books. Part of the contents had been hastily packed but abandoned. Captain Tisdale with his company was assigned to provost duty. Captain Cornwell was still acting regimental quartermaster; Captain Mitchell, acting assistant adjutant general of Colonel Birge, whose brigade head-quarters was near Opelousas ; Captains Comstock, Blinn, McCord, Finley and Fuller, were absent sick ; Captain Grosvenor, present, sick ; Captain Sprague, the only captain present for duty, was in command of the regiment.

April 23, the Military Governor of Louisiana, Gen. Shepley, paid us a visit. April 24, Lieutenant Meissner was thrown from a disloyal mule, and his collarbone fractured. April 25, General Weitzel and staff and Colonel Birge visited us.

April 26, Chaplain Upson preached in the Methodist church, the first Union sermon heard in that town for years. The text was, "Fight the good fight of Faith," with special emphasis on the first word.

Many soldiers and negroes and a few poor whites constituted the congregation. An officer's diary contains the comment, "It was a Jewish and not a non-resistant discourse; in which the preacher fully coincided with the Psalmist in imprecating vengeance on his enemies, and gave an edifying description of what he considered to be a *good fight.*"

April 27, private John Fogarty was shot at ten P. M., while endeavoring to escape from the officer of the day, whose repeated commands to halt he was disobeying. His sudden death was a subject of painful recollection to his company, commander and comrades. A Court of Inquiry, of which Captain Cornwell was president, fully justified the shooting. Next evening at dress parade where Lieut. Wells commanded, an order of the Military Commander was read, reciting the occurrence and warning soldiers of the penalty of disobedience.

April 30, our senior captain, Comstock, rejoined us.

Friday morning, May 1, we marched ten miles from Washington to Barre's Landing on the Bayou Courtableau, where we arrived at noon. Company E, as provost guard, and the sick, were left behind at Washington. Among the latter was Lieutenant Bradley, who appeared to be at the point of death from fever. His condition was long critical, but he finally recovered.

May 2, Lieutenant Deming, Company H, was assigned for duty to the First Louisiana Engineers (colored), Colonel Hodge's regiment. Hours for duty were announced as follows: Reveille, sunrise; sick-call, 6 A M; breakfast, 6:30; drill, 7:30 to 8:30; picket-guard, 8:40; camp-guard, 8:50; drill, 10 to 11;

first sergeants, 11:45; dinner, 12; drill, 3 to 5; retreat, sunset; tattoo, 8:30; taps, 9.

Paymaster Sherman's clerk, William Bragg, Company D, arrived May 3, and paid the regiment next day to March 1.

May 5, the brigade started at one o'clock P. M., and went to Washington and five miles further towards Alexandria. May 6, the regiment marched twenty-two miles on the dusty road to Alexandria, keeping alongside the Little Bayou Boeuf. Owing to the state of the roads, the heat, and the insufficient food, this march was very severe. May 7, we marched twenty miles on the same road and halted at two P. M. in a field of oats, just cut by the rebels. Much of the cotton in the country was still burning or had been secreted, at our approach. All the valuable horses, mules, cattle and pigs had been driven out of our way. However, fresh meat and sugar abounded. An infinite multitude of snakes, bugs, fleas, wood-ticks, and spiders, beguiled our weary hours. We ate some honey here, but its effects were like those of the book in Revelations.

May 8, we marched seventeen miles along the same bayou, passing through Cheneyville. We saw what was said to be the terminus of the railroad from Alexandria, and the remains of a small stern-wheel steamer, which the rebels had saved us the trouble of burning. The road was hot and dusty beyond expression, and the feet of company officers and men were parched and blistered; but the Thirteenth were as proud of their marching as of their fighting. Only twenty-two of our number this day "fell out" sick and disabled, so as to be carried in ambulances;

though there were seventy such in the Twenty-fifth Connecticut, and the One Hundred and Fifty-ninth New York entirely disappeared in vehicles, except the major and two color-bearers! We reached a place known as Thomson's Plantation, where we lay two days and heard heavy cannonading all night at a distance.

Monday, May 11, the regiment left its bivouac at six A. M. and marched four miles to Stafford's Plantation on the bayou, thirteen miles from Alexandria. Here Colonel Warner and two other regimental commanders were put under arrest by General Grover for permitting soldiers and negroes to seize poultry, and carry off fence rails for beds. A bed of rails is made by putting two rails side by side. We slept wedged in between them. Something should be pardoned to the hungry and shelterless. This day a mail reached us, the first for some weeks. Could the fathers, mothers, sisters, wives, and friends of our volunteers, have beheld the intense interest felt in these missives, the joy at receiving them, the sorrow at disappointment, the agony of torture at the least suspicion of unfaithfulness in those they loved, fewer tears would have wet faces that never blanched in battle.

May 12, we were saddened by the report of Hooker's great defeat at Chancellorsville on the third of May.

May 13, the anniversary of our arrival in New Orleans, Lieut-col. Warner, Surgeon Clary, Chaplain Upson, and Captains Comstock and Cornwell, rode a dozen miles to Alexandria, and, after the most classic model, watered their steeds in this Xanthus. Orders were received by Captain Sprague in their absence to hold the regiment in readiness to move at four o'clock next morning with two days' cooked rations. Capt. Finley arrived at evening after several months' absence in the North, where he had gone from Thibodeaux in consequence of a terribly severe sickness. Lieutenant-colonel Warner was released from arrest this day.

Next day we marched seventeen miles back to Cheneyville. Here in the depot was an immense quantity of sugar belonging to the Confederate government, all of which was soon made into candy by our soldiers.

May 15, we marched fourteen miles, toward Simsport, to Enterprise, a place which some wag must have named on the *lucus-a-non-lucendo* principle.

May 16, we marched sixteen miles and encamped alongside the Bayou Rouge. Peter, colored servant of Lieut. Perkins, was tied up and flogged by Provost Marshal Cowie for taking a handful of rebel sugar from a hogshead for his master.

May 17, we marched twelve miles, the last eight of them along Bayou de Glaze to its junction with the Atchafalaya at Simsport. We crossed the Atchafalaya on large flat-boats, rowed by negro boatmen, who sung a plaintive song as they plied the long oars. The Thirteenth had the honor of crossing first. We then marched half a mile to the music of our unequalled band. Finding no one to report to, we sat down alongside the fine mansion of Senator Sims (called also by the contrabands, General Sims, or Semmes). The house was made Headquarters, Department of the Gulf.

Orders were received at night to " have full rations

cooked, reveille at four A. M., and march at five ;" but when morning came these orders were countermanded. Almost immediately, however, we were marched across the road, and into the field between the houses of Mr. Sims and Mr. Tishins. We had just established ourselves in camp, if a prostrate regiment, a few of whom have blankets stretched over them, can be called a *camp*, when we were moved again to another part of the same field, and there went into a similar form. At three P. M. we "fell in" to move again. A detail was now made from every company to carry back rails, and rebuild the distinguished rebel's fence, from which our soldiers had taken a few sticks for fires or beds.

May 18 and 19, our troops were still crossing the river. Col. Warner, Chaplain Upson, Captain Cornwell, Adjutant Whittlesey, and several other officers, among whom was Quartermaster Bromley, visited one of the few elegant mansions, and were hospitably received by the ladies. After some time spent in agreeable conversation, one of the ladies volunteered to execute some music on the piano. She commenced the *Bonnie Blue Flag*. When she reached the close of the line, "*As long as the Union was faithful to her trust*," her emotions overcame her, her voice faltered, tears streamed down her cheeks, and hastily rising she left the room. Much sympathy was felt for the beautiful woman in her grief, and the hearts of our susceptible officers softened towards the lovely and melodious impersonation of rebellion. The dignified matron "improved" the occasion as follows: "Alas! we are no longer united! Once we had one country, one people, one nation. Now we have a northern country, and a southern country, a northern people, and a southern people, a northern nation and a southern nation!" "Allow me in this connection, to remark, Madam," interrupted Bromley in his blandest, politest manner, "that the *second* nation you so beautifully allude to, is a mere *imagi-nation!*" This convulsed the listeners with merriment and restored good feelings at once." "What's the real object of this expedition?" asked Mrs. Semmes." The real object of the expedition," replied the Chaplain, "is to protract the expedition until the quartermasters and contractors all get rich. I verily believe if they had their way they'd keep us in these swamps as long as the children of Israel were kept in the wilderness." "Chaplain Upson," responded Bromley, "I can tell you why the children of Israel were detained so long in the wilderness. It was because they had too many chaplains and too few quartermasters!"

Continuous cannonading was now heard nearly every night. Reports reached us that several heavy guns had been silenced by our fleet at Port Hudson.

These days of rest, though few and brief, were like an oasis in the desert, after our toilsome marches in the burning heat with the enemy forever in striking distance. The fields were covered with blackberries, which our soldiers gathered by the bushel. The river Atchafalaya, believed by some geologists to be the original channel of the Mississippi, was at this season broad, deep, swift, abounding with alligators ; yet our men greatly enjoyed bathing in it.

May 21 was signalized by a free fight in the Thirteenth, principally between members of Companies H and D. Privates Shannon and Doyle of H met in single combat; private Blake undertook to part them; he wouldn't have any fighting, if he had to whip them both. He would conquer peace. Lieutenant Wells, officer of the day, mistook Blake for an active combatant, which indeed he seemed to have become. Wells endeavored to arrest Blake. Private Cashin, another peace man, came to the defence of Blake and drew a bayonet on the lieutenant. Corporal Herbert and several other members of Co. I rushed to the lieutenant's assistance. Other members of H assisted Blake, Cashin and Doyle. Captain Fuller, of Co. D, drew his pistol and rushed into the *melée* to aid the lieutenant; but getting thrown on his back, other members of Company D supported their Captain. Lieut. Norman now sprang to the help of the two officers, whereupon members of Co. K ran to the help of Lieut Norman. So the fight became general. Swords were drawn, pistols flourished, and bayonets thrust. Captain of Co. H, field officer of the day, took the guard and marched rapidly to the spot, bringing the pieces to a *charge bayonet!* The crowd dispersed instantly. No one being much hurt, it passed off as a huge joke. Louisiana rum was at the bottom of it.

The same day our brigade embarked on the steamers *Empire Parish* and *Saint Maurice* for the siege of Port Hudson. Our course was up the Atchafalaya to Old River, thence out to the Mississippi, and down to Bayou Sara. This is some twenty miles above Port Hudson. Near the mouth of Red River we saw the flag-ship *Hartford*, and the two iron-clads, *Lafayette* and *Switzerland;* when the brigade gave three cheers for Farragut. At midnight we arrived at Bayou Sara.

We disembarked, and lay an hour on the wet ground without blankets, a slight rain adding to our discomfort. The regiment then crept cautiously along the streets and out of town in the deep darkness. As we passed one large dwelling house the front door opened. A figure in white appeared, and asked in the sweetest of tones, "What regiment is this?" Some of our boys replied, "The Thirteenth, my darling!" "Ah! the Thirteenth Georgia?" she tenderly asked. "No, my dear; the Thirteenth Connecticut," was the reply. The door shut with a heavy slam. The seraph in white had vanished,

> "As an angel's wing, through an opening cloud,
> Is seen and then withdrawn."

Halting now and then, and, as it were, feeling our way, we finally turned aside half a mile from town into a field which, ominously enough, proved to be a cemetery. The scant baggage of officers on the march had been left in wagons, and we slept as best we might, without fires or blankets. Ex-governor Wickliffe, reputed at that time the handsomest man in Louisiana, was arrested this night in Bayou Sara as a prisoner of war. Here we found people who did not know what greenbacks were. When we explained, they refused to take them and insisted on receiving confederate paper in payment for butter, honey, corn-bread, and milk.

At nine o'clock, A. M., we marched out on the road towards Port Hudson, our skirmishers feeling their way, and the troops making halts about once every half mile. About twenty men of the Thirteenth were hastily mounted and detached as advance guards.

From time to time they engaged the guerilla cavalry of the enemy. In one of these skirmishes private Flannery of Company B, received a ball through the leg, and was borne past us on a stretcher, the first man wounded of the army approaching Port Hudson from the north. Lieutenant Perkins was reported killed, but we were delighted soon after to find him "all right." On this march General Banks commenced picking up all the able-bodied negroes, and mounting them on mules, to the great distress of Governor Wickliffe, who accompanied us on foot. About noon General Banks passed us. We were at a halt. He was alone, and riding towards the front into danger. Our men liked this unpretending manner and his personal bravery, and for the first time they gave him a rousing cheer. Captain Mitchell volunteered as a temporary aid to the General, who exhibited a fearlessness that almost amounted to recklessness.

This day, May 23, we reached a point six or seven miles from Port Hudson. Towards dark a little episode occurred in the camp of the Thirteenth. A certain Dr. Whicher, surgeon of the Confederate line, stationed at Port Hudson, was arrested. He had been seen on horse-back during the day, taking notes from time to time on the road, inquiring the names of regiments and brigades. His appearance and manner excited suspicion. He looked about thirty-five years old, evidently a man of some education and ability, a little under the influence of stimulants, and a perfect embodiment of chivalry. As night approached he was seen riding slowly in a buggy, the orderly of Colonel Bissell, Twenty-fifth Connecticut, accompanying him. Inquiring of our soldiers where the pickets were, he attempted to pass them. Not being permitted without a pass from General Grover, he returned. Two or three officers, hearing the statements of the men, made known their suspicions to Colonel Warner, who called him back and asked him who he was.

"I want to see General Grover," he answered.

"Who are you?" said the Colonel.

"What business have you to ask me that question?"

"I command this regiment, and I have a right to know who's in my camp. Your conduct has been very suspicious, and I demand to be answered, and answered in a respectful manner."

"It's none of your d—— business. I shall go to General Grover, d—— you, and report your d—— insolence," replied Dr. Whicher.

"You are my prisoner, sir, and you need not try to intimidate me," said the Colonel.

"*I* try to intimidate *you!* I swear that's a —— —— bright idea, by ——! I try to intimidate you in presence of the whole Yankee Army! That *is* a d—— pretty idea! In the middle of the whole Federal army! —— —— your army! —— —— you and your army!"

"You infernal puppy!" said Colonel Warner, "you shut up your mouth. Lieutenant Norman, are you officer of the guard? Take this man to General Grover with my compliments. Tell him that he refuses to disclose his name, and I suspect him of being a spy."

"By ——" responded Dr. Whicher, "I'm not afraid to disclose my name. My name's Whicher. I'm a surgeon of the Confederate line, by ——.

I'm not afraid of any d—— Yankee that ever breathed! —— —— your cowardly soul! By —— I'd like to fight you. I dare you to fight! By —— I'll fight you with pistols, I'll fight you with rifles, I'll fight you with bowie-knives, I'll fight you with any d—— weapon you choose." Springing upon his feet in the buggy, he struck his right fist violently into the palm of his left hand, gesticulating fiercely, defying us all and spitting out a torrent of curses. It was suggested by the writer to Colonel Warner to examine his pockets for papers. Norman's guard having arrived, the doctor was searched, and on him was found a paper signed by the commander of the Confederate picket inside Port Hudson, ordering, "Pass Dr. Whicher at all hours;" also, a letter purporting to come from the daughter or niece of a rebel prisoner, praying some friend to intercede with General Banks, humbling though it might be, to rescue her relative from the horrid Yankees.

The horse and buggy were given to Dr. Clary for transportation of the sick. Of the roast chicken and corn-bread inside the vehicle it was rumored that Adjutant Whittlesey made a good evening meal. Dr. Whicher's shirts also were confiscated; a practice not to be justified under any circumstances. Dr. Whicher himself was delivered into the custody of the provost marshal.

This night it rained, and the officers sleeping under the thorn trees, without blankets or even shelter-tents, passed a most dreary night.

Next day we moved, with the rest of Grover's Division, three or four miles to the cross roads leading to Jackson from Bayou Sara and Port Hudson. Here we met Grierson's cavalry. Weitzel was reported closing in on our right; Dwight, between us and Weitzel; Auger, on our left next the river. Augur was reported to have had a sharp fight in which he drove the enemy a day or two before. At the forks of the roads we hastily constructed breast-works of fence rails, logs and earth, to repel any sortie. Had the enemy been wise they would have evacuated the place before our arrival, and the rebel general, Johnson, did send a courier with such orders, which were either intercepted or disobeyed. Sergeant Steele, Company A, was here injured by rails falling on him.

At half past nine, A. M., Sunday, May 24, 1863, the different converging columns drew nearer, and the investment was complete. Birge's brigade moved three miles. The first shot at our advance on the Jackson road, in which our regiment marched, was just before noon. Sharp skirmishing ensued. A labyrinth of woods, lanes, and ravines afforded cover for defensive operations. We carried several outer earth-works and rifle-pits on the Jackson road, and pressed the enemy back within their main parapet. Advancing, the Thirteenth, near the last bridge, struck off diagonally to the right into the woods, and took a position half a mile from the principal line of works. Here we were treated to shell and grape, and two or three received slight wounds. The bugs and vermin were quite as disagreeable as the rebel projectiles. The whole of the woods for miles bore traces of having been a rebel camp, and confirmed the report that at the bombardment in March they had not less than eighteen thousand men. Captain Fuller was sent in command of Companies A, F, D, and I. Holding A as reserve, he sent Lieuts. Strickland, Beckwith and Wells forward with the three other companies to skirmish. Sharp fighting ensued, the officers and men pressing forward with the utmost gallantry, until they were outflanked and obliged to retire. Here fell that brave and true man, Sergeant Torrence, Co. F. He was leading his men, when a bullet pierced his forehead. Three days later we found his body, then swollen and blackened in the sun, far to the front where he fell.

Next morning, Cos. A, F, D, I, H, under command of Captain Sprague, were pushed forward to a thicket on the left of the Jackson road, and about a hundred and twenty rods from the parapet; the other half of the regiment remaining in the woods with Col. Warner. The captain threw out twenty-five skirmishers under Lieut. Wells, with orders to press the enemy's sharpshooters and at night constitute a picket. They forced the enemy back to their rifle-pits, and in the afternoon put a stop to most of the sharp-shooting that had been so annoying in the morning. A shower of balls saluted any one who stepped from behind cover.

We were startled by rapid and tremendous volleys of musketry close to us on the right, mingled with discharges of artillery. It was the regiments of Dwight firing by company, and the rapidity seemed to indicate serious work. It soon ceased, however, at a bugle signal.

A decayed tree in our front by the road-side appearing to be a guide for their artillery, it was suggested to Col. Birge to cut it down. He sent pioneers, who felled it that night.

By direction of Col. Birge, privates Sidder, McGrath, and Ellis Robinson, all of G, were selected by Captain Sprague and sent out at midnight with instructions to crawl up to the parapet, examine the intervening ground, the width and depth of the moat, and the practicability of scaling the works. We supplied them with pistols. They were unable to reach the ditch, but they passed the rebel pickets. Their investigations were valuable, and their courage deserved reward. The pickets of the Twenty-fifth Connecticut fired on them by mistake.

Sergeants Aldrich and Ward, of H and D, were sent to open communication with Augur's infantry on our left. With some difficulty and danger they succeeded. Thenceforward these bases were in constant connection.

From tree-tops we could see miles of fortifications, heavy guns mounted, tents, huts, houses, the rebel flag, regiments and companies marching, and what appeared to be inner earthworks. May 26, Colonel Birge's pioneers constructed a ladder on the main look-out tree at our place of regimental bivouac. Sergeants Huntley, Ward, and other intelligent non-commissioned officers were kept constantly on the watch at the top with powerful glasses. At the foot of the tree was General Grover, or one of his staff. Frequent messengers from Augur inquired about the enemy's movements, and the effect of our heavy shot.

From a captain's diary the following is extracted: "May 27, about half-past ten A. M., the Thirteenth was ordered to the support of Weitzel who was reported pressing into the enemy's works on our right. We moved in that direction half or three-quarters of a mile, through the woods which contained many dead and wounded. The enemy's projectiles were still shrieking through the woods. Here we halted and lay all the afternoon in line of battle, expecting the order to charge, while the dead and wounded were borne in long procession past us. The Twelfth Connecticut is reported to have fought bravely and conspicuously, some of them scaling the parapet. Weitzel's whole brigade behaved finely. Three of his staff were killed. One of them was his Adjutant General, Captain Hubbard, formerly of the First Maine Battery, one of the finest looking and best officers in the army ; another was the accomplished Pole, Wrotnowski, one of the most skillful of our engineers, the builder of Fort Butler at Donaldsonville. The Twelfth Maine charged across the moat and lay all day on the slope of the breastwork. The negro regiment of Colonel Nelson fought with reckless daring, and the most extravagant tales of their heroism are related by the correspondent of the *New York Herald* and others. There was no need of exaggeration The simple fact is, the negroes fought well, and thei heroic conduct reflects honor on their race. Generals Sherman and Dow were wounded. Two or three of the Thirteenth were slightly wounded."

The shower of balls was so severe that some of our cooks dared not bring dinner or supper. Happily we were allowed to lie down behind logs, while the long storm wreaked its vengeance on trees and horses. But the regiments of Weitzel suffered terribly. After his own desperate onset had failed, he is said to have sent word to General Banks, "I have yet to learn that any other general has co-operated in the assault, which was ordered to be simultaneous."

May 28, there was an armistice of several hours, to allow the burial of the dead. We moved at evening a quarter of a mile to the left, to support Duryea's and Bainbridge's batteries. We were here placed temporarily under Acting Brigadier General Paine, commanding a division. This night we slept on arms in line.

Next morning we moved back to the position of the preceding day. Again we received all day a smart sprinkling of rebel balls. They had a cross-fire on us, as the writer learned when, seated with back to a tree, a ball tore off the bark under his ear. Corporal Finnegan, Co. G, received a ball through the arm. To venture from behind cover was sure to engage the skill of the rebel sharpshooters. We became accustomed to being shot at. We were strikingly reminded how vast a quantity of lead and iron may fly through the air and alight on this wide world, without hurting a human being! Some of these visitors came close. One bullet passed through Colonel Birge's coat. A rain at night soaked everything, and we thought how old Cromwell trusted in God, and wondered if he really kept his powder dry. A brisk artillery fire at night awoke us from dreams of home.

May 30 was a busy day. The continued rattle of musketry and artillery indicated that we were getting well-acquainted. This interchange of civilities indicated no personal hostility. We did not feel like hurting one hair of a rebel head. Never did men march to battle with less hatred than the Union soldiers.

The Thirteenth remained all day, and for two weeks thereafter, in a ravine, under and behind the two batteries. Two thirty-pound Parrots of th Twenty-first Indiana were mounted on the right. Th shot were continually sounding past us from the vol canic works in front. The noise was singularly varied sometimes, a buzzing like a bumble-bee; sometimes a fine sharp tone like a musquito's; sometimes, a great rush like a train of cars; sometimes, a real shriek or scream like the whistle of a locomotive; sometimes an intermittent squeak like an ungreased cartwheel The last was the case with the eleven-inch shells o one gun mounted on the turn-table at the railroa depot, which fired all around the horizon every night The Thirteenth boys christened it *The Demoralizer* Further along on the right it was known as *The Lad Davis!* The shells being often empty, their swi rotation caused them to observe a *crescendo* an *diminuendo*, which the soldiers translated into, *Wher is he? Where is he?* till they finally exploded into loud, HERE! The strange sounds were caused b still stranger projectiles; for they fired not only th regulation shot, but such curiosities as explosive bu lets, cane-knives, flat-irons, spikes, bolts, nuts, hat cl ets, ramrods, pig-iron, and wooden plugs wound wit cotton!

The Thirteenth busied themselves in constructin rude huts and caves in the soft, steep slope of tl ravine, the crest of which was crowned with batte ies. The chief fear was that some of these guns, i their recoil, would come crushing down upon our sha ties, for they often fired all night. The writer sle with perfect soundness within twenty feet of on piece of artillery which was constantly firing over h head.

Meantime our sharpshooters were busy at work in front, and rebel bullets sang incessantly through the brush roofs of our huts. The pieces of shell often struck with a heavy *thud* among us. All day the gigantic game of battledoor and shuttlecock between frowning batteries! All night the meteoric shower of bombs!

Sunday, May 31, Lieut. Beckwith, while trying his skill in shooting, was struck by a bullet which carried away one toe. His language on the occasion would have led a bystander to infer that he thought, if profanity were ever justifiable, it was precisely then.

Sergeant Eugene Ward's commission as lieutenant arrived this day.

June 1, Col. Warner and Adjutant Whittlesey were taken sick, and departed in ambulances for New Orleans. Captain Comstock, as senior captain, succeeded to the command. Lieut. Gardner was appointed Acting Adjutant. Large guns and mortars were constantly arriving. We were busy every moment; cutting trees, removing obstructions, making military roads, digging rifle pits, raising counter breastworks, mounting heavy artillery, perfecting our connections, or sharpshooting. The coils of the anaconda were growing tight.

Lieutenant Beaton arrived this day with Co. E from New Orleans, where they had made their way from Washington, La., with a loss of a few who were taken prisoners. Captain Tisdale was left sick in New Orleans. He shortly afterwards secured the position of Assistant Provost Marshal in that city, and the regiment lost his valuable services.

June 2, expecting a sally, our regiment, by order

of Colonel Paine, formed line just after dark on the brow of the ravine, and slept on arms. There was the usual cannon and mortar practice.

June 3, we were occupied with cutting a military road through our ravine, under the supervision of Colonel Paine. This night the enemy shelled us with unusual accuracy.

June 4, Lieutenant Tibbets, one of our best officers, rejoined us after a long sickness. Colonel Paine, for whom we had conceived a hearty respect, was sent to the rear with two brigades, to watch the enemy reported hovering there.

June 5, Captain Grosvenor returned from New Orleans, where he had been a month sick.

Several marine batteries of heavy guns from the fleet were in process of erection. One remarkable battery, called the nineteen-gun battery, was built by Hodge's colored regiment, of which the writer had been commissioned lieutenant-colonel. It was on the extreme left, opposite one of the so-called citadels of the rebels. Everything pointed to the coming bombardment preliminary to a great assault. Rifle pits, saps, mines, and parallels, were preparing.

General Sherman's force was on our extreme left; Augur, on the left centre; Grover, the centre; Weitzel, the right centre; the colored brigade, on the extreme right; Farragut and a portion of his fleet, on the river above; the mortar schooners and the rest of the fleet, on the river below; across the river, and behind the levee, the batteries of the Twenty-first Indiana, and Carruth's Massachusetts battery.

June 10, at midnight, there was lively fighting along the entire front. A continuous line of skirmishers had been formed to feel the enemy's strength on all points, ascertain the position of the rebel artillery, and, if the aspect were favorable, scale and carry the fortifications. Heavy cannonading commenced about half an hour after midnight, and continued two or three hours. A thunderstorm came on with blinding lightning and stunning crashes. The gods seemed mingling in the battles of men, as of old on the plains of Troy. The Thirteenth "fell in" under arms, and stood exposed to the hostile fire, but not participating actively in the engagement. Only one man, private Jacob Kehr, Co. F, was wounded seriously. The Twelfth Connecticut were ordered into the hottest fight, and behaved with the utmost gallantry. A portion of them even crossed the breastworks; but not being supported by the other regiments of Weitzel's division, they were forced to retire with heavy loss. The assault failed on every side.

A tedious, though not copious rain fell next day, which passed rather gloomily; all sorts of rumors prevailing about the assault of the preceding night, and the coming general attack. The rebel sharpshooters were rather more active than usual, and the writer remembers with satisfaction several narrow escapes with Lieutenant Averill.

In anticipation of the expected storming of the works, Colonel Paine, who had returned to his former quarters in rear of Co. A, gave instructions to a large number of soldiers in the use of the hand-grenade.

June 12, private Adam Bach, Co. H, was buried by the falling in of his earth house. With difficulty he was extricated alive, entertaining new views on the subject of architecture! Lieutenant Baker, one of our best-drilled officers, who was sick, occupied a bomb-proof, constructed by engineer John Ryan, Co. G.

The inconveniences to which most of the officers and soldiers were subjected before Port Hudson can hardly be exaggerated. Among other privations there was a great scarcity of water. It was difficult to get enough to drink, and almost impossible to procure enough to wash with. Little of clothing indeed had we; a shirt, pair of drawers, and pair of socks constituting the whole of our underclothing. The most troublesome plague was vermin. The ground had been a Confederate camp, and was filled with rebel lice. When Captain Grosvenor returned, June 5, he asked first-sergeant Sterry, "How are the men?" "Pretty well," replied the sergeant, "only very lousy!" "What!" said the Captain, "lousy? We must get rid of *that!*" Evidently the Captain was not posted. "Captain," said Col. Holcomb to the writer, on the twelfth of June, taking him aside with an air of great mystery and with many apologies, "I have noticed that you—ah—in short—that you—I hope you'll excuse me, for I'm troubled that way myself—I noticed that you—ah—*scratch* a great deal! Now probably you think it's a sort of camp *itch!* But I tell you, its nothing more nor less than—*lice!* The ground's full of 'em, wherever these blamed rebels have been!" "Colonel," was the answer, I've fought 'em an hour a day for weeks past! This morning Col. Birge and staff caught me at it, and asked me, 'Captain, what do you find?' to which I answered in the language of Orpheus C. Kerr, 'only a few harmless insects!'" From the Brigadier-General to the private, every man must give an hour a day to exterminate that vile race. Musquitoes are decent and rattlesnakes quite respectable; but no man can apologize for lice!

The arrangements for the bombardment had been completed; the great batteries on every side converged on the obstinate fortress; the ships with their volcanic freight were in position; the sappers and miners had run their parallels and concealed approaches far up towards and, in some cases, beneath the rebel works; the hand-grenades were filled and distributed to picked men.

June 13, at 11 o'clock, A. M., a furious general bombardment commenced, which the rebels as furiously returned. It lasted two hours, and made considerable havoc among the rebels, dismounting a number of their cannon. It ceased on the appearance of a flag of truce. In vain! The surrender was demanded. A defiant answer was returned. The seven thousand defenders of Port Hudson could not fly and would not yield.

The night following was unusually quiet, as the writer had occasion to note, being up on duty as Officer of the Day. Lieut. Strickland, destined to fall in the early morning, was Officer of the Guard. Together we visited the different parts of the line, and his cheerful animated conversation gave no augury of his swift-coming doom. He had been slightly wounded at Irish Bend; but slight wounds only make a brave man braver; and he spoke of the coming engagement with confidence.

Colonel Holcomb, who fell by Strickland's side, was ardently in favor of the storming. "It's no use to dilly-dally," said he to Dr. Clary, as he was moving his brigade to its position the evening before the battle; "We'll take the place, even if we leave half of our officers dead on the field!"

By some ill-advised calculation Sunday was fixed upon for the assault. Sunday attacks are seldom successful. This was no exception.

At 3 oclock, A. M., Sunday, June 14, 1863, the regiments moved to take the places assigned them for the bloody drama. Some of them lost their way in the dark maze of woods and lanes. The Thirteenth groped to the left till it reached the Jackson road, where we awaited the rest of the Third Brigade, Grover's Division. We were to be the right of the brigade line. The brigade of Colonel Holcomb was in front. We were to act as a reserve. Some regiments were late in reaching the posts assigned. The Twelfth Connecticut was detained more than an hour through the ignorance of a staff officer who undertook to conduct them. The Ninety-first New York carried hand-grenades. The Twenty-fourth Connecticut, each man carrying two gunny-bags filled with cotton, followed the Twelfth Connecticut. The latter were deployed as skirmishers to the left; the Seventy-fifth New York, to the right. As we lay next the road waiting for orders we got a little hot coffee.

It was intended that the assault should be simultaneous on several points, and should be a surprise. The favorable moment, of course, would be the first dawn of day. But before this, the deafening roar of cannon far and near, and the hiss of shot tearing through the trees, told us that the enemy comprehended the movement.

At daylight the Thirteenth passed into the road and marched across the bridge up to a sort of plateau swept by the enemy's guns. We were halted there and ordered to lie down. As we lay there, a large number of wounded were brought past us, and a hospital was hastily established on the slope. The presence of the groaning sufferers, and the rather rough performances of the surgeons, were not calculated to whet the appetite for battle. We looked on in silence.

It is impossible to convey in words any adequate idea of the difficulties, natural and artificial, presented by the ground between us and the enemy. There were forty or fifty rods of standing timber, and then many precipitous, crooked ravines, filled with a tangled mass of felled trees, vines and brambles; and the level ground was scarcely less obstructed; all being in clear view and point-blank range of the enemy's works, from which arose incessant puffs of smoke, as their men fired from safe cover. A winding path, three or four feet wide, occasionally protected by logs, sand-bags and earth, had been dug and cut from the edge of the woods thirty or forty rods along the gullies towards the rebel works, but even this was exposed in part to a hostile fire, and terminated abruptly many rods from the fortifications. Such was the ground in front of the Federal center.

Nothing looks so formidable to an enemy as even and steady lines of infantry, in successive waves advancing with unbroken front and covering the ground from right to left. This was the formation in which we had been so successful at Labadieville, Irish Bend and Vermilion Bayou; but it was utterly impracticable here. There could be no swift deployment; no regular nor rapid advance, if deployed.

At sunrise the Thirteenth was slowly pressing its way by the right flank between stragglers, wounded men, trees and stretchers, to the entrance of the narrow path above described. The place should have been surprised; but the different onsets were not well-timed. The hand-grenades, from which so much had been expected, proved a failure; some were thrown too soon, others did not explode; some were picked up inside and hurled back at the besiegers. A few did their work, and killed several rebels. The head of the column staggered, and finally melted away, under the fire from the fortifications. Owing to the obstructions on the ground, the supports which were ordered up arrived too late, and each successive body of troops had to sustain the whole weight of the rebel fire.

The Thirteenth reached the edge of the wood, between which and the enemy lay the mass of felled timber. Two or three rods from the narrow channel which formed the only practicable entrance to the irregular ground in front, sat General Weitzel on a fallen tree. There was a few minutes' halt. The onward movements of the regiments in front ceased. A report was just circulating that our troops had effected a lodgment inside. The writer asked Weitzel if it were true. He answered with a despondent look, "No. We've not got a foothold inside." "Why can't we go in at once?" asked the writer. "We can go in," he replied, "if the officers and men will only do their duty." "Have the enemy massed their troops at this point?" "I don't think they have," he replied; "and if they have, we've got more men right in here between us and the works than their whole garrison." In this the General was much mistaken, but he probably said it for effect upon the listeners. An aid from General Banks now came up, breathless with haste. "General," said he, "General Banks orders that you force an entrance at once into the rebel works at all hazards." Yes," replied Weitzel; and then, to a staff officer, "Give my compliments to Colonel Holcomb, and tell him to go in immediately." His cool, yet unsatisfied and discouraged air, astonished some of us, who looked for an impetuous charge by the favorite young general. We had unbounded confidence in him, and would have followed him anywhere. But Weitzel was an engineer, and engineers are slow. He did not favor bloody and hazardous assaults, either at Port Hudson or at Fort Fisher. He had no faith in storming columns. It was currently reported that he said to General Banks, "I can take Port Hudson without losing a man; and I should consider such a victory as evidencing higher generalship than to carry the place by storm and lose a thousand men." We left Weitzel sitting on his log, with the shot flying over his head, and we pressed forward to support Holcomb.

The narrow path, in many places a mere ditch, was obstructed by dead and wounded, by men carrying stretchers, and by stragglers making their way to the rear. Every available cover behind stumps, logs or earth, every little depression of the ground that could shelter from the enemy's fire, was occupied. Hand-grenades were scattered along the path; also muskets, bayonets, cartridge-boxes and belts, gunny-bags filled with cotton, and here and there pools of blood. We crowded along by the flank in four or two ranks, or in single file, towards the indescribable din. The van of the Thirteenth issued from the dry ditch into the open space, and the regiment caught a glimpse of Colonel Holcomb, who had just received Banks's last order through Weitzel, and had commenced a brief speech to his men. "There's Colonel Holcomb!" shouted a score of voices, and a cheer, long and loud, rose from the Thirteenth Connecticut as they recognized their old major. They rushed forward at the instant on the sloping broken ground, to where Holcomb was haranguing his men. The fire from the breastworks perceptibly slackened at the voice of the regiment, and the writer saw a few rebels turn and run from the parapet. But the blaze of musketry was soon re-kindled, fierce as ever. An unsteady mass of men of different regiments, a mob rather than an army, the various commands seeming blended, some enthusiastic and eager, but most of them evidently disheartened and shrugging their shoulders, were listening to his fiery emphasis His speech was like the growl and roar of a lion; upbraiding some, threatening some, encouraging others; and concluding with, "All I ask of you is to follow me! Will you follow me?" "Yes! Yes!" shouted fifty voices; but far more were silent. The majority sat sullen and cowed. Not satisfied with the response, he turned to the Thirteenth Connecticut, about half of whom had now arrived, and he exclaimed, "There's the glorious old Thirteenth Connecticut! I know they'll follow me! Thirteenth, I'll lead you!" Glancing round and seeing nothing of the senior captain, the writer, being next in rank, answered in a loud voice, "The Thirteenth Connecticut will follow Colonel Holcomb anywhere." A rousing cheer sanctioned the promise. The following, from the writer's diary, was written next day:

"After urging the officers and soldiers of other regiments, all of whom were huddled together in the narrow hollow, or piled behind logs and stumps, he [Holcomb] called on the Thirteenth to follow him. Our regiment at this moment was somewhat broken and scattered, and the companies were partly mixed with those of other regiments. Some of our best companies on the right were separated from us: the broken ground and mass of logs in the gullies and on the hillside, near the top of which Colonel Holcomb and other officers stood, prevented anything like a regimental front. My immediate attention was, of course, given to my own company, which had kept together admirably, one sergeant and three privates only having become separated from the rest and left behind in the melée. Not seeing our regimental commander, who was supposed to be on the right, and who, we thought, had perhaps fallen, I asked Colonel Holcomb to delay the charge a moment, until I could get the left wing into position to make a united movement. He assented. I immediately commenced moving my own and the other companies obliquely to the left and front, to give breadth to our advance and secure something like a line of battle; meanwhile endeavoring to encourage the men by exhortation and example. I tried to bring the men, every man, as far to the front as possible, before starting, without exposing them too much; in order that, at the word, each might have the least practicable distance to pass while making a simultaneous spring on the rebels. But before these arrangements had been completed, and almost before they had begun, Col. Holcomb, swinging his sword, gave the command, "*Forward!*" The Thirteenth leaped to the front, mixed with the troops of Holcomb's brigade. The impassable portions of the ground instantly destroyed the unity of the advance. The right of the regiment was upon and beyond the bluff; the center, near Holcomb, but moving diagonally to the left with infinite difficulty. The portion of troops nearest Holcomb, not having so much rough ground to pass over, got in advance of the others, and became instantly exposed to the hottest fire. For the most part they were shot down at once. Colonel Holcomb dropped dead: Lieutenant Strickland fell near him, each pierced through the head by a musket ball. Captain Grosvenor received a bullet through the arm. Acting Adjutant Gardner, of the Thirteenth, was wounded in the throat. Colonel Gerard, Twenty-second Maine, Colonel Morgan, Ninetieth New-York, each commanding a brigade; Colonel Hubbard, Twenty-sixth Maine, Major Burt, One hundred fifty-ninth New-York, and some other field officers, were present; but no one took the place of Colonel Holcomb, who alone of the field officers seemed to do anything effective, or have any heart or faith in the movement. The left wing, still struggling forward, now got in advance of the right and of the troops massed about Colonel Holcomb, who were fast falling, when private Blake of my company came running to me, and exclaimed, "Captain, Col. Holcomb is killed!" "Get back to your place, sir," I replied; It's no such thing!" "But Captain, he certainly *is* killed! See, here are his brains all scattered over my coat!" A glance confirmed the terrible fact; but we hoped still to reach and scale the parapet, and I instantly repeated, "Get back to your place in the ranks, sir. Forward! men. Forward!" But the troops on the right had almost vanished. All were thrown into confusion by the unforeseen obstacles, trees, gullies, logs; yet we still pressed obliquely forward towards the enemy's works, a goodly number from other regiments being mixed in with and following the Thirteenth. We reached a ravine not previously known, almost under the breastwork, and nearly parallel. Into this ravine we poured pell-mell. It arrested our progress. Most fortunate for us was the shelter it afforded; for we had not men enough with us to maintain ourselves long, had we reached the inside of the works. An increasing tempest of every species of shot and shell now tore the broken plateau, over which we had charged, and no supports could reach us. Colonel Holcomb having fallen, and almost the whole of the advancing column being thrown into confusion by the well-nigh insuperable obstacles, and most of the storming party greatly retarded by logs, bushes, briers, and gullies, and the leader of the movement killed, the assault failed. The right of my company was within a few feet of Colonel Holcomb when he fell; privates Blackman, Johnson, Blake, and sergeant Adams being almost within touching distance of him."

Whoever came up to this point was obliged to run the gauntlet of the enemy's fire; but under the urgent orders of General Banks, when we had partly silenced the rebel guns, from five hundred to a thousand had been pushed forward to it before ten o'clock, A. M. We lay within thirty yards of the breastwork.

We immediately commenced re-forming our companies, and separating the Thirteenth from the fragments of other commands. A rebel redoubt, known as *The Priest's Cap*, projected from the parapet just on our right. The fire from a salient angle of it proving very troublesome, the writer sent Company E under Lieut. Beaton to take post behind a large log on a knoll, and silence the enemy's sharp-shooters. Hardly had they got into position, when Capt. Comstock, who now arrived on the spot, ordered their recall; alleging that they were too much exposed. About the same time Colonels Gerard, Hubbard, Morgan and Putnam, and Major Burt arrived. Captain De Forest came up, an accomplished officer of the Twelfth Connecticut, who richly deserved a brigadier general's shoulder-straps, but was both too modest to urge his claims and too honest to pull the wires and bribe the politico-military authorities. Captain Fuller of the Thirteenth now came, bringing the edifying intelligence that he had just seen and examined the dead body of the writer of this history!

The sunshine was now burning like fire. We suffered greatly from thirst. A peremptory order came from Banks to the senior officer of the troops at this point to enter the works at all hazards. Again and again similar orders came.

> "Those behind cried *Forward*,
> But those before said *Back!*"

Col. Hubbard expressed a readiness to follow, but not to lead. He considered it "a perfect slaughter pen." Major Burt offered to follow with a portion of the One hundred fifty-ninth New York, but did not believe we could hold the ground, if we took it. Col. Gerard said, "If General Banks wants to go in there, let him go in and be d——! I wont slaughter my men in that way." Col. Morgan said, "If General Banks or any staff officer will examine this ground, and then say we ought to make the assault, I'll make it. Tell General Banks I've sent for an engineer to examine the position." Col. Hubbard asked: "Col. Gerard, If I'll lead with my brigade, will you follow and support me?" He answered in the affirmative. But Col. Hubbard did not lead. Capt. Comstock said he was ready to follow with the Thirteenth Connecticut, but thought it nonsense to undertake it. Col. Day of the One hundred thirty-first New York, came up with his coat off. Said he, "I started out this morning with the determination to be a h—— of a fellow! I've been a h—— of a fellow long enough. If anybody else wants to be a h—— of a fellow, I've no objections! But it's too d—— risky!" Cols. Gerard and Morgan were soon afterwards dishonorably dismissed for disobedience of orders.

So the assault was not renewed. Meanwhile the lead and iron rained around us, and the accuracy of the shots was truly astonishing. Some of our men were hit lying in the very bottom of the gully, as if the balls dropped from the sky!

Repeated orders to renew the assault on the works in our front, which General Banks seemed to consider the key to the town, having been disregarded, he sent Lieut. Francis, former Adjutant of Wilson's Zouaves, with a request for the formation of a storming column of two hundred men to lead the attack, promising promotion to every officer and man who should volunteer. Col. Hubbard promulgated the order. Lieut. Beaton, of Co. E, Thirteenth Conn., was the first officer to volunteer. Private Blackman, of Co. H, Thirteenth Conn., was the first enlisted man. An officer of the One hundred fifty-ninth New York came forward, and said he had twenty men who would follow him in. Capt. Sprague notified Col. Hubbard and his company that he would be one of the number. Volunteers were fast coming forward, and the two hundred would soon have been obtained. Meanwhile a sort of council of war was held among the regimental commanders, every one of whom opposed the scheme. Capt. Comstock well expressed the prevailing views by saying, "I think, if we're going in at all, we ought to go in by regiments under the senior officer; and this talk of a storming column of two hundred men is all boys' play." In the midst of this discussion, and when the requisite number had been nearly made up, an aid of General Banks came in haste, countermanding the order; assigning as a reason, "Two heavy lines of rebel infantry have been discovered, lying back a little distance inside the works, at this point."

On the summit of a hillock in rear of our right wing, and near the spot where Col. Holcomb fell, was a little breast-work of cotton-bags, which some of our union soldiers had rolled before them as a protection against rebel bullets. Behind these, some half-a-dozen brave men kept firing on the enemy. One by one they were struck by the shot, which constantly knocked up the dust around them. For a long time this continued, until the cotton took fire, either from a shell or from their own muskets. As it burned we saw it apparently consume the clothing and the bodies of the dead and dying. As it reached their cartridge-boxes, we saw the quick explosions of ammunition. Here and there in sight lay some of our soldiers behind stumps, the perpetual target of the rebel riflemen. One soldier in particular lay on his back, perfectly straight and motionless behind a little stump; but, about once every half-hour he would cautiously turn over, aim, fire, and re-load! We could not go to their assistance, nor could they stir from their perilous position.

Of all that fell on this fourteenth of June, no one was more sincerely lamented than Charlie Merwin, drummer of Co. A; a handsome boy of seventeen years, brave, amiable, patriotic, a favorite with all. Before light he had voluntarily gone to the bloody front, to assist in carrying off the wounded. At eleven in the morning, while carrying a wounded man on a stretcher, to get him out of the reach of bullets, a rifle ball shattered his leg. It was amputated on the field. He was taken to New Orleans. A second and a third amputation became necessary, and he sank under the terrible suffering.

The day passed slowly—a long, exciting, mournful day. The fierce sun above us, we were tormented by thirst. We were faint with hunger. Every heart was sad at the loss of comrades. But we kept the enemy on the *qui vive*. Cos. A and B were stationed on the brow of the ravine, just below the rebel line of fire. Here they acted as sharp-shooters. Not the smallest part of an enemy could be exposed without receiving a volley of bullets. At dusk Cos. C, I, H and K relieved them, and crawled up to within two or three rods of the parapet.

At ten o'clock at night a staff officer crept up to our position, and whispered to us that the enemy were supposed to be massing on the right, to cut their way out, and that the Thirteenth was to move back in silence to the position of the preceding night, and hold itself in readiness to assist in repelling them. This change was noiselessly executed. No sortie was made. Next morning saw us in our old position under the two batteries.

Such was the action of the Thirteenth Connecticut in the combined assault on Port Hudson, June 14, 1863. Surely, it was by no fault of ours that it did not succeed. We had done all that was required of us, and more. We had been ordered to act as a *reserve;* but by the sheer force of enthusiasm and without positive orders, the Thirteenth rose equal to the emergency and worked their way up to the "fore-front of the hottest battle."

And now came the fearfully depressing realization that all these efforts, all this heroism, and all this appalling carnage, had failed. Yonder still floated the rebel flag. Their batteries still dammed the great river. From their bands inside, we could hear their jubilant secession music. We were defeated! With bitter anguish we thought of this, and then of the unavailing slaughter of our near and dear friends. Two thousand men, young, gallant, brave, the flower of our army, had fallen. In the gloomy hospital, or still under the rebel fire on the scorched field, they were sleeping their last sleep or writhing in agony! And all in vain!

No, not in vain! For home, country, honor, freedom, civilization, they had indeed poured out their blood like water. On our right lay the bleeding form of Col. Paine. Besprinkling the garments of our soldiers were the brains of the gifted Holcomb. The thirsty earth drank the life-blood of our loved Strickland, and McManus, and Carey, and Cramm, and Burns, and Merwin; and how many more! In the dense thicket, in the deep gully, in the tangled ravine, in the open field, on the hostile ramparts, wherever the mimic lightning blazed, or the hissing bolt flew, or the huge shell thundered in showers of death, they cheerfully gave their lives. Many a heroic deed of that eventful day will forever remain untold. Many a manly form sleeps in an unknown grave beneath those crimsoned battlements. But, thank God! each patriot name, each self-sacrificing soul, forgotten here, yet "liveth evermore!" And, long as the Mississippi shall roll its mighty volume to the sea, the memory of Port Hudson shall kindle the loftiest emotions of every lover of the human race.

June 15, we rested.

Capt. Blinn, who had been two months separated from us by sickness, in New-Orleans, now re-joined us.

June 16 was memorable for the publication of the famous order of General Banks, calling for the formation of a "storming column of one thousand men;" and memorable, too, for the ready response which the Thirteenth Connecticut gave. No truer, sharper test of the spirit of the army could have been devised.

In the Union ranks all was gloom. The very sun

seemed to shine in mockery. Three weeks previously Gen. Banks had issued a flaming order, concluding with the high-sounding promise that in three days the Union flag should float from the rebel bulwarks! But the determined onset of May 24, and the great struggle of May 27, had both met a bloody repulse. The incessant sharpshooting by day and shelling by night had not lessened the energy of the besieged. The midnight assault, June 10, had been terribly disastrous. The furious bombardment of June 13, had been as furiously defied. And the fourteenth of June! Its smoke had hardly cleared away. Its hundreds of corpses were still blackening in the sun. The groans of its wounded were yet heard on every side. The heart sickened at the horrors of that day, and its great catalogue of victims. The long-continued, elaborate preparations, and the prodigious slaughter, seemed useless. The belief became almost universal that only by the slow process of starving out the garrison could we capture the stronghold. The army had seen enough of assaults and of storming columns.

But could we spare the time? Was there not danger that the bold and skillful Johnson, hovering in rear of Grant's besieging army at Vicksburgh, would suddenly strike a blow at us and raise the siege of Port Hudson?

The Thirteenth Connecticut believed itself almost invincible. We felt that a swift onset by a few hundred men, every one of whom knew how to die but not how to retreat or surrender, would surely effect a lodgment inside; and we believed there were brave men enough who would spring to their support, if properly handled, and give us Port Hudson in two hours.

Such were the reasonings of the officers and men of the Thirteenth when the inspiring call of Gen. Banks, always more potent in rhetoric than in arms, rang out like a trumpet. "To the bold men" of the army and navy, thirty thousand strong who, for weeks had fixed their eyes on the frowning battlements with a determination to plant there the flag of liberty, he appealed with singular eloquence and power. He promised a medal of honor to every soldier and promotion to every officer, who should volunteer to form a "Storming Column of One Thousand Men" and lead the final charge. The Thirteenth neither asked nor cared for these rewards, nor ever murmured because the promises so lavishly made were never kept. A few of us were brevetted in the summer of 1866 for gallantry at Port Hudson in the summer of 1863.

The different companies were called up and the order (General Order No. 49, Headquarters, Department of the Gulf,) was read to them. Volunteering immediately commenced. Three days after its publication one hundred and fifty men of the Thirteenth Connecticut had volunteered. When it became known that our old Colonel, Birge, was to lead them, there were many other accessions. In three weeks, sixteen officers and two hundred and twenty-five enlisted men of the Thirteenth had joined this *forlorn hope!* This comprised more than half of those who were present for duty. No other regiment, nor even any other whole brigade furnished so many men for the enterprise as the Thirteenth Connecticut alone. The nearest approach to this was made by the two colored regiments, which together gave two hundred men. The Twenty-fifth Connecticut, never lacking in patriotism or courage, sent but one officer and three enlisted men; whose names were several times published, as evincing remarkable patriotism, in the Annual Report of the Adjutant-General of the State of Connecticut. Of the companies in the Thirteenth, G did the best, nearly every man present for duty having volunteered. This was due in part to the active exertions of first-sergeant Charles B. Hutchins, afterwards lieutenant in the Corps d'Afrique. Among the non-combatants who volunteered for this perilous work was Hospital Steward William Bishop, Thirteenth Connecticut, as brave a man as ever faced death in battle.

It is not to be supposed that all were actuated by patriotism alone. Possibly none were entirely free from selfish promptings. Some were ambitious of distinction; others may have believed they could not honorably refuse. Some perhaps were quite unaware of the fearful risk. A few may have been weary of life. A few too were suspected of designing to recede at the last moment, on some pretence; meanwhile, and perhaps always, enjoying the reputation of being brave, patriotic men.

But the majority knew the situation, reverenced the call of their country, and freely offered to sacrifice on her altar even life itself. It was the fruit of no sudden impulse, no thoughtless folly, no reckless desperation. Calmly and widely they surveyed the field of danger and of duty, weighed the considerations, calculated the contingencies, and prepared for either fate,—to share the reward of the victorious brave, or die like the nameless three hundred at Thermopylae.

The author of this history wrote out the last will

and testament of some of these men; witnessed the transfer of money, watches, jewelry, and keepsakes to their comrades who were to remain behind; and wrote letters giving what they feared were their last messages to the loved ones at home. From an officer's diary is extracted the following memorandum, dated June 16, 1863, just after he had volunteered in the storming column: "I have in my possession about two hundred and twenty dollars in Treasury Notes, of which, in case of my death, I wish to have two hundred sent to my wife, * * * * * * * * * * * * * For her sake I wish my remains to be sent, sooner or later, * * * * for interment. Dr. Clary or Chaplain Upson is requested to see to the execution of the foregoing."

June 19, the Thirteenth moved circuitously to new ground two miles to the right, and within about a mile of the negro brigade. Here those who were not of the storming party remained till the surrender. Volunteering for this forlorn hope was still going on.

June 25, Lieutenant Kinney and another officer prepared a petition to General Banks as follows:

"*Thirteenth Regiment, Conn., Vols.,*
Before Port Hudson,
June 25, 1863.

GENERAL:

The undersigned, comprising all the officers of the above-named regiment, present for duty, having volunteered as members of the Storming Party called for by General Orders, No. 49, Headquarters, Department of the Gulf, beg leave respectfully to request that the intended assault may not be made on a Sunday."

Two captains and one lieutenant refused to sign it.

June 26, the storming column marched to the ground designated for its camp. The place was half a mile from the camp of the Thirteenth. It was separated from the rest of the army and organized in two battalions, which were carefully drilled, instructed, and held in readiness to move at five minutes' notice. Scaling ladders and other requisite implements were preparing.

All the officers present having volunteered as stormers, except the sick, it became necessary to appoint some officer to the command of those not included among the stormers. Captain Comstock, senior officer commanding, accordingly detailed Captain Sprague to perform that duty, who appointed Lieutenant Kinney acting adjutant. Both of these officers were amongst the stormers, and declined the appointment until assured by Colonel Birge that whenever the storming column moved, they should join it.

By request of the enlisted men, non-stormers, Captain Sprague on the twenty-seventh of June obtained from Colonel Birge a promise that the remainder of the regiment should follow immediately in rear of the stormers, as their first support; a position hardly less perilous or less honorable than the storming column itself. This showed that the remnant of the regiment had no intention of lagging behind in the momentous struggle. So the whole of the Thirteenth was *virtually* in the assaulting column.

There being no company officers present for duty with the non-stormers, Captain Sprague consolidated these temporarily into five companies under the command of sergeants. The same day, it being reported that the stormers were immediately to make the assault, he obtained written permission from Colonel Birge for himself and Lieutenant Kinney to act as his staff officers in the expected movement. The band of the Thirteenth Connecticut played this evening at the dress parade of the selected storming brigade. It being again rumored that the enemy were intending to cut their way out this night, the regiment slept on their arms.

June 29, sharpshooters were called for, under the name of "crack shots," to report at Grover's Headquarters. Captain Sprague sent from the Thirteenth privates Maloy, McWilliams, Rice, Adams, Richmond, Austin, Gardner, Haight, Peck and Mathews. At four o'clock, we "fell in" for review by Gen. Banks. He not appearing, we broke ranks, and again "fell in" at six o'clock. Waiting in line till eight o'clock, word came that he was "indisposed;" but would review us next day at ten o'clock. Accordingly, June 30, he reviewed and addressed the stormers and Birge's brigade. His speech was remarkably eloquent and appropriate. In it he promised us we should celebrate the coming Fourth of July inside Port Hudson.

Lieutenant Beckwith arrived from Hospital and immediately entered the storming column. Captain Sprague mustered the Thirteenth for pay.

July 2, the names of the Thirteenth officers in the forlorn hope were taken as follows:

Field and Staff—Colonel Henry W. Birge, commanding the column.

Company A—Lieutenants Charles E. Tibbets, John C. Kinney.

Company B—Captain A. Comstock, Lieutenant Louis Beckwith.

Company C—Captain C. D. Blinn, Lieutenant N. W. Perkins.

Company D—Captain C. J. Fuller, Lieutenant Perry Averill.

Company E—Lieutenant Charles S. Beaton.

Company G—Captain D. H. Finley.

Company H—Captain Homer B. Sprague.

Company I—Lieutenants Frank Wells, Louis Meissner.

Company K—Lieutenants W. F. Norman, Charles Daniels.

This day was signalized by the capture of Springfield Landing, our principal base of supplies on the river a few miles below Port Hudson. A guerilla party held the place an hour, cut off our communications, and took a number of wagons. The wagoner of Company B, "Dutch John," was taken; but had the shrewdness to deceive his captors by pretending to be lame! Getting permission to ride a mule, he rode away at the first corner and soon rejoined us!

Sergeant Brown, Company H, seeing privates Cashin and "Big Dugan" absent without leave, disguised himself as a guerilla, captured them both, and to their astonishment marched them back into the camp of the Thirteenth!

July 3, we received orders to be in readiness to make the grand attack at fifteen minutes' notice.

July 4, we held a meeting of officers, at which resolutions were drawn up by the writer in honor of the lamented Strickland.

At noon Farragut fired a national salute with shotted guns into the rebel works. Quartermaster Bromley was sent to look after our baggage stored at Bayou

Boeuf and Brashear City. These places had been captured by the rebels.

July 5, and no assault by the storming column!

Experienced miners were now called for by General Grover. We sent privates Warner, Wagner, and Barnes.

July 6, a large force of the enemy was reported in our rear. The non-stormers of the Thirteenth were moved back by Captain Sprague a mile and a half near the Bayou Sara road, to repel any attack from that quarter. It rained on us at night, but we had become used to that. No hostile demonstration was made against us, except by a furious and most boisterous bull. But a "strong bull of Bashan" is no despicable foe.

July 7, the regiment returned to camp. The order to keep on hand two days' cooked rations and be in readiness to move at fifteen minutes notice, was revoked by a circular from General Grover. This was in consequence of the glorious intelligence of the fall of Vicksburg on the fourth. An unutterable weight was now lifted from our minds; for we knew that we were safe from any attack by Johnson, and that the capture of Port Hudson was only a question of time.

In company with Chaplain Upson, Captain Cornwell, and Lieut. Kinney of the Thirteenth, and Quartermaster Ives of the Twenty-fifth, the writer rode to Col. Nelson's head-quarters. He commanded a colored regiment. We found him in high glee at receiving a hundred Confederate dollars, which he had just won in a bet with a rebel major inside the works. He had laid a wager that Vicksburg had surrendered. The understanding was that the Confederate paper should be replaced by greenbacks in New Orleans. His interview with the rebels was amusingly told. He had been in the habit of conversing during the siege with the rebel officers in his front, and had delighted in telling them the most egregious lies. Among other things he had gravely informed the major that the besiegers were so pleasantly situated they had no desire of terminating the siege! that nothing would suit us better than to remain before Port Hudson until winter, and we should regard it as a positive misfortune to capture the place! that consequently, we had never assaulted the place in earnest! that we were abundantly supplied with every luxury the New Orleans market could afford! that most of the officers had little gardens near their tents, which furnished lettuce, radishes, onions and all kinds of garden sauce daily! and, particularly, that the Sanitary Commission had established beautiful pavilions, a quarter of a mile apart, all around our lines, where the weary soldier could at any time obtain ice-creams, iced lemonade, and other liquors and luxuries, all *gratis!*

A cessation of hostilities was now proclaimed along the whole lines.

Three commissioners, of whom Colonel Birge was one, met three rebel commissioners and agreed upon terms of surrender.

Towards evening the writer rode with Lieut. Baker along the rebel works, where many a mouldering corpse, a clotted mass of corruption, told how dreadful had been the struggle. Everywhere was wild excitement. White flags, white handkerchiefs, strips of canvas, and balls of cotton, were hung on every part of the works. The long, long agony was over. Here at least the demon of war should be drunk with human blood nevermore.

As a special mark of honor the storming brigade entered Port Hudson the morning of July 9, to receive the surrender. A deserved recognition of the distinguished services of the Thirteenth was seen in the fact, that our colors and our band were selected from all others to grace the triumphal pageant. We marched down near the railroad depot and then turned to the right past the long line of six thousand prisoners. These looked ragged and rough, but in good flesh and healthy. They appeared to be rather taller and larger than the average of our men. We could hear them mutter repeatedly in low tones, "D— you! You couldn't take us by fighting! You had to starve us out!" At the command, "Ground Arms!" they flung them spitefully down.

The ceremony over, our two hundred and forty stormers rejoined the remainder of the regiment. Here we found two rebel prisoners, Lieut-col. Lee, Fifteenth Arkansas, and Captain Hardee, Miles' Legion, Louisiana. They had been intercepted in attempting to escape, having been two days in the swamps without food, trying to pass our pickets. Giving them as good a dinner as we were able to provide, and furnishing Capt. Hardee with a copious supply of whiskey, the writer sent them to General Grover under charge of Sergeant Aldrich. Col. Lee was one of the few rebel officers who never drank a drop of liquor.

With Lieuts. Tibbets and Beaton, and Lieut-col. Weld of the Twenty-fifth, the writer visited the inside of the stronghold.

> "Juvat ire et Dorica castra
> Desertosque videre locos litusque relictum,
> * * * * * * * *
> Classibus hic locus; hic acie certare solebant."

Cannon shot had sadly mangled the church and some other buildings. The ground was everywhere scooped out in enormous hollows, where the vast bomb-shells of the fleet had fallen and burst. The logs which in many places surmounted the parapet, were packed full of lead from our muskets. The rebel artillery bore remarkable testimony to the accuracy of ours, a great proportion of their heavy guns being dismounted. Where our approaches came nearest, extraordinary precautions had been taken. Torpedoes had been thickly planted outside and inside the parapet. Our mines had been met by countermines. Where our column had penetrated with the Thirteenth Connecticut at its head on the fatal fourteenth of June, the inside had been thick set with pointed stakes inclining towards the parapet. But a description of these and a thousand kindred things belongs more appropriately elsewhere.

Such was the part taken by the Thirteenth Connecticut in the eventful siege of Port Hudson. By its heroic conduct in every emergency, and especially on the fourteenth of June, and more especially still in the grand Storming Column of one thousand, the regiment placed itself far in advance of all rivalry. No spot dims the brightness of that page. The regiment stood alone. For days and weeks two hundred and forty-one of its members looked death in the face, and offered all on their country's altar. Full well they knew, for hard experience had taught them, the ground over which they must pass, the wall of fire and steel they must climb, the whirlwind of shot they must face. When all other regiments shrunk back and clung to life, the Thirteenth Connecticut pressed forward, and with the sublimest courage and self-sacrifice they dared the issue!

How delightful the repose that followed! The siege had been one long-continued battle; a battle that lasted forty-four days after the investment was complete. Vicksburg was not so bloody. Seven millions of projectiles had been fired by us since we started for Port Hudson! But now the seemingly endless din had ceased, and we felt how sweet was rest! how prophetic, too, of that "nobler rest above!"

"No rude alarms of raging foes;
No cares to break the long repose;
No groans to mingle with the songs
That warble from immortal tongues!"

CHAPTER V.

On the eleventh of July, 1863, the Thirteenth Connecticut, with the effective men of the brigade, the Twelfth Maine and Twenty-fourth Connecticut, marched through Port Hudson and down the bluff to the steamer *Laurel Hill*, on which they embarked for Donaldsonville. Arriving at this town we bivouacked near the levee, Colonel Birge being in command of the division.

July 13, Colonel Morgan's division, lying on both sides of the Bayou La Fourche, was attacked by a heavy force of the enemy and driven back on the town with a loss of several pieces of artillery, and many killed, wounded and prisoners. The Thirteenth, at sound of the cannonade, fell rapidly into line and marched with the rest of the brigade to their support. We met them as they were retreating in good order. On our way we came upon Colonel Dudley falling back with his brigade. He said to Colonel Birge who had just halted us, "You'd better fall back. You're too far to the front. I'm going back to a position I can hold." Colonel Birge, with a glance at the Thirteenth, replied, loud enough to be heard by the regiment, "I can hold this position." We formed line along the levee. Colonel Morgan was brought past us to their rear in a wagon, having been "sun-struck!" From the levee we could see the enemy at the bend in the bayou, and received a few parting shots, which flew harmlessly over us or fell short in the water. The enemy retiring, Colonel Birge formed the division in line of battle in rear of the town, the right resting on the bayou and the left on the Mississippi. Here we slept on our arms. On this line the division remained some days.

The battle of Donaldsonville was substantially over when we arrived. The engagement was creditable to our soldiers, who displayed their usual gallantry. But the feeble condition of Colonel Morgan and perhaps of some other officers, gave the advantage to the enemy.

It appears that the rebels had come in while we were concentrated at Port Hudson. On the twenty-first of the preceding June they had captured Brashear City and Bayou Boeuf. Fights occurred at Brashear, Bayou Ramois, Chockahoula Station, La Fourche Crossing, and Donaldsonville. At the last-named place a small force of our troops in Fort Butler, mostly invalids, repulsed twenty times their number. All our stores at Brashear and Bayou Boeuf, were lost. The sugar mill and contents were burned. The loss fell heavily on many of us. The government made no recompense. In the affair at Bayou Ramois, Sergeant Blanchard, Co. E, was killed on the bridge by a volley from the enemy.

The military situation in the La Fourche country being similar to what it had been on our previous campaign in that region, it was thought that a suitable land and naval force might intercept the enemy at Brashear, as had been vainly attempted the preceding autumn. Accordingly, orders were said to have been received by General Grover to send two of his best regiments to Brashear by steamer. The Twelfth and Thirteenth Connecticut were selected.

July 18, they received notice to cook two days'

rations and be ready to embark. July 21, at six o'clock P. M. we went on board the ocean steamer *Crescent*, with the Twelfth. We expected to fight the rebels who held Brashear ; yet we left Donaldsonville without regret, having suffered much during our ten days there, for want of tents, baggage, clothing, and food.

Steaming down the river, we arrived in New Orleans early in the morning of July 22. Lieut-col. F. H. Peck, Twelfth Connecticut, was senior officer in command of the troops. At New Orleans, where we lay at anchor a day and a half, off Canal street, we were visited by Col. Warner and Capt. Grosvenor. Adjt. Whittlesey here rejoined the regiment.

During the night of the twenty-second, as we lay at anchor, a singular panic occurred on the hurricane deck, which was crowded with sleeping soldiers. One of them, dreaming we were suddenly attacked by the rebels, leaped up with loud shrieks and alarmed his companions. Half-naked, confused, bewildered in the darkness, they sprang to their feet, four or five rushing overboard. Two were drowned in the swift stream; private Alger of A and a soldier of the Twelfth. The remainder were picked up by a boat from a French war steamer.

In the afternoon of the twenty-third we steamed down the river, and out of South-west Pass at night. Next day we made fine progress till noon, when we got into shallow water, where the steamer left a long muddy wake and often grounded. Finally we were obliged to lie quiet all night about two miles from a light-house. The weather being hot and the troops crowded, we found the steamer a most uncomfortable place. Next day, July 25, we steamed along, getting aground occasionally. We arrived at Brashear at three o'clock P. M. We went ashore. The rebels had hastily evacuated the town previous to our arrival, pitching some of their artillery into the river, burning the cars, smashing their locomotives, and setting fire to some of the large gun-carriages, which were still burning. They had done a great deal of fortifying during the month they had held possession. Fort after fort, one of them with embrasures for eighteen guns, had sprung up for miles along the river on both sides. They were clever in their wit, too. In conspicuous capitals, on the walls of one room at the depot, was the significant inscription, " Office of Major-General N. P. Banks, Chief of Ordnance for the C. S. A. forces south of Red River, and Ex-commissary of Stonewall Jackson !"

We lay two days in a muddy, filthy field near the railway and not far from the depot. The ground had been a camp. At night musquitoes swarmed in numbers and vigor unparalleled ; an indescribable torment.

July 27, we moved three-quarters of a mile to a delightful green plot on the river bank, close to an extensive sugar mill.

Sunday, August 2, our pickets at the bend, nearly a mile above our camp, had an exciting skirmish with a party of twenty or thirty rebel horsemen across the river. Being field-officer of the day, and riding with Lieut. Baker on the bank where there was no cover, the writer was the recipient of close and numerous attentions from their rifles. Deserters coming in reported an intended attack.

August 4, a flag of truce, escorted by a large number of cavalry, made its appearance on the other side of the river. As they came leisurely along, they had a capital opportunity to reconnoitre our position. Annoyed beyond measure at their cool audacity, we had yet no means of stopping their advance. We were delighted when at last a big gun on the steamer *Clifton* thundered the wished-for, "Halt!" Their business being trivial, Col. Peck thought it prudent to withdraw the Thirteenth from its exposed position. Next day we returned in a rain storm to our former mud camp.

While at Brashear, Lieut. Wells, with company I, went on a two days reconnoitering expedition. They embarked on the gunboat *Estrella*, and passed up the Teche, and into Grand Lake in pursuit of a steamer, the presence of which was betrayed by its smoke. On the Teche they were attacked by guerillas, whose fire they answered with artillery. In the midst of Grand Lake they ran aground, an accident for which they believed themselves indebted to a disloyal pilot. After twelve hours they were pulled off by the *Clifton* which had come to their assistance.

Through the frailty of Dr. B., Surgeon of the One Hundred and Thirty-first New York, the two regiments were now left without a physician. The swamp malaria, the rain, mud, lack of shelter from the scorching heat of mid-day, and the heavy dews, and not least, the unutterable nuisance of musquitoes began to tell on the health of the regiment. More than half fell sick. At one time but a single officer was fit for duty. The consequences were lasting. Eleven of the Thirteenth are reported to have died in University Hospital in September. Hospital Steward

William Bishop rendered invaluable service. On the eleventh of August we were rejoiced at the appearance of our tried and faithful physician, Dr. Clary, who had been absent sick for several weeks.

August 12, the long railroad bridge over Bayou Ramois, four miles from Brashear, was completed by workmen under charge of Sergeant Maddux.

August 13, General Weitzel and staff came in the first train from Algiers. A salute was fired by the fleet in honor of his arrival. A scene of great hilarity followed in the car, where mirth and conviviality ruled the hour. All were in good *spirits* for some time.

August 16, Lieut. Perkins was sent with Company C on picket to Bayou Boeuf. Here they lived three days on nothing, while the musquitoes lived on them! August 19, the *Clifton* took them off to Brashear, whence the remainder of the regiment had just started for Algiers by rail.

At nine P. M., the regiment arrived at the Algiers railroad depot, where they remained all night. Next day at three P. M. we embarked on the steamer *Jatan* (not Satan, as often improperly spelled), and went up the river near to Carrollton. Here, for the first time in five months, we were allowed tents. The poorest house is better than a tent, as the poorest tent is better than no shelter at all.

Next day we went into camp on ground formerly occupied by the First Louisiana, a part of our old camp Kearney.

August 23, private Secille, Company F, was drowned while bathing in the Mississippi.

August 26, Assistant-surgeon L. W. Clarke, opportunely arrived. There was much sickness, and he was remarkable for his unremitting attention to his patients, as well as his skill in the treatment of disease.

August 28, orders came at dusk for the regiment to be ready to move with one day's cooked rations at seven next morning. At nine A. M. the regiment left by steamer for Algiers; thence by rail at five P. M. to Terrebonne station on the New Orleans, Opelousas and Great Western Railroad. We arrived at eleven P. M.

Sunday, August 30, the regiment marched three miles to Madam Guion's plantation, lying alongside the Bayou La Fourche, and in the edge of Thibodaux. Madam Guion, though an ardent secessionist, was a kind, true-hearted woman, a lady of the highest respectability and moral worth.

Much sickness prevailed; the result of the hardships and exposures of the five preceding months. For illustration: August 30, Company H had twenty-four nominally present for duty, but all being really greatly debilitated; ten present sick; twenty-five absent sick and wounded.

September 1, Captain Sprague, Lieuts. Wells and Beckwith, Sergts. Wheeler and Sterry, and Corpls. Brown, Baldwin, Murphy and Gay, were directed to proceed to New Haven, "to receive and conduct recruits to the regiment." This detachment left Thibodaux September third for New Orleans; thence, via Mississippi river to Cairo, and by rail to New Haven.

For some months the regiment enjoyed much-needed rest, and gradually recovered health and strength. Under the judicious care of Captain Comstock, the camp was beautifully laid out, the company streets were handsomely paved with brick, the tents were neatly floored, a drum-corps of remarkable skill was trained by Principal Musician Hadley, who had returned from desertion, and the regiment was drilled in the various company and battalion movements. Time passed rapidly and pleasantly.

September 19, 1863, Colonel Birge was promoted to be brigadier.

October 5, Capt. Blinn was promoted lieut-colonel, and Capt. Sprague, major. November 5, Blinn was promoted colonel; Sprague, lieut-colonel; Comstock, major. In November, Sprague received a commission as colonel of the Eleventh Regiment, C. D. A.

The detachment sent to New Haven was detained there at Conscript Rendezvous, on courts-martial and other duties, till near mid-winter.

December 31, Capt. McCord and the writer rejoined the regiment at Thibodaux. We found the men as comfortable as the intensely cold weather, and the pond of mud and water, in which each tent was an island, would allow. Col. Blinn was in command. Major Comstock had left for the North. Captain Cornwell, with Lieut. Meissner had formed a mounted detachment of thirty-five picked men of the Thirteenth, for duty at Gen. Birge's head-quarters. This detachment always appeared well and rendered good service on several important occasions.

The same evening a pleasant scene was enacted at Thibodaux. It was the presentation of a magnificent sword, belt, sash and spurs to General Birge, the gift of the officers and soldiers of the regiment. Captain McCord had selected them with exquisite taste at

Tiffany's, at a cost of about five hundred dollars. The presentation speech was made by Colonel Blinn, to which the general briefly and modestly responded. Other speeches followed and toasts were offered. Captain Darden, a citizen, was present, and in a very happy frame of mind. He had been drinking of a peculiar liquor entitled "Perfect Love," which "casteth out fear" and sorrow! "Gentlemen," said he, "I propose a toast—'*The Mayflower! May she live!*'" Then, after a moment's pause, "Gentlemen, go slow. I am Captain Darden, descended from an ancient family, known in history as the *Dardanelles!* The *Mayflower* was the first ship that came to this country. I came soon afterwards, and selected this beautiful spot for my residence,—the finest country in the world. Go slow, gentlemen! I speak from observation. I have traveled extensively. I have seen the animals in the geological gardens in Europe. Go slow! I have passed through the Duchess of Saxe Weimar. Therefore, I proposed the health of the *Mayflower!*"

January 2, 1864, at dress parade, the regiment was formed in double column and listened to a neat, brief and touching speech from General Birge, who thanked them for their beautiful presents, and bade them farewell as he was going North on leave of absence. Colonel E. L. Molineux succeeded the general in command.

January 4, Lieut. Col. Selden, formerly of the Twenty-sixth Connecticut, arrived, an authorized agent to secure the re-enlistment of the men as *veteran* volunteers. The orders of the War Department not having been laid before the regiment, and it being generally supposed that the Thirteenth had not been long enough in the service to entitle them to re-enlist, little interest had been felt in the subject, and nothing had been done. The time limited was January 5. But one day therefore remained. In that one day, wet, cold and stormy, each company was called up separately in the rain, and the matter was urged upon them. Four hundred men accepted the proposition to re-enlist for three years or during the war; and we only waited for the arrival of proper blanks. This hearty, spontaneous, almost universal enlistment of those men who were accessible, there being but four hundred and six men present for duty, is hardly paralleled in the history of the war. It was fitting that the regiment, which had been so conspicuous for heroism at Irish Bend and Port Hudson, should surpass others in the alacrity with which they volunteered for another three years of hardship and death. The want of blanks was a very serious hindrance. Fortunately the War Department extended the time to the twelfth of January, and again till the first of March.

The re-enlistment was effected under three promises: first, that the men should receive a thirty days' furlough in Connecticut; secondly, that the Thirteenth should be turned into cavalry; thirdly, that they should be promptly mustered out at the close of the war, if it happened within three years. None of these promises was fulfilled.

January 25, Mr. Tobias Gibson called for a guard over his negroes. He had two sons, graduates of Yale in 1853 and 1854; one being then a brigadier in the rebel service. Scores of similar applications were made, some of which were granted.

The wholesome respect felt by the citizens for the Federal officers is illustrated by the instant compliance of a wealthy planter with a demand by a negro woman for her wearing apparel, of which he had unjustly deprived her. She presented the following solemn document:

Head-Quarters Co. A, 13th Conn. Vols.,
Thibodaux, Jan. 29, 1864.

General Orders, No. 1.

Lucinda, colored, is hereby appointed Laundress of Company A, 13th Conn. Vols. She will be obeyed and respected accordingly.

J. C. KINNEY,
Lieut. Com'd'g Co. A, 13th C. V.

January 29, a photographic picture of the Thirteenth at dress parade was taken.

January 30, a General Court Martial, of which the writer was president and Capt. McCord one of the members, was convened at Thibodaux. It sat several weeks. Among the cases tried was that of private Nugent, who had assaulted "Capt. Perry Averill, formerly Lieut. of old D," while Field-officer of the Day. Nugent had seized the captain's horse by the tail, and attempted to stop him by tugging thereat; failing in this, he dragged the captain from the horse and tried to choke him.

The One hundred Fifty-ninth New York occupied ground adjoining ours on the left. The Twenty-sixth New York Battery was half a mile distant on the Terrebonne road. The Ninetieth New York was along the railroad. The One hundred Thirty-first was at Brashear. The First Louisiana was at Donaldsonville. Barret's Cavalry were at Napoleon.

Tuesday evening, February 9, there was a grand *Soirée Dansante*, or *Mardi Gras* ball, at the Court House in Thibodaux. Many of the officers were surprised to find their names in the list of managers on the cards of invitation. One Lieutenant-colonel, having a stye on his eyelid, declined to join in the movements of the light fantastic toe. These were days when our officers were fond of "going down to Terrebonne to shake the foot."

Lasting impressions were made upon the soft hearts of some. Lieut. Daniels married Miss K——s, daughter of the worthy postmaster at Thibodaux.

February 12, a Board of Survey, of which the writer was president, was ordered to investigate the losses of the regiments at Bayou Boeuf and Brashear in the preceding June. Their efforts were laborious and thorough. They strongly urged upon the Government to reimburse the men; but in vain.

February 17, there was a large political gathering at the Court House. Speeches were made by Hon. Michael Hahn, and Messrs. Lynch, Lombard, and Shannon. At evening, Bromley, who had been honorably discharged the service, gave a "scientific supper" at the hotel! He ordered stuffed birds of paradise, the tongues of nightingales and the brains of humming-birds. He avowed himself a representative of the interests of Mr. Flanders, the rival candidate of Mr. Hahn for the gubernatorial chair; Flanders and Bromley being both in the Treasury Department. An animated political discussion arose, in which Captain Darden, one of the *savans*, challenged Bromley to point out the difference between the Hahn principles and the Flanders principles. He instantly replied,

"It's the same as between *char*coal and char*coal!*" Captain Raymond, another of the philosophers at the "scientific supper," interfered, and finally grew personal. "I want to know," said he to Bromley, "how a quartermaster-sergeant can send home eighty dollars a month!" "Why, the deuce!" said Bromley; "I'm surprised! Don't you know the *facilities* we have for sending home money? Send it by *Adams Express*, of course." "But how can he *make* the money?" said the captain. "Make it? Why, that's a reflection upon your sagacity! Make it out of his regiment, of course!" Capt. Darden now chimed in: "Dont you Flanders men mean to put the negro on an equality with the white man?" "Put the negro on an equality with the white man?" echoed Bromley with an air of indignation; "Why, *no!* We consider the negro to be infinitely *above* the white man! We wouldn't degrade the negro, by bringing him down to the low level of the white man!" "Where does the Tombigbee river empty?" interrupted Capt. Raymond, who prided himself upon his geographical knowledge. "The Tombigbee river," said Bromley; "The Tombigbee river empty? Why, where do you empty a bottle of whiskey? Into your mouth! Well, the Bigtomby river empties into its mouth!" So fared it at the "scientific supper."

March 7, a brigade of cavalry marched through Thibodaux, commanded by Colonel N. A. M. Dudley, who had been known by the *sobriquet* of "The Great North American Dudley," but who afterwards, from the splendor of his uniform, was called "Gold-Lace Dudley." They were the advance guard of the Red

River army on their way overland through the Teche country to Alexandria.

Saturday, March 12, Major Comstock returned from a two and a half months' absence North. Lieut. Wells also came, bringing fifty recruits from the State rendezvous. The next week he was mustered as Captain, and Second-lieutenant Kinney was mustered as First-lieutenant.

March 13, General Grover arrived at Thibodaux, and assumed command of the Second Division, Nineteenth Corps. Next day, by General Order No. 1, he brigaded the division. The Second Brigade, under General Birge, comprised the Ninetieth New York, Thirteenth Connecticut, One hundred Thirty-first New York, One hundred Fifty-ninth New York, and First Louisiana.

March 15, orders came to be ready to march at half an hour's notice. March 19, we moved to Terrebonne station; thence, in the morning by rail to Algiers, where we arrived at noon. Here we bivouaced near the railroad. At night a cold rain storm came on, which soaked the regiment and made the ground a lake of mud. March 21, the Thirteenth marched into the old Belleville iron-foundry on the principal street in Algiers.

Friday, March 25, 1864, we embarked on the steamer *Alice Vivian*, a captured blockade-runner. At dusk we steamed across to New Orleans, where we lay till nine o'clock, P. M., and then moved up the river. Next day, at seven, we passed Donaldsonville; at one, Baton Rouge; at four, Port Hudson. At night we tied up to the river bank. On the 27th we entered Red River. At noon we saw Fort DeRussy, which A. J. Smith had captured two days before the arrival of General Banks. At night we again tied up to the river bank.

At seven A. M., March 28, we reached Alexandria. We went into camp half a mile above town on the right bank, quarter of a mile from the high bridge spanning the Bayou Rapides. Along this bayou that morning the long lines of the Nineteenth Corps, under General Franklin, were moving out by the flank. Close to this place of bivouac, some weeks later, was built the celebrated Red River dam. Hardly had we reached this position when we saw a fine large Mississippi steamboat strike on the rocks at the rapids just above us, and settle a few feet in the water. It was a hospital boat, and lay there partially submerged for some weeks. Lieut. Stanley of the Thirteenth was sent with a guard of ten men to protect it while patients and stores were removed.

Friday, April 1, we moved with the rest of the brigade at noon to the other side of the bayou nearer the town. The regiment was engaged in picket duty. April 4, General Birge arrived on the steamer *Battle*. April 7, a heavy rain fell, completely flooding our camp. The eighth and ninth were clear and cold, and the pond of water vanished.

Monday, April 11, at ten o'clock, P. M., the regiment left Alexandria on the steamer *Ohio Belle*, bound for Grand Ecore. The captain of the boat expressed some doubt of being able to reach his destination at the time appointed. General Birge suspecting him of disloyalty, notified him in very emphatic language, that he must bring his boat to Grand Ecore at the designated hour. Private Henry Robinson, of G, was lost overboard and drowned at night.

About three P. M. next day, as we steamed up the river, a sharp fire was opened by guerillas upon the troops who were crowded upon the upper and hurricane decks. It was a complete surprise and caused a great stampede to the lower deck. Our soldiers vigorously returned the fire. The scramble to get out of the way of the rebel balls was amusing. One sergent jumped down through the covered top of a telegraph wagon. The pilot house was riddled, and the negro pilot expressed great wonder at the small dimensions into which a field officer compressed himself. The frantic ejaculations of one captain to another, "Don't delay me! Don't delay me! Get out of the way! Let me skedaddle!" were an inexhaustible subject of merriment to his fellow officers. Two men of Company H were wounded. One of them, Henry Smith, as neat and faithful a soldier as any in the regiment, lost his leg.

Guerilla-firing on boats was a daily occurrence on the Red River. Every steamer must run the gauntlet. The upper works of many were honey-combed by rebel shot. The stream was so low between the high banks that the large guns of the fleet could not effectively return the fire.

At seven P. M., Tuesday, April 12, we disembarked on the left bank opposite Grand Ecore. Here we threw out pickets and slept on our arms in a ploughed field. Next day at noon, as we were pitching tents, Colonel Blinn rode up and said, "Get ready for a fight!" We immediately "fell in," crossed the river on a pontoon bridge, and went through the village, and nearly a mile back from the stream into the woods. Here the regiment formed part of a continuous line of troops, which extended circularly around Grand Ecore, the right and left resting on the river. Below the town on the river bank was the Corps d'Afrique, which General Banks did not allow to do any fighting. Next came Lee's cavalry division, of which Lucas's brigade lay next the colored troops. Then Dudley's brigade; alas! no longer "Gold Lace Dudley!" Then Fox's New York battery; the Thirty-eighth Massachusetts; the One Hundred Twenty-eighth New York; the Thirteenth Connecticut; First Louisiana; Twenty-fourth and Twenty-sixth Iowa; several New York regiments; Forty-seventh Pennsylvania; batteries from Missouri, Vermont and Delaware; Duryea's Zouaves; and others, extending quite to the river.

We found the army greatly depressed. The battle at Sabine Cross Roads, April 7, in which all the beautiful uniforms and all the precious champagnes of the long trains, some miles of wagons, changed owners in the midst of much noise and confusion, "the mules resolutely facing the enemy;" and the drawn battle of Pleasant Hill, April 8, where both armies sent flags of truce which met on the battle-field from which each had retreated; placed our invading army on the defensive.

Grand Ecore, as its name indicates, is on high bluffs. The village is composed of forty or fifty houses, picturesquely situated. The place is easily fortified. It is four or five miles from the old town of Nachitoches.

Shreveport was the objective point of the expedition. What General Banks would have done, had he captured it, is matter of conjecture. It was at that time the rebel capital of Louisiana; but of little importance in a strategic view. It was said he intended to effect a junction there with General Steele pushing a column from Little Rock. Much cotton grows in the Red River country. Grant was appointed Lieutenant-general, March 9. At that time the expedition had already commenced, and Dudley, with his miles of wagons, and "mules resolutely facing the enemy," was far on the road to Alexandria. There certainly appeared to be danger that Banks would capture Shreveport and penetrate Northern Texas. We conjured up visions of *El Llano Estacado* and hordes of swift Camanches. Let us hope it was true, as commonly reported, that Gen. Banks was not the originator of the Red River campaign, but acted in obedience to orders.

It was essential to the success of this romantic expedition that the Red River should rise. The old geographers say it annually overflows its banks in April. Had such been the fact in 1864 we might have run a brilliant career of conquest and gained new views of *El Llano Estacado* and the Great American Desert. Our wooden gunboats and ironclads could easily have penetrated to Shreveport; nay, reached the great rafts! General Banks, had he returned in time from the illimitable plateaus, might have been President! But the genius of the stream lay low with the alligators in the red ooze of the bottom; disloyal, or heedless of almanacs and geographies and distinguished political generals!

"*Heu! nihil invitis fas quenquam fidere divis!*"

The night of April 13 we slept on our arms in the woods. Next day we commenced throwing up strong breastworks along the whole line. Grand Ecore became at once a vast fortified camp similar to Port Hudson. Thousands of negro soldiers, were employed cutting down trees in front of the fortifications on every side.

At night the officers of the Thirteenth Connecticut and First Louisiana used to meet around a large camp-fire and relate amusing anecdotes.

April 15, the enemy were reported driving in our pickets. Captain Averill and Lieut. Miner with a detachment from the Thirteenth embarked with rebel prisoners for Port Hudson. These two officers were taken sick. After some two or three months Averill rejoined us for duty at Algiers ; Miner, at Morganza.

April 19, we received orders to be ready to move at an hour's notice against the enemy. All colored persons, except officer's servants, were removed. We were evidently preparing for active service of some kind.

This day the number of officers present for duty in the Thirteenth was twelve; of enlisted men, three hundred and seventy-nine.

Wednesday, April 20, A. J. Smith's command moved out at four P. M., on the Nachitoches road.

Thursday was a quiet, beautiful day. Occasional cannonading was heard. At five o'clock, P. M., we marched out rapidly from Grand Ecore in a southeasterly direction along the banks of Cane River. Birge's Brigade, preceded by a cavalry force, took the lead, and the whole army followed. The road was long and dusty. As darkness came on the way was occasionally lit up by burning houses and barns ; a disgraceful and needless barbarism, which excited our disgust but could not be wholly suppressed. The march was very rapid and severe and continued till three o'clock next morning without pause, except for a few minutes where the roads were obstructed by the enemy felling trees. We made twenty-five miles that night. A large proportion were left utterly exhausted on the road. Officers fell asleep on their horses. Birge's "style" of marching was too rapid. We were obliged to wait until ten o'clock A. M. for the rest of the army to come up.

This forced march from Grand Ecore looked like a precipitate flight. As we resumed our retrograde movement on Friday morning at ten o'clock, the soldiers struck up the song, more truthful than poetic,

> " In eighteen hundred and sixty-four
> We all skedaddled from Grand Ecore !"

This day we marched slowly along Cane River about ten miles, the roads being much obstructed by felled trees, and the enemy constantly skirmishing with our van. Lieutenant Lyman, in command of the rear-guard of the Thirteenth, performed his duty admirably. No one of our men lagged behind. The enemy were reported several thousand strong, mostly mounted. The country was generally level, interspersed with woodland, and well adapted to cavalry evolutions. In the afternoon our advanced guard reported the enemy falling back in line of battle. Our regiments were kept perfectly compact and well in hand. Here and there for long distances the rebels had carefully moved round as on a pivot each length of fence rails, so as to allow unobstructed passage to their horsemen. Their numbers were constantly increasing; they began to press our rear and hover on our flanks. It became evident that we were to have a battle.

Towards sunset we reached a point about a mile from Monet's Ford, better known perhaps as "Cane River Crossing." The stream runs here between steep banks, some forty feet high, and perhaps a hundred yards apart. The river itself varies in width according to the season. At this time it was about a hundred feet wide. It was shallow but not easily fordable, except at the point where the Alexandria road crosses it. Here, if anywhere, the enemy would make a stand.

At night we lay on our arms while the brigades in our rear, and the wagon trains, were arriving. The situation was rather serious. A heavy force of rebel cavalry with artillery was posted in our front, prepared to dispute the passage of the stream. A like force of unknown numbers was pressing our rear. They were elated by their splendid victory of Sabine Cross Roads, and our hasty retreat from the impregnable stronghold of Grand Ecore. Our troops were sulky but full of fight, only asking a chance to meet the enemy on equal terms.

The morning of Saturday, April 23, 1864, opened with a slight rain. A heavy cannonade commenced directly in front. The enemy's artillery, advantageously posted to sweep the ford and all approaches, opened a vigorous fire of shell on our advancing columns. Our own artillery quickly responded, and the frequent cheers from the gunners told how well it was served.

The Thirteenth moved at six o'clock, advancing a short distance and then awaiting orders, while the reconnoitering and the artillery duel went on. The men were clamorous to be led to the charge; for, ugly as the place looked, it was far better than Port Hudson. If we could once get at them with the bayonet, we felt that all would be well.

To avoid the needless effusion of blood, and gain possession of the ford with the least loss of life, it was decided to send a strong detachment across the stream a mile or two further up, and by a circuitous route take the enemy in flank or rear. General Birge was selected to lead the detachment. He moved the Thirteenth Connecticut, followed by the First Louisiana, Thirty-eighth Massachusetts, One Hundred Twenty-eighth, One Hundred Sixty-fifth, and One Hundred Seventy-third, New York, Thirteenth Maine, and other regiments, a mile back. A negro woman pointed out the best place for crossing. The Thirteenth first waded the stream, the water being waist deep. Some non-commissioned officers who tried to cross dry shod in a canoe, were capsized in the middle of the stream, to the great amusement of the other soldiers. Forming line the Thirteenth moved up the precipitous bank. Throwing out skirmishers and flankers, we penetrated the woods and advanced slowly in line with caution and silence, about a mile over the unknown ground. Occasionally, in this forest, to avoid obstacles, we passed into a flank movement by the right of companies, but immediately came again into line. The mounted men of the Thirteenth accompanied us, as a sort of body guard to General Birge, under command of Lieut. Meissner; Captain Cornwell having remained at Alexandria, distributing commissary stores to the destitute and starving citizens.

Emerging from the woods we saw across a wide field what first appeared to be earthworks. As we drew nearer, it proved to be the red soil of ploughed ground. Penetrating another hilly forest, the regiment followed a winding path, until our skirmishers came upon the enemy's pickets. Sharp fighting ensued which developed the rebel position. It was the crest of a well-wooded, rocky, precipitous ridge, quarter of a mile from the ridge on which our skirmishers now took post in front. The Union regiments in the rear of our skirmishers were out of view of the rebels, whose bullets, however, were dropping among us, occasionally hitting a man. Between us and the enemy were a few acres of smooth cleared land.

The troops were formed in two lines; the first containing the First Louisiana on the right, and the Thirteenth Connecticut on the left. Colonel Fiske, outranking Colonel Blinn, commanded this line. Behind us were the New York regiments and the Thirty-eighth Massachusetts. At some distance on our right was the brigade of the gallant Fessenden, which was to advance on the enemy's left, while we charged the centre.

All arrangements having been completed, Colonel Fisk commanded, "Battalions! Forward! March!" General Birge's instructions were to descend the wooded slope, cross the open ground, fire not a shot, but carry the rebel position with the bayonet. The line moved forward with great regularity in quick time. Lieutenant Kinney shouted, "Come on, boys! The paymaster is on the other side of the hill!" Up we went over the hill where our skirmishers stood. Detecting the movement the enemy commenced a furious discharge of small arms and artillery, more noisy than destructive. The line, not at all disconcerted, moved steadily forward without returning it, though anxious to be doing execution with their beautiful rifled muskets. A heavy fire on our right told us that Fessenden was hotly engaged.

Descending into the open field our ranks were disarranged by a rail fence and an irregular gully. Hastily passing these and reforming line without halting, the Thirteenth pressed forward in beautiful style, with perfect confidence and steadiness. On our right the boundary of the open field in front of the First Louisiana, was such as to continually force them to the left, crowding and doubling their ranks upon the Thirteenth, and compelling us to move obliquely to the left. "Give way to the left! Take room to the left! Touch lightly to the right!" resounded along the whole line, and finally, "Left oblique! March!" amid the stunning roar of musketry and cannon. This noise was stimulating rather than intimidating; our forty-four days under fire at Port Hudson having taught us a contempt for the mere thunder of battle.

Reaching the foot of the ridge from which the enemy were pouring down their bullets, we found another rail fence and gully! This would have been a little discouraging, had not the hostile fire perceptibly slackened before our determined onset. We heard a clatter and rattle as of steel in front. Were they fixing bayonets? Up the hill we started, our pace quickening almost to a run, as we clambered up the steeps, laying hold of the bushes, and finally scaling the summit. Notwithstanding the advantage of the rebel position, we captured several prisoners; one of whom, a handsome Texan youth of seventeen summers, protested that he had been conscripted and that he served most unwillingly. A few dead and wounded lay here and there, victims of our skirmish fire, for in our charge and assault we had rigidly enforced the order not to fire a shot. Neither in this nor in any other battle did any of the Thirteenth kill a man with the bayonet, the enemy always giving way before it became a hand-to-hand fight.

The Thirteenth and the First Louisiana, having reached this position with ranks broken and disordered by the nature of the ground, but not in the slightest demoralized, formed line for another advance. Total strangers to the locality and liable to be ambushed, we waited till the lines in our rear came in sight, when the order, "Forward—March!" was again given. We moved among the trees down the opposite slope and in the direction the enemy had fled. General Birge with a few staff officers and Meissner's cavalry, passed to the front on our right. We had thus advanced in line thirty or forty rods down the slope, and were just on the point of reaching the edge of the wood. Here was an irregular ravine ten or a dozen feet deep, with a rivulet in its bed and a bridge across it on the right of our regimental line. A rail fence was on its bank next the woods, and a little cleared land in front. Suddenly the thousand-fold rattle of musketry and rapid discharges of artillery, the foe being invisible and yet apparently within touching distance, struck a momentary consternation into our ranks. They halted as if paralyzed. The moment was a trying one. We had been ambushed, and were completely taken by surprise. A Braddock's defeat stared us in the face. There was no time for deliberation. We could not stand under that withering fire, and we would not retreat. "The Thirteenth never retreats!" we shouted, and "Forward! Forward! At them with the bayonet!" We leaped over the fence, into and out of the ravine, one or two companies on the right dashing across the narrow bridge. Halting an instant, and partially reforming line without delay, and shouting "Forward! Forward!" we rushed rapidly towards the rifle smoke and flash. Sooner than it can be told a great commotion occurred on the right of our regiment and the left of the first Louisiana. Some twenty of Meissner's cavalry came dashing pell-mell back through the ranks. Many of them were covered with blood; horses and riders were falling, Meissner himself shot through and through, General Birge borne along hatless by the tide, Captain Young of Banks' staff with limbs horribly mangled by a shell, eighteen of the thirty troopers being killed or wounded, the whole scene tending to strike a panic into the two regiments. Many of the men fell flat on their faces to escape the storm of shot; some started to retreat. The voice of Colonel Fiske was heard above the din exclaiming, "Stand up! For God's sake, stand up like men! Stand up and do your duty like men." Most of the officers joined in the same commands and a universal shout of "Forward! Forward!" again rose. The two regiments wavered but a moment, and then plunged wildly on towards the enemy. A crooked ravine running diagonally across the field, and filled with interlacing vines, brambles and trees, arrested our disorderly advance and afforded cover. For ten or fifteen minutes the firing continued. The writer being the only mounted officer present, found it expedient to make frequent " changes of base " by galloping from one end of the line to the other, the bullets singing in his ears like a swarm of angry bees! A most unmelodious sound; and yet the advantages of ubiquity, of correct observation, of a husbanding of strength, and of a good example, more than compensate for the additional danger arising from being on horseback. Soon the fiery rain ceased. Our second line was in sight. The enemy appeared to occupy another ridge fifteen or twenty rods in front, similar to the first, and like that covered with trees and a thick undergrowth of brush, the usual gully and rail fence being at its base. While preparations were going on for a third advance, we busied ourselves in ministering to the wounded and dying.

The plan adopted was for the second line, now comparatively fresh and a short distance in our rear, to rush to the fence and tear it down. The Thirteenth Connecticut and First Louisiana were to follow closely, charge over the other line and then carry the place with the bayonet. As before, not a shot was to be fired. We could not afford the time. A brief death-grapple was to decide the conflict. No skirmishers.

The movement commenced. The second line moved silently forward. The Thirteenth advanced quickly about five rods in rear of the other line, eager to make the final spring and finish the struggle. But not a shot greeted us! The enemy had vanished!

Thenceforward our progress to Alexandria could

hardly be seriously impeded. Flushed with victory the Thirteenth marched with streaming banners to Cane River Crossing.

In this battle the Thirteenth lost but one officer and twenty-four enlisted men killed and wounded. The whole Union loss was but about two hundred. Our experience here and in other battles proved that the bravest policy is the safest; and the number of killed and wounded is no criterion whatever of the gallantry of a regiment. On the contrary, a large list of killed and wounded oftener indicates the opposite. For nothing is so fatal as retreating. It is while turning the back to the enemy, or running away helpless and defenseless, that the severest losses are suffered, and not while marching straight into the face of the foe, giving blows as well as taking them. So true is the advice of Napoleon: "Boys, you must not fear death! *When soldiers are not afraid of Death, they drive him into the enemy's ranks!*"

Yet in this sharp conflict we lost some true men. Meissner, Reynolds, Matthews, Britz, Garcia and Gunter, were among the bravest of the brave, and gallantly upheld their country's flag. They died victorious, while their comrades' tears mingled with huzzahs; and long as life lasts, will their memories be cherished and rêvered.

April 24, at ten A. M., we marched away from Cane River Crossing. The sun was very hot and the road dusty. We moved slowly till three or four P. M., forming line of battle twice in expectation of an engagement. At four o'clock we commenced marching fast. We entered an extensive forest of large pine trees, the passage through which occupied us nearly four hours. Near eight o'clock we issued from the forest and marched two hours in the darkness in a southerly direction. This journey was very fatiguing. Heavy artillery firing at intervals during the day told us that the gallant hero of Fort De Russy, was covering our retreat, and hurling defiance at the rebels in our rear.

With sorrow and shame it must be recorded that our march was lit up at night with the conflagration of buildings burnt by our stragglers. Large rewards were offered by General Banks for the conviction of the perpetrators of these outrages.

April 25, at nine A. M., we started again. A heavy rebel force was reported pressing our rear guard, and the cannon of old A. J. Smith, who seemed the very incarnation of war, thundered all day. At one time the firing waxing hot, General Banks is said to have sent back a courier to inquire if he needed assistance to which Smith is said to have responded, "Go to ——! I've just whipped three thousand and I can whip thirty thousand!"

Endless rumors, all false, reached us, of the capture of Alexandria, of the destruction of our fleet, of A. J. Smith trapping the pursuing enemy by thousands of the advance of the rebels on New Orleans, and the like.

The wounded officers and men occupying the ambulances and wagons, the sick and the exhausted were obliged to drag along their limbs as best they might Some of our men were killed by hard marching. Thi was the case with Corporal James Malone, Company H, one of the most faithful and uncomplaining o all. He sank rapidly, and died a few days after reaching Alexandria.

We marched fifteen or twenty miles that day, the latter portion along the Bayou Rapides, and reached Alexandria at nine P. M. Here we groped a long time in the intense darkness endeavoring to find our old camp ground. Few of us will ever forget the weary hour we were led back and forth, around and around, to our final place of bivouac, after the tiresome work of the four or five days past. We were too much worn out to enjoy the grand scene of the shelling of the woods opposite Alexandria by the gunboats, the extreme darkness lending vividness to the meteoric shower that streaked, flashed and thundered till near midnight.

April 26, we rested and were broiled in the sun without shade or shelter. Frequent heavy firing announced the activity of General Smith or the gunboats above us on the river; we knew not which. The whole rebel army was reported arriving to give us battle. Alexandria was fortified with breastworks, redoubts and abattis, the streets were barricaded, and everything appeared to indicate an approaching engagement.

April 27, the cannonade was continued all the morning, and appeared to be coming nearer. April 28, the arrival of General McClernand was reported. Dr. Clary received orders from the Medical Director to take possession of the *Ice-House Hotel*, and prepare it for the reception of a thousand wounded.

This day the greater portion of the army was drawn up in two vast lines of battle in concentric semi-circles half a mile apart, with reserves in town. Cavalry and infantry pickets and scouts were on every side. The Thirteenth was near the center of the second line. The level plains in rear of the town gave us a fine view of the lines. We were never in higher spirits than this day, when we hoped the enemy would attack us in force. We did not ask for odds; but wished that, once for all, they would meet us on the open field. Hour after hour we awaited their attack; but in vain.

They chose rather to blockade the river below Alexandria and cut off our supplies. At night the great sugar mill and adjoining buildings on the Bayou Rapides, nearly a mile from Red River and a mile from town, were set on fire. The flames lit up Alexandria, and semed to make what a rebel paper termed Harriet Beecher Stowe, a "pandemonium."

This day Captain Wells was sent with fifteen men of Company I to conduct a hundred rebel prisoners on the steamer *Sallie Robinson* to New Orleans. Expecting to be attacked as usual by guerillas, Wells placed the rebels conspicuously on the hurricane deck, making a sort of breast-work of the "grey-backs!" He was not fired on! Returning, he reached Fort DeRussy. Here authentic reports came of the blockade above, and fragments of gunboats drifted down to confirm it. He declined to advance further, but soon joined us at Simsport.

April 29, we received orders to cross the river on the pontoons to Pineville, which had been so thoroughly shelled a few evenings before. We passed over after dark with the One hundred Fifty-ninth New York, First Louisiana, Cornwell's Cavalry and a section of a battery. Colonel Molineux, being in command of the whole, sent the writer at ten o'clock P. M. to post a large picket around the brigade; a work which required some hours, the night being exceedingly dark, and the woods an intricate maze of lanes, thickets, marshes and hillocks, the locality utterly unknown and the enemy near. Next day we threw up strong works.

Every morning we turned out under arms, half an hour before light, in readiness for an attack.

Within two miles of us was the State Military Academy, of which General William T. Sherman was Principal at the breaking out of the war.

We lay for some time at Pineville, awaiting the completion of the great dam which floated off the gunboats. The plan of a dam to raise the water so that Porter's fleet could pass over the rapids was discussed weeks before it was attempted. The writer recollects that before we left Alexandria for Grand Ecore, an "intelligent contraband" suggested almost the precise mode that was afterwards adopted. The river was made to pass through a narrow space between the two ends of the dam. On the eighth of May two Monitors floated through. That night, or early the next morning, it broke, and several days were required to rebuild it.

May 1, Lieut. Kinney was detailed as Acting Signal Officer.

May 4, heavy firing was heard. Fighting was vaguely reported on the Bayou Rapides. May 5, rapid and continuous artillery discharges were heard down the river. At night ten or a dozen persons arrived at our camp, who had escaped from the gunboat *Covington* and the steamer *John Warner*, which had that morning been captured and destroyed by the rebels twenty or thirty miles below Alexandria. Some of them were wounded. Dr. Clark supplied them with refreshments and surgical treatment. General Nickerson, who had started with his brigade to march down the bank of the stream, returned on learning of the disaster.

The situation began to be interesting if not alarming. The river was completely blockaded by the rebels, who sunk steamers in such a way as to obstruct the channel, and erected batteries to throw plunging shot down through the decks. A large force was known to be concentrating between us and the Mississippi. We had no doubt we could cut our way through, but we did not like to have our enemies stop our supplies and force us into action prematurely.

Being short of forage, orders were issued that the horses should be supplied, as far as practicable, by pasturage. Alexandria was fortified. We were curious to know whether it would be retained or abandoned. If not worth keeping, why should we have captured it?

May 9, Banks's purpose became evident. All the gunboats were to be got below the dam, and the whole army and navy were to move. Orders came to hold the Thirteenth ready to march at two hours' notice. No baggage in wagon was to be allowed.

May 10, Col. Fisk, Col. Sprague and other field officers were ordered to remove all *cotton* from transport steamers, and load them with army stores; an order that brought many a worshiper of the "southern king" to grief! General McMillan was in command of this working party. His instructions were explicit: "Fling overboard every d—— pound of cotton, and fling the d—— proprietors over after it!" Till past midnight we labored, throwing off the regal fabric and loading with army stores the "*Ginnie Hopkins*," "*Silver Wave*," and other steamboats.

May 11, the regiment marched with the First Louisiana and One hundred Fifty-ninth New York, under Colonel Molineux, seven miles along the right bank. As we halted, General Grover and staff came riding up at considerable speed. He ordered us to return three miles. At three o'clock next morning we were under arms in line of battle. Lord Byron sat up all night to see the sun rise! There were good reasons why we should not wish to be caught napping. At seven o'clock this P. M. the "long roll," as potent if not as sweet as the music of Orpheus, brought the brigade in a twinkling into line of battle. Our pickets exchanged shots with the enemy. Orders came to move at seven next morning.

May 13, we moved at nine, and marched slowly seven or eight miles along the river. The day was sultry. Cannonading was heard in the distance. The rear of the army left Alexandria. That portion of the town next the river was fired by some such vandals as disgrace every army, and a terrible conflagration ensued.

At six A. M., May 14, we resumed our march. Heavy skirmishing went on the first hour in front and on the right flank, as indicated by the incessant rattle and smoke of small arms. We made fifteen miles, holding ourselves in readiness to form line at any moment. Before dark we arrived at the point where the Confederates had destroyed and sunk several of our gunboats and transports across the channel. Articles innumerable had been brought ashore and scattered every where along the banks. Among other things were the remnants of a large mail we had sent a few days before. Capt. McCord found his Ordnance Returns. Several soldiers recovered letters they had written home. The writer looked in vain among the scattered documents for an account of the battle of Cane River, which he had sent a few days before for a Connecticut newspaper, and which was probably at that time edifying a select circle of rebels. Here were gun-carriages burning; and rifle-pits, lunes and breastworks. Here, too, were fresh camp-fires, where the "Johnnies" had roasted their meat and baked their inevitable corn-bread.

At eight o'clock next morning, Sunday, we left Red River, and marched southeast two or three miles through the woods to a little bayou, where we halted an hour till a pontoon bridge was thrown across, when we passed over, and continued our advance. Hot skirmishing soon commenced. We moved slowly and cautiously several miles through a forest, and reached an extensive open plain skirted with woodland. Here we formed line of battle, our brigade immediately supporting the cavalry, who were skirmishing heavily in full view of us. As the brigades successively arrived, they formed on the colors to right and left. The batteries moved at a gallop and threw themselves into position, while the squadrons of cavalry hovered lightly to and fro as if on wings. The scene was one of extraordinary beauty. There was ceaseless clatter of musketry like the popping of corn when a thousand kernels burst into whiteness. The far-stretching cloud of smoke in front of us, and anon the heavy round-shot falling like the first big drops of a summer shower, gave indication of an approaching storm.

The enemy largely outnumbered us in cavalry. Prisoners and deserters reported that they had fifteen pieces of artillery, twenty-five hundred infantry, and twenty-two regiments of cavalry ; the last under command of the celebrated Prince Polignac.

When our dispositions were completed, we made a general advance in line of battle. The sight inspired us with the feeling of irresistible strength.

> " The host moves like the deep sea wave,
> Where rise no rocks its pride to brave ;
> High-swelling, dark and slow."

The enemy prudently declined a pitched battle, but retired, obstinately skirmishing, knowing their superiority in mounted troops.

We drove them through Marksville. Our cavalry occupied the town just before sunset, the infantry halting half an hour before dusk in the suburbs. We improved the time by attempting to replenish our canteens. The soldiers began to boil a little coffee. They had suffered severely, the black muddy water of the occasional shallow circular pools seeming to aggravate rather than allay thirst. General Grover, commanding our division, had placed a squad of guards over the large rain-water cistern nearest us in the edge of the village at a house he had just selected as his head-quarters. Our men were swearing lustily at being deprived of the precious beverage, which the writer and other officers were endeavoring to procure for them, when up rode Captain Finley, Co. G, then on Grover's staff as Division Mustering Officer. He communicated orders to Col. Molineux to move his, the second, brigade instantly with all speed to the front, for the enemy were driving our cavalry back. "I asked the General," said Finley, "if I should not bring the first brigade, as it lay nearer." He answered, "No; the first brigade is too small, too d—— small! I want the *second* brigade."

"Fall in! Fall in!" echoed instantly along the brigade line. Leaving the steaming coffee, we were off without a moment's delay. By the right flank at a double-quick we penetrated the town, traversed the length of the main street, more than two miles through choking dust. "*File right!*" and out into the open plain we rushed, guns on the right shoulder, at the same rapid pace. Winding along like a huge serpent with glittering scales and the banners of the Thirteenth for his crest, we moved parallel to our cavalry line which was just ahead of us and actively engaged. The enemy shelled us. "Halt! Front! Fix bayonets!" rang out the stentorian voice of Col. Molineux. Grover came up at the instant. "Boys," said he, "very likely the cavalry will charge you. If they do, take it cool. Fire by rank. Remember the rear rank fires first." The Thirteenth answered with a tremendous hurrah, which our cavalry caught up and repeated. The enemy replied with one of their peculiar yells, like the screech of a thousand wildcats.

But they did not charge. It was getting dark. Our cavalry knowing they were now supported, plied their Spencer carbines with unwonted vigor. The batteries on both sides got at work; the vivid, uninterrupted sparkle and infinite roll of fire-arms, and the shouting of the combatants, clearly revealing the hostile position in the deepening darkness.

At ten o'clock the battle ceased. We lay on our muskets in line, utterly exhausted by the severe ordeal. A long march without dinner or supper had been followed by three miles at a double-quick, while the men's feet were raw with blisters, their tongues parched with thirst, their throats and nostrils filled with stifling dust. Yet hardly a man of the Thirteenth had fallen behind, though the extraordinary haste of the movement betokened savage work ahead, and the rebel artillery sent us its howling defiance. We sank to sleep, and never was rest sweeter.

Morning came, beautifully clear and sunny. The enemy had retired a mile or two, and were drawn up to give us battle on Mansura Plains. We moved at once. As on the day before, the cavalry preceded, and our brigade led the infantry. Arriving in sight of the enemy, Grover's division was deployed in two lines. General A. J. Smith, looking like the very god of war, was sent to make a detour to the right. The rest of the infantry was drawn up in successive lines and massed columns. The plain was immense; slightly rolling and fringed with trees on three sides. Fences obstructing our advance, Grover commanded, "By the right of regiments to the front;" and the line immediately broke into beautiful moving parallels, which advanced steadily under an artillery fire from the front and right. Reaching ground that permitted it, the regiments again came into a magnificent line of battle. The artillery duel waxing warm, Grover's line was halted. Fox's battery on the right of the Thirteenth, and a section of Rogers's on the left, maintained a steady cannonade. Our regiment was mostly in rear of a rail fence, which stood on a bank of earth a foot high. This afforded protection to those who preferred to lie down, as most of us did, while the rifled projectiles were screaming and bursting. A considerable number, however, mounted the fence, unable to restrain their curiosity to gaze on the truly sublime display. Glancing back, almost the whole army was seen, resplendent in steel and brass; miles of lines and columns; the cavalry gliding over the ground in the distance with a delicate, nimble lightness of innumerable twinkling feet; a few batteries enveloped in smoke and incessantly thundering, others dashing swiftly to salient positions; division and corps commanders with their staff officers clustering about them, watching through their glasses the hostile army; couriers riding swiftly from wing to wing; everywhere the beautiful silken flags; and the scene ever changing with the involutions and evolutions of the vast host!

> "'Twere worth ten years of peaceful life,
> One glance at their array!"

To us the spectacle was thrilling and glorious: to the enemy it must have given point to the scripture simile, "terrible as an army with banners."

While we were impatiently awaiting the order to charge, there were many narrow escapes from death, the enemy having a cross fire on us. But no man of the Thirteenth was seriously injured that day. In the midst of the battle General Grover rode rapidly straight out in front of the Thirteenth some fifty rods. Halting on a little knoll in full view of both armies, he raised his glass to his eyes and looked long and steadily at the rebel position, heedless of the hissing of bombs. Making a signal, Fox's battery galloped to the spot, and immediately opened a fire of spherical case. At the same instant, far to the right, we recognized the familiar sound of A. J. Smith's cannon, always rapid and tremendous. Grover's division now rushed to the charge. The enemy wavered, broke, and we saw them in rapid retreat. We followed them closely four miles, but their preponderance of cavalry enabled them to make good their escape without heavy loss. Prisoners reported the celebrated Polignac among the wounded.

After the battle we marched leisurely to Bayou Rouge, and thence to Bayou de Glaze, on the bank of which we encamped, six or eight miles from Simsport.

Next morning, May 17, 1864, we marched at seven o'clock, reaching Simsport at noon. It was along this identical bayou that we had marched exactly one year before, on our way to Port Hudson. A mile from Simsport, we passed some new and strong fortifications on Yellow Bayou, the principal of which was called Fort Lafayette. The rebels evacuated them at our approach.

The wagon train was attacked this day, to the great discomfort of our new Quartermaster, Bishop; whose strenuous exertions, however, preserved the baggage of the Thirteenth.

A slight rain fell next morning. The weather was hot at noon, when a very sharp artillery firing was heard, apparently two or three miles west of us, said to be on Yellow Bayou. Here an attack of the enemy in force was handsomely repulsed. Our loss was about two hundred killed and wounded; that of the enemy, much greater.

At one o'clock we moved across the Atchafalaya on a magnificent bridge of twenty large steamboats, lying side by side. Another such bridge this country has rarely if ever seen. We went into camp on precisely the same ground as a year ago that day. At eleven o'clock at night there was an alarm. We "fell in," and were moved two miles up the river bank.

At five o'clock next morning, orders came to march instantly in light order to battle. We proceeded a mile and a half to support our troops in case the attack by the enemy should be renewed. In the afternoon we marched two miles above the Sims house and bivouaced.

At six o'clock P. M., May 20, 1864, we were suddenly ordered to fall in to march immediately. We left at seven and a half, and marched till midnight, making about twelve miles towards Morganza. At eight A. M., next day, we marched again through terrible heat and dust to a point just above Morganza, on the Mississippi. Several men, one of whom was private Klein, Co. B, were sun-struck. The sight of the great swift-rolling stream was hailed with loud and long-continued shouts. It was like looking on a powerful friend, whose protection we needed and in whom we could perfectly confide, but whose face we had feared we should see no more.

We lay at Morganza several weeks in "a camp chiefly memorable for its dust and intense heat." The army extended several miles along the right bank of the river. The fine penetrating dust by day, and the musquitoes by night, were two great and constant plagues. The enemy hovered in small parties about our camps, sometimes driving in our pickets.

May 29, a hostile force was reported approaching. The regiment fell in under arms, with orders to be in readiness to march at a moment's notice. No attack was made.

June 1, the regiment received orders to go with the brigade into camp a mile and a half down the river, in a thicket of young willows, poplars, and cottonwoods. Welcome enough was this announcement; for we had lain ten days without much shelter on the scorching sand, constantly powdered by the fine dust, and amidst the unceasing din and tramp of hundreds of men and animals. A fatigue party cleared and prepared the narrow regimental streets in the dense growth. The Thirteenth Connecticut, One hundred Fifty-ninth New York, and First Louisiana moved next day to the new grounds on the river bank. The soldiers ingeniously constructed bowers and beds of the slender trees, and enjoyed the delicious shade. The principal draw-back was the swarming insects, to which no language can do justice.

June 3, 4, 5, 6, 8, we had copious showers. A large detachment of the Thirteenth was daily sent on picket duty.

June 6, reports came of fighting between the irregular troops of the enemy and one of our gunboats, above us near Morganza; an affair of frequent occurrence.

June 8, the Fourteenth New Hampshire arrived, bringing an immense quantity of baggage and nice new clothes. They were brigaded with us; their Colonel, Wilson, assuming command by right of seniority. Their men, who had never seen active service, looked with evident alarm upon the rough veterans of the Thirteenth. They could not believe that just two years before, we were "Butler's dandy regiment," and wore finer clothes, and whiter gloves, and brighter boots than they.

June 10, the Nineteenth Corps was reviewed at four P. M. by General Emory, two and a half miles from our camp. A heavy shower thoroughly drenched the army during the parade.

The two great questions with the regiment in these days were: "What will be the success of Grant in Virginia?" and "When will the Thirteenth receive its *Veteran Furlough?*"

June 14, General Sickles reviewed all the troops at Morganza.

June 18, Paymaster, Major Mann, made his wished-for advent. The officers had found it difficult to subsist, prices being enormous and money scarce. Potatoes were sold us by the sutlers at twelve dollars a bushel. Some of our officers pretended to trace the pedigree of these sharp traders back to the Garden of Eden, quoting, "Now the serpent was more *subtler* than any beast of the field!"

June 19, the enemy were reported in force at Tunica Bend and old Fort Adams. We moved up to give them battle. The Thirteenth embarked at ten P. M. on the steamer *Ohio Belle*, with the One hundred Fifty-ninth New York, and a detachment of cavalry. Several transports and gunboats accompanied us, all being loaded with troops. We steamed up the Mississippi to Tunica Bend, where, next day, we sent a detachment ashore. They encountered a small party of guerillas, and made a few prisoners. At night we moved up to Fort Adams, where we disembarked at six A. M., June 21, and sent scouts in different directions. The enemy had fled. No trace of them could be seen from the summit of the hill, several hundred feet high, on the slope of which the old fort stands. The officers who climbed to the top gained an extensive and enchanting prospect of the surrounding country.

At five P. M. we re-entered the steamer and quickly returned to our camp near Morganza. We reached it at ten P. M., pretty thoroughly baked by the heat; for a Mississippi steamer, crowded with troops at this season, is an oven.

June 26, the Second Division was brigaded anew; the Second Brigade comprising the Thirteenth Connecticut, One hundred Thirty-first New York, One hundred Fifty-ninth New York, First Louisiana, and Third Massachusetts Cavalry.

July 2, orders came for our brigade to be in readiness to go at an hour's notice on board steamer for New Orleans. At ten P. M. the Thirteenth embarked on the large new boat, *Mollie Able*. The sick of the division were left in care of Dr. Clark at Morganza. It will be recollected that in the haste of departure the Dr.'s celebrated mule disappeared; also Col. Sprague's famous high-spirited sorrel mare, with sore back; a loss that nearly broke *Noah's* heart!

That night and all next day we glided down the river, reaching New Orleans at ten P. M., July 3. Next day at ten we went into camp in Algiers.

Great dissatisfaction existing because our veteran volunteers were not allowed the promised furlough of thirty days in Connecticut, though six months had elapsed since re-enlistment, and some had been killed in battle and others had died in hospital, the writer, upon the solicitation of several officers, drew up an earnest petition that the furlough might be granted forthwith. This application, at first opposed by several officers, was finally signed by all. It was granted.

Accordingly, July 13, orders came for the veteran volunteers, and a portion of the non-veterans to embark on the screw steamer *Cumbria*, Captain Blanchard, with sealed orders. At noon, July 14, we went on board; leaving a hundred and fifty non-veterans at Algiers under Capt. Wells. The captain was himself a veteran, but had been in the North much of the time for a year before.

These non-veterans remained a week in Algiers. They then went aboard the *Karnak* for Fortress Monroe, and thence to Washington. They proceeded to Tenallytown where they remained two or three days; thence to Washington, where they took the cars for Monocacy Junction. Here they joined the Twelfth Connecticut, and remained about a week. Thence they went by rail to Harpers Ferry, and lay one night on Maryland Heights. Thence they advanced to Halltown, where they remained some days; thence to Cedar Creek; thence back to Winchester; thence again to Berryville. Much of the time they were in presence of the enemy, and are said to have behaved well. Private Reltrath was captured. They finally rejoined the veterans early in September near Berryville.

At two P. M., July 14, we bade a final adieu to New Orleans. The paymaster paid the men on board, and accompanied us as far as Quarantine. At dawn, July 15, we passed the bar at the mouth of the river, and the regiment saw the receding shores of Louisiana for the last time. The sealed orders, when opened, were found to command Colonel Blinn to leave the non-veterans at Fortress Monroe, and proceed with the veterans to Hartford.

Our progress on the *Cumbria* was slow. July 23, we reached Fortress Monroe at eight A. M. Here the non-veterans, about sixty in number, were left under command of Lieutenants Miner and Squires. They soon joined the Twelfth Connecticut for temporary duty. At ten P. M. we steamed away from Fortress Monroe. July 25, we came in sight of the heights of Neversink. Soon the machinery, which had been several times out of working order, broke down altogether, and we were obliged to rely wholly upon sails. A tug finally towed us in. A refreshing supply of coffee and soft bread was brought to the soldiers by the efficient State Agent, Colonel J. H. Almy, while we lay at anchor. The regiment was transferred to the Sound steamer *Elm City*, and arrived at the New Haven landing before light, July 27.

A cordial reception was tendered by the citizens of New Haven, and the veterans marched through the streets to the sound of music, bells and cannon, and under the escort of the Governor's Horse-Guards and other local military companies. At the State House, where a bountiful collation had been provided us by the beauty and patriotism of New Haven, eloquent speeches of welcome were made by Governor Buckingham, Mayor Tyler and others. The arms and accoutrements were stored in the State House, and the veterans dispersed under orders to re-assemble at the recruiting rendezvous in Fair Haven, on the twenty-seventh of August, 1864.

CHAPTER VI.

THE happy days of our veteran furlough flew swiftly by. The regiments that had preceded us, had each enjoyed several months in the State. It was universally expected that the same would be the case with the Thirteenth. Consequently there was much delay in assembling at the rendezvous. But the pressing necessity for more troops at the front defeated their hopes of an extension of the holidays. The Thirteenth was wanted immediately in the Shenandoah Valley.

On the twenty-ninth of August those who had assembled at the recruiting station in Fair Haven, only eighteen officers and one hundred and forty men, were ordered immediately away. At eleven at night we embarked on the steamer *Continental*, leaving behind Major Comstock and the remainder of the veterans. At five A. M. we arrived in New York. From Jersey City at four P. M. we took the cars for Philadelphia, where we arrived at ten and a half P. M., and received a good collation at that model establishment of its kind, "The Union Volunteer Refreshment Rooms." At one o'clock at night we took the train for Baltimore, where we arrived early in the morning. August 31. Here we were furnished a lunch at "The Soldiers' Rest. Again taking the cars we reached Washington at four P. M.

Next day at noon, we left Washington. The cars moved slowly to the Relay House and thence to Harpers Ferry, where we arrived about midnight. We remained in the cars until day, when Colonel Blinn crossed the bridge to report for orders. Captain Averill, "formerly Lieutenant of old D," in leaping from the cars, sprained his foot, and was left in hospital.

After waiting till five P. M. we marched across the bridge into and through the village, and up the long steep hill past the fortifications. Going through Halltown, we moved four or five miles towards Charlestown and bivouaced. The road was very dusty; the soldiers tired. Report reached us that Capt. Wells, whom we had left in Algiers, lay sick in Hospital at Sandy Hook below Harpers Ferry, and that the non-veterans had done good service with the rest of the Nineteenth Corps in saving Washington during the dark days of August.

Next morning, September 3, 1864, at eight A. M. the regiment left its place of bivouac, and marched rapidly forward. We passed the jail where John Brown was confined; the court house where he had his trial as he lay bleeding and helpless; the field, rendered forever historic by the offering of his life for the liberty of the African race. Five years had not passed; but the edict of freedom for that race had been proclaimed at Washington, and a million bayonets were putting it in force! The martyr's body indeed lay mouldering in its lowly grave at North Elba; but with what gigantic strides his soul was marching on!

Our army had this day set out to fight the enemy. We passed the baggage wagons which had been ordered out of the way of battle. We must hasten, or be too late, and there were those in our regiment who thought it a disgrace to have a fight and the Thirteenth not to be in it. Others felt differently.

Corporal Strange, Co. F, at our first halt this day, shot off the first two fingers of his right hand. Such an accident had not occurred in the Thirteenth since Port Hudson, where it was quite common for soldiers of some regiments to shoot off the right fore-finger.

By a forced march the Thirteenth that afternoon reached the army, some twenty miles from Harpers Ferry and two from Berryville. We halted on the left of the pike. Within two hours we were ordered forward into battle as a part of Molineux's brigade. The enemy had fallen back in good order from Charlestown as we advanced, and were making a stand on the road from Berryville to Winchester. About two divisions of troops on each side were engaged. The transition from the quiet and cheerful scenes of home to the smoke-wrapped fields and hellish noise of war was rather startling; but the Thirteenth went in with its accustomed alacrity. We crossed the pike and advanced under an artillery fire to the front and right, where the musketry was raging. Halting in brigade line, the Thirteenth were sheltered by a slight rise in the ground, while the enemy's shot and shell passed over us to the road on our left. Night closed round us, only illumined by the flashing powder. The shelling and the musketry firing in the darkness recalled many similar scenes in Louisiana. Rain commenced falling and stopped the fighting. We lay in line on the battle-field—a hard night for the Thirteenth.

Next morning the contest was renewed with artillery; the firing being very brisk half a mile in front of us. The enemy soon gave way and withdrew towards the Opequan Creek, which crosses the Winchester pike.

Retiring quarter of a mile our brigade commenced throwing up breastworks. The same was done along the entire line of the Nineteenth Corps. While busied in this work, the writer was detailed at half-past two as field-officer of the day. Taking out the relief of seventy-five men, we met our pickets and sharpshooters in full retreat. A rebel battalion in line with colors flying had attacked and driven them in. The enemy were closely following. Deploying, we succeeded in arresting the retrograde movement. Several companies arriving as re-enforcements, we re-established the picket line after two hours of sharp fighting. The pertinacity with which they pressed every advantage and clung to every position, surprised us. They meant to make a desperate struggle for the rich valley of the Shenandoah. A few men were wounded on our side. Several of the enemy were killed, as we learned from inscriptions at their graves a few days later.

Picket duty and reconnoissances in force now occupied our time. September 5, the whole of the Thirteenth were on picket. The same day a heavy reconnoitering column found the enemy massed on our right, and our lines seriously threatened. Cold rains at night made us particularly uncomfortable. Every morning, for an hour before daybreak, the army stood in line.

September 6, rain fell all day.

September 7, Molineux's brigade at ten A. M. joined a reconnoitering column, and moved towards

Winchester. We returned at evening, having found the enemy in force near the Opequan. Major Comstock rejoined us.

September 8, it rained all day.

Sunday, September 11, religious services at brigade head-quarters were broken off by a thunder storm.

September 12, a soldier was drummed through the army to "The Rogue's March," escorted by seven men with muskets and bayonets, some of which followed inconveniently near. He wore a hard-tack box, through which his head appeared. On one side was written, "THIEF;" on the other, "STOLE PROPERTY WHILE GUARDING IT."

September 13, the regiment was ordered to the extreme left of the works across the Berryville pike. On our right was a section of field artillery; and next was the Twenty-second Iowa, their right resting on the road.

Our brigade at this time comprised the Eleventh Indiana, One Hundred Thirty-first New York, Thir Massachusetts Cavalry, Thirteenth Connecticu Twenty-second Iowa, and One Hundred Fifty-nint New York; all under command of Colonel Molineux

Thursday, September 15, the regiment was ordere to be under arms at four and a half o'clock A. M Notice was given by the brigade commander that an attack was every moment expected.

Saturday, September 17, General Grant was reported to be visiting Sheridan. The battle of the following Monday was the result.

Sunday, September 18, after regimental inspection, religious services were conducted at the camp of the Eleventh Indiana by Chaplain Ames of that regiment. Orders were received to move at two o'clock A. M. next day to the Berryville pike and there join the remainder of the brigade. No wagons were to accompany the movement, nor any baggage.

At half-past two o'clock A. M., September 19, 1864, being Monday, the Thirteenth moved out to the road. Colonel Blinn was in command. In an hour the whole army was in motion. The enemy was known to be in strong force six or eight miles distant on the Winchester side of the Opequan Creek. From Limestone Ridge, which is a long line of high ground bordering the Opequan on the eastern side and crossing the turnpike, the First Connecticut Cavalry had driven the enemy the night before.

We marched along in the darkness, much of the way through woods, making frequent halts. At daybreak the pause lasted longer, and we formed line of battle. Soon we passed into a flank movement, marching for the most part on the right of the pike, which was crowded with artillery and ambulances. Rapid cannonading indicated that the fight had commenced.

It has often been remarked that what passes under the observation of one man in a great battle is necessarily of very limited extent and imperfectly seen. It is only by comparing the accounts of many eye witnesses in different parts of the field, that a view, at once accurate and comprehensive, of a general engagement can be obtained.

As we neared the Opequan, word came to the regimental commanders that the Nineteenth Corps was wanted immediately at the front, and that General Sheridan expected much of it; that the men must hastily fill canteens at the stream, and press forward, losing no time. Before reaching the Opequan, Colonel Blinn, who had been sick for several days with chills and fever, was obliged to resort to one of the ambulances, leaving the writer in command.

Having waded the shallow creek the Thirteenth advanced rapidly a mile along the pike which led through a narrow wooded gorge. Then the regiment filed to the right in a straight road leading up a long hill and nearly perpendicular to the general direction of the pike. Along this branch road, on the side farthest from Winchester, the Thirteenth first formed line, the other regiments of the brigade being on the right and left.

After standing here half an hour, we marched by the right flank across the road and into a wood lot, perhaps a quarter of a mile in the direction of the enemy; thence obliquely to the left into an open field, which commanded an extensive view to the left and front; but the right was hidden by woods. The regiments moved separately some distance to the front and there the brigade again formed line, connecting with other brigades of Grover's Division. We were moving off to the left down a slope, when Gen. Grover rode up rapidly and ordered us further to the right The regiment was now on high ground. To the lef we saw a portion of the Sixth Corps, which was postec on a hill, breaking and running to the rear under a hot fire of musketry; and we saw supports rapidly passing to their assistance. In rear of the Thirteentl was a little hollow in which Surgeons Clary and Clark commenced establishing a hospital for the wounded but the shells came so thick that they were compelle to remove it to a Quaker's house, half a mile back. The artillery fire waxing warm, and everything pointing to an extensive engagement, the writer delivered letters with money into the hands of Dr. Clary; a wise precaution as the event proved.

The regimental commanders had received no information of the plan of the battle. It appears to have been as follows: The Sixth Corps to form on the left, the Nineteenth on the centre and right. These were to amuse the enemy and cover well the mouth of the gorge, from which the whole army had to issue. The Eighth Corps was to come up, pass round the rear of the Nineteenth, mass upon its right, and then hurl itself against the rebel left wing.

The danger in this programme was that the enemy by a determined charge would strike for the mouth of the gorge, cut Sheridan's army in two, and hold the only practicable road for the retreat of that portion which should have arrived on the field. This was precisely what Early attempted to do, and he came fearfully near to its accomplishment.

He allowed the Sixth Corps to debouch from the long narrow road between the hills, to come out into the open rolling country and deploy on his right with little resistance. Grover's Division did the same in front of the rebel centre, where Early had massed his troops. Dwight's division, was still coming up. The Eighth Corps was struggling along the bottom of the gorge.

To gain ground to the front and give room for the evolutions of the troops in our rear, a general forward movement was commenced. Grover's (second) division was at first crowded, the battalion intervals being obliterated, and the regiments overlapping one another. The lines of advance from the defile being divergent, a large gap was soon made between the two corps, and also breaks occurred in our division front. The irregularity of the ground aggravated these unfavorable features.

A heavy fire of musketry was now added to that of artillery. This only seemed to increase the enthusiasm of Grover's men. Our advance commenced with steadiness and in a beautiful line, but gradually quickened into a rapid charge.

One of our first men struck was that brave and faithful first-sergeant, Samuel B. Dunn, Company K, both of whose hands were sadly torn by grape shot. The writer recollects throwing a cord to form a compress, as the Sergeant held up his mangled hands. A small, crooked brook thick set with bushes, broke the regiment near the centre, it being impossible from the noise to hear the commands. Major Comstock was directed to look after the companies thus temporarily separated on the right, and keep them to the colors, the forward movement still continuing.

The Thirteenth was now advancing up something like a little valley, raked longitudinally by a hostile battery about quarter of a mile distant, and by a line of rebel infantry, whose position was indicated by the incessant jets of smoke. The rapidity of our advance allowed no time for observation. A tremendous fire was tearing every portion of the field.

The rebel general seemed to have waked up at last. He must have been puzzled at the impetuous onset of Grover's division, in front of which he had concentrated his best troops to pierce our centre. The time for action seemed to have come.

Grover's division in the wild excitement charged too far, it being impossible to restrain the men, who had got the idea that this was to be the final and decisive assault. The Thirteenth, though broken at times by the irregularities of ground, discharged its duty with unwavering fidelity. "Colonel, your horse is wounded," said orderly-sergeant Maguire to the writer. The blood spirting from the animal's flank, the writer leaped down, and continued to press forward with the regiment, which was moving at a double quick.

The enemy's first line recoiled before our swift advance, but his batteries kept up their tremendous firing.

Orders finally came to halt. We stopped under a heavy fire. The Thirteenth, farther to the front than most of the line, was at a dry channel, two feet in depth and width, worn by a small brook. Here the men were allowed to load and fire at will, each man creeping up about a rod from the ditch to deliver the fire. Quite an interval separated us from the other regiments.

Passing to the left and giving instructions to the men to husband their ammunition and not fire without careful aim, the writer noticed several men on the right starting up and running to the rear, and at the same instant Lieut. Handy of Colonel Molineux's staff, on his horse, his face pale, his hands uplifted, apparently communicating orders; the men starting to their feet. "What are those orders?" the writer demanded. "Retreat! Retreat! Get to the rear as fast as possible!" he answered, throwing up both hands Early's masses were coming!

" Rise up. Face to the rear. Battalion—About face. Forward—March! Not too fast. Slower. Keep dressed on the centre. Guide on the colors. Slower." Such were the commands given.

Hardly had the retrograde movement commenced, when one of Sheridan's staff officers came riding up at a tearing speed, his horse covered with foam. The regiment had passed two or three rods. The writer had not yet started but was angrily calling out to some of the officers to stop their men from running. " For God's sake!" said the *aide*; " What does this mean? This retreat must be stopped. This position must be held. It must be held at all hazards." " Battalion—Halt!" commanded the writer at the top of his voice. Those of the Thirteenth who heard the order hesitated a moment, and some obeyed; but the great majority did not hear it, or were swept along in the ever-increasing speed of retreat. " I'll bring them back,' said the *aide*. " Our brigade commander ordered the retreat," replied the writer. " It's a mistake. This position must be held to the last extremity. By —, if we lose this, all's lost. Hold it, I'll bring support immediately." Plunging his spurs into his horse he disappeared in the direction of the retreating regiments. A hail storm of metal poured after him.

Quite a number of members of other regiments clustered to the little group, till we had about seventy men. Forming these in line, and causing bayonets to be fixed, the writer waited the return of our brigade. Minutes seemed hours. We knew that great efforts would instantly be put forth to retake the abandoned ground; for if Early once got possession of the entrance to the gorge in our rear, it was all over with our army. We looked every moment for our brigade. It came ; but too late for us!

Emory, Grover, Birge, Molineux, and many other officers made almost incredible exertions to stop the retreat, which had now become a precipitate flight. The right of the Sixth Corps like the Second Division of the Nineteenth had given way before Early's tremendous charge. His veteran regiments, however, were broken as our own had been by their impetuosity and the irregular ground; and when they reached the First Division, Nineteenth Corps, which had just formed line and advanced to meet the shock, the tide of retreat began to be rolled back and the Second Division rallied.

Captain De Forest, of the Twelfth Connecticut, in his admirable description of *Sheridan's Battle of Winchester*, in Harpers New Monthly Magazine, presents the following picture:

"Grover's and Rickett's (First Division, Sixth Corps) commands reached the base from which they had advanced, in a state of confusion which threatened wide-spread disaster. Sixth Corps men and Nineteenth Corps men were crowding together up the line of the Berryville pike, while to the right and left of it the fields were dotted with fugitives, great numbers of them wounded, bursting out of the retiring ranks, and rushing towards the cover of the forest. Some regiments disappeared for the time as organizations. Early's veterans advanced steadily with yells of triumph and constant volleys of musketry, threatening to sweep away our centre, and render our struggle a defeat, almost before it became a battle. It was the bloodiest, the darkest, the most picturesque, the most dramatic, the only desperate moment, of the day. General Emory, General Grover, with every brigade commander and every staff officer present rode hither and thither through the fire, endeavoring by threats, commands and entreaties, to halt and re-form the panic-stricken stragglers."

All this came of the unfortunate order to retreat, while exposed to a heavy and destructive fire. Men may face such a storm with steady and grim defiance. The Thirteenth had done it many times. But no soldiers can turn their backs to such a tempest, and march slowly away. An irrepressible panic seizes them. They *will run!*

But we who had remained in position when the red waves of battle were sweeping towards us and the grey foam was dashing past, were engulphed before we knew it, in the surging flood. The first party approached our left. The writer commanded, "*Fire!*" but the cry arose, "Don't Fire! They're deserters coming in!" A glance convinced to the contrary, and again the writer commanded, "*Fire!*" But it was too late. We were prisoners!

The rallied division of General Grover, and the fresh division of General Dwight, now made a determined stand. Splendid deeds of heroism were performed, by the enemy as well as by our own men; and many a gallant officer and hundreds of gallant soldiers fell to rise no more. The well-nigh fatal charge was at last arrested. The rebels were forced back far enough to allow the Eighth Corps to come from the defile, pass behind the Nineteenth, and form in dense column on the right. Here, at four P. M., in conjunction with the cavalry, they made that long-intended and brilliant charge which turned the enemy's left. A simultaneous advance of the three corps now drove the entire Confederate army from the field.

In this engagement the Thirteenth lost six killed, thirty-nine wounded, and thirty-two prisoners; among the latter Lieutenant Gardner. The Nineteenth Corps lost nineteen hundred and forty-six killed and wounded.

About sunset the Thirteenth moved a mile or more to the left of Winchester and bivouaced. Next day they accompanied the rest of the brigade in the pursuit. They reached a point near Strasburg. To the left of the highway a mile from town they occupied the crest of a high hill. Here they threw out pickets and passed a very cold night.

September 21, the regiment moved with the brigade several miles to the right and took position about half a mile from the railroad.

Next day was signalized by the splendid victory of Fisher's Hill. The Thirteenth was engaged till past midday in erecting earthworks, under the constant fire of the rebel pickets and sharpshooters. It was difficult to get shovels, and our men would much rather fight than dig, yet waited patiently.

The Richmond papers announcing that Early's position at Fisher's Hill was impregnable to the whole Yankee army, must have been received by him just about the time he started in headlong flight down its slopes!

Cannonading had been going on most of the day, when the Thirteenth, late in the afternoon, were ordered forward along the pike. Passing through Strasburg, they charged at first directly up the road, and then to the right, where they received orders to halt and lie down. A severe fire of shrapnel, shell and solid shot was opened upon them, during the charge, and their preservation was truly marvelous, only two being wounded. Dr. Clark, who was present says, "It was like going through hell!" The Eighth Corps, which had so nobly turned the enemy's left at Winchester, now performed a similar and equally gallant service. Creeping on hands and knees half a mile, they sprang at one bound inside the rebel works. At the same instant the Thirteenth, with the rest of the division and corps, made a simultaneous rush on the stronghold, and the stars and stripes were borne to the summit.

After the battle the regiment pushed on rapidly in pursuit. The road was strewn with broken and burning wagons, ambulances and the debris of a defeated army. Report spread that we had captured every piece of rebel artillery except one. The men were just felicitating themselves on the good news, when they were suddenly opened upon with both musketry and artillery! This was some three miles from Fisher's Hill. The regiment halted, formed line of battle, and advanced to charge; but the enemy had fled. Pursuing through Tom's Brook, Hawkinstown and Woodstock, the regiment halted on the left of the road at four A. M., September 23, just after passing through the last named town. Rations were issued, and after four or five hours' rest, they resumed the pursuit, passing through Edinburgh to Mount Jackson. Here the enemy attempted to make a stand; but the Second

Division passing around their left forced them to evacuate the position. The Thirteenth pressed on, occasionally coming in view of the flying rebels. The regiment kept in the fields to the right of the pike. Wherever a piece of artillery could be brought to bear on the enemy, it was done ; until the Thirteenth reached New Market. Here our men rested through the night, and then marched to Harrisonburgh. The view of the multitudes of camp fires at Harrisonburgh by night was one of great beauty ; the whole amphitheatre of hills being illuminated for many miles around. Resuming the march next morning, the regiment reached Mount Crawford ; the furthest point reached by the Thirteenth ; some twenty-one miles distant from Staunton.

Remaining twenty-four hours in Mount Crawford, the regiment returned, September 27, to Harrisonburgh. Here they remained in camp about two weeks. The nights began to be severe, only shelter-tents being allowed to soldiers, and a tent-fly to officers. The regiment was engaged here in the usual picket duty, and was occasionally drilled. Several alarms were had, and the regiment repeatedly "fell in" with all haste. Every morning, an hour before day-light, they stood to arms and remained until sunrise, shivering, but full of fight.

October 7, the regiment marched back to Strasburgh, and went into camp not far from the spot where they had thrown up works just previous to the battle of Fisher's Hill. About this time privates Schweikart and Fuller, while out foraging for the officers' horses, were captured by the enemy's scouts. In two or three days the command moved back several miles to CedarCreek.

October 15, the regiment moved out rapidly half a mile to support the picket line then warmly engaged. The Eighth Corps was attacked in force, and two or three hundred were killed and wounded. The Thirteenth remained out through the frosty night beside a stone wall. Fires being prohibited, they suffered severely. Here they remained next day, exposed to the skill of the rebel sharp-shooters. It was at this time that the commissioners, who had been sent from Connecticut for the purpose, took the votes of the soldiers for the approaching presidential election. It is due to these public functionaries to say, that, being under the rebel fire, they performed their duties with great alacrity, appearing to feel that time was precious. In the afternoon the troops moved back to their position near the creek.

October 18, twenty-seven conscripts arrived from Connecticut. They were assigned to Company K, under command of Lieut. Perkins.

The same day orders were received by the regimental commanders of the Second Division, Nineteenth Corps, to have coffee for the men at three o'clock next morning, and to be in line before daybreak, ready to march on a reconnoissance in force. This order was fully observed.

In the morning of October 19, 1864, the following was the disposition of Sheridan's army before daylight:

The three corps d'armée were posted in echelon, descending from the left, each corps being on a moderate elevation of ground and thus forming one of the three grand steps. First, on the left of the Strasburg pike was the Eighth Corps. Second, on the right of the same road was the Nineteenth, half a mile to right and rear of the Eighth. Third, to the right and rear of the Nineteenth was the Sixth. Crook commanded the Eighth, Emory the Nineteenth, and Wright the Sixth. Wright, by seniority, commanded the whole army until Sheridan's arrival on the field. The extremities of the wings were three miles apart. The ground on the right of the Sixth Corps was occupied by Torbert's cavalry. A small division of infantry, known as Kitching's Provisional Division, lay on the left of the Eighth Corps looking outward. Our batteries were posted along the front, where a strong line of earthworks and extensive abattis had been constructed. The Second Division, Nineteenth Corps, was under arms, ready to go on their expected reconnoissance.

The enemy, reenforced by twelve thousand fresh troops, was supposed to be lying entrenched on Fisher's Hill.

Three days previously a brigade of our cavalry occupied the ground over which Early now led his men to turn our left. Two days previously General Emory had reconnoitered the spot, and suggested that it was possible for the enemy to flank us there. But no one dreamed that the rebel commander had the audacity to attempt the perilous enterprise. It was a truly Napoleonic feat.

From the summit of the Massanutten mountain, with a good glass, the position of the whole union army could be seen.

Before midnight on the eighteenth of October the rebel army commenced that flank movemant, to which history furnishes no parallel. Giving orders to his cavalry and light batteries to amuse and threaten our right wing at the proper moment, the remainder of Early's army, not less than twenty thousand, descended into the ravine that stretches along the base of the Massanutten peak, crossed the north branch of the Shenandoah, and crept stealthily two or three miles, passing around the Eighth Corps in perfect silence, and sometimes within easy talking distance of Crook's pickets. Hour after hour the long stream of troops in grey flowed on. They had left their canteens, in order that the tinkling sound might not betray them.

Half an hour before daydreak the division of General Gordon, whose genius is said to have devised this master-piece of strategy, had passed quite around the Eighth Corps, and was massed in close column facing obliquely the left and rear of the Nineteenth! Opposite Kitching's Provisional Division, and facing squarely the left flank of the Eighth Corps, were the two rebel divisions of Generals Ramseur and Pegram. Facing the front of the Eighth Corps were the two divisions of the confederate Generals Kershaw and Wharton. Thus lay this doomed corps just at daybreak, all unconscious of danger, with rebels to the number of twenty thousand on three sides and less than half a mile distant, crouching and eager to pounce upon their sleeping prey!

On a sudden a terrific roar of musketry and the yells of ten thousand infantry! It was Early's "Good morning" salutation! His veteran lines moved steady and swift, the little resistance they encountered serving only to keep the charging columns compact. The gallant Eighth Corps, which had won so glorious a name on many a battle-field; the corps which Sheridan had swung round that great semi-circle at Winchester, like a rock in a huge sling, smiting Early a blow which sent him reeling back to Strasburg; the corps whose lion-spring, swift as a thunderbolt, had landed it in the monster's fiery lair on Fisher's Hill, on the twenty-second of September; was now rolled up, trodden under foot, and swept away as easily as the whirlwind drives the autumn leaves. In twenty minutes from the firing of the first gun, the Eighth Corps was a panic-stricken flying mob.

The retreating mass of fugitives first apprised the officers of the Nineteenth Corps how terrible was the blow that had fallen. Almost at the same instant the dense masses of Gordon's division struck McMillan's brigade of the First Division, Nineteenth Corps, which had been hastily pushed to the left rear by Emory, who comprehended the fact that the enemy were outflanking us. The Twelfth Connecticut was in this brigade, and most gallantly did that noble sister regiment uphold the honor of the state on this, as on every other occasion. They fired three vollies, but the far superior weight of the enemy crushed them, as an elephant would trample down a bull-dog. Two other brigades successively shared the same fate in a few minutes. Still onward pressed the rebel columns, and ever rose and rung their terrible battle-yell. They threw out no skirmishers, for they knew the ground perfectly.

Emory threw several brigades of the Nineteenth Corps on the outer side of their own breastworks, as the bullets now came from the rear. Wright pushed the Sixth Corps rapidly to the left and rear to gain full possession of the Winchester and Strasburg pike.

The part taken by the Thirteenth Connecticut was not peculiar. They moved with the remainder of Grover's division, the whole of which was under arms for the expected reconnoissance. Had fifteen minutes' notice of the real state of things been given, the division could have been faced to meet the shock. But almost simultaneously with the first roll of musketry, the fugitives of the Eighth Corps came rushing up and across the pike, and bullets began to fall from the front, left, and rear. By Molineux's order, the Thirteenth, with the rest of the brigade, stepped into the trenches at the first firing. In a few minutes the inrolling tide of fire and steel reached them, and chaos came with it. By some misunderstanding, the right wing moved off with Col. Blinn; the left, with Major Comstock. Many determined stands were taken by our veterans, who seized every opportunity to hurl back death and defiance at the avalanche of rebels. But every successive position had to be abandoned. In some disorder all the regiments were retreating. Towards noon the two wings of the Thirteenth were re-united.

General Wright, not feeling safe till the Winchester and Strasburg pike was securely held, kept pushing the Sixth Corps towards this important avenue of communication. At last it got into position on the left of the Nineteenth and in connection with it. The pursuit seemed to have ceased. The enemy were gathering up the fruits of victory. Only their artillery continued firing. It was five hours since the action had commenced. The army had been driven about four miles.

The Sixth Corps had gained the pike, and the army had began to assume a formidable attitude fronting the enemy, when Sheridan came with flying speed from Winchester on his superb black charger. Everybody recognized him as he rode from regiment to regiment with animating words. The troops were resting in line. Sheridan's presence acted like a charm. They felt that they had been taken at a great disadvantage. After infinite difficulty they had once more got into a position to strike back. Even the shattered and dispersed fragments of the Eighth Corps began to crystalize. The cavalry formed a long line across the field, stopped all stragglers, and compelled them to fall in with the nearest organization.

The Nineteenth Corps was for the most part posted in a large piece of woods. They threw out skirmishers, the Thirteenth being deployed under command of Colonel Blinn. The skirmishers were ordered not to attempt to rally on the battalion, but to join the final charge, each man falling in with the movement wherever he might be.

After two or three hours, every moment of which was most industriously employed in re-forming, reorganizing, and preparing, word was brought to Emory that a column in mass was advancing against him. The Nineteenth Corps was all ready for them this time. They struck it near the centre. A steady roll of musketry followed, which lasted several minutes. The enemy retreated in the utmost confusion. This was the first repulse they had received this day.

Another pause of an hour, and the army impatiently awaited the signal for the grand advance which was to restore the fortunes of the day. Sheridan's order came at last: "The entire line will advance. The Nineteenth Corps will move in connection with the Sixth. The right of the Nineteenth will swing towards the left so as to drive the enemy upon the pike."

So the Sixth Corps were to charge squarely up the pike; while the Nineteenth, outflanking the confederates, were to make a gigantic wheel to the left. The two corps would form an enormous V, inclosing a great portion of the enemy within the angle.

When all was ready the movement commenced. General Birge is said to have seized a flag, rode out in front of our skirmish line, and pointing to a hostile battery, given the signal for charge. With shouts that seemed to shake the hills, fifteen thousand men moved forward in quick time against the sheets of flame that blazed from the long grey ranks and roaring batteries. The shocks were quick, repeated, terrible. From height to height, from wood to wood, from wall to wall, the broken ranks of the enemy retreated, making a stand for a few minutes at successive wooded ridges, which had been hastily fortified by rude breastworks of rails and earth; and then recoiling again before the steady and resistless advance; until five thousand cavalry, led by such men as Torbert and Custar and McIntosh, thundered upon their heels, and the lately victorious and magnificent army of Early became a routed rabble!

Forty-nine pieces of artillery, about half of which were captured from us in the morning; sixty-five ambulances, and a proportionate number of wagons, small arms, and the thousand implements of war; fifteen hundred prisoners, and two thousand rebel killed and wounded, were among the fruits of this great victory so wonderfully wrested from defeat. But its chief importance was its crushing effect upon the already reeling confederacy.

The loss of our army was very severe; not less than thirty-five hundred killed, wounded and missing. The Thirteenth lost two killed, eighteen wounded and nine missing. Among the killed was our brave color-sergeant, Geo. A. Winslow. He fell pierced through the forehead by a rifle ball, beneath the folds of the flag he bore so gallantly and loved so well. Among the wounded was Major Comstock, whose hand was badly cut by a fragment of shell.

Captain Wells deserves especial mention, for going into battle and sharing the perils of the regiment through the day, though he had in his pocket a leave of absence.

That night the regiment slept in the camp it had vacated in the morning. Next day it moved half way to Strasburg and bivouaced. On the twenty-first it returned to Cedar Creek. After a few days there, it retired six miles towards Winchester, and went into winter-quarters with the rest of the army. Strong earthworks were immediately thrown up, and soon after log-huts were built. The place was christened *Camp Russell.*

December 1, 1864, the regiment moved from Camp Russell to Martinsburg as guard to a wagon train. There on a high hill they remained a week in camp, and then returned to Camp Russell. Two weeks later the non-veterans, one hundred and twenty-five in number, left for New Haven to be mustered out of service. Fifteen officers accompanied them, rendered supernumerary by the consolidation of the veterans into a battalion of five companies. They were Colonel C. D. Blinn; Quartermaster William Bishop; Adjutant F. N. Stanley; Captains J. J. McCord, C. H. Cornwell, D. H. Finley, Perry Averill; First Lieutenants, Robert A. Ripley, J. S. A. Baker, William F. Norman; Second Lieutenants, J. J. Squiers, George E. Fancher, Charles H. Beaton, J. M. Lyman, E. S. Dunbar.

This consolidation was completed on the twenty-ninth of December, and the Thirteenth Regiment proper ceased to exist as an organization.

The Veteran Battalion, Thirteenth Conn. Vols., being composed chiefly of those who had re-enlisted in the preceding winter for three years or during the war, contained a large proportion of the patriotism and courage of the old regiment. Its members still clung with pride to the battle-torn flags they had so often borne to victory and looked confidently forward to new fields of danger and glory.

December 30, the day after the regiment was consolidated, the battalion moved with the remainder of the army five miles from Camp Russell to Stevenson's Depot, the terminus of the Harper's Ferry and Winchester Railroad, where the battalion was detached to guard the ammunition train of the Nineteenth Corps. A snow storm came on at evening, and next day was terribly bleak and wintry. The intense cold will long be remembered, the thin shelter-tents being entirely inadequate to keep out the cold, as the men lay without fires on the frozen ground. Monday, January 2, 1865, another snow storm came on. Our men stood shivering, silent and helpless. January 3d, the battalion moved to higher ground half a mile distant. January 4, another snow storm came and with it much suffering. The battalion at last obtained materials for building houses, and were just getting them into a habitable condition, when they received orders, January 5, to move by rail with the rest of the Second Division. A cold rain storm came on, soaking the clothing of the men who were kept eight hours in the storm on platform cars. Some had feet frozen; others, ears and fingers. Proceeding by rail from Harper's Ferry, they arrived at Baltimore, Saturday morning, January 7. Here they were crowded into barracks at Camp Carroll, a mile from town. They were packed in like sheep, with hardly room to stand. Private Lantry shot private Black, both of A: cause, rum.

Next day was clear and cold.

January 10th, the first and third brigades marched in a cold rain through the mud, and embarked under sealed orders. January 11, the battalion went on board the steamer *Manhattan*. At midnight, January 12, they were transferred to the steamer *Illinois*. Friday, January 13, they were towed to sea by tugs. Touching at Fortress Monroe and taking on board rations, they steamed out to sea the same night. The water was rough, but the *Illinois* came to anchor at evening, January 16, off the Savannah bar. January 17th, they waited all day for a pilot. Wednesday morning, January 18th, they weighed anchor and stood off in the direction of Hilton Head; but soon meeting the steamer on which was General Grover, they returned at his signal to the mouth of the Savannah. January 19th, they landed at last in the evening, two lighters having taken them up to the city. January 20, they went in a rain storm to the Central Railroad Depot, which they occupied a week. January 26, they moved a mile to the fortifications on the south side of the city and went into camp there. January 27, at night the great conflagration occurred in the city, reaching a magazine of shells, of which the explosions resembled the noise of a bombardment.

At Savannah, Captain Bradley commenced a series of inspections, and used extraordinary efforts for improving the condition and appearance of the men. He enforced the most rigid discipline and displayed many admirable traits of a commander. The battalion soon assumed the beauty and good order which had so distinguished the Thirteenth in its early history, and which their constant hard service in the field had to a great extent rendered impracticable for nearly three years. The weather being mild the battalion recovered from the hardships of the preceding fall and winter. The principal work was picket duty.

Wednesday, March 8, the battalion received orders to be ready to move at a moment's notice with three days' cooked rations. Sunday, March 12, reveille was had at three and a half A. M. At nine P. M. the battalion embarked on Steamer *Yazoo* for Morehead City, North Carolina. Monday, March 13, they arrived off the mouth of Cape Fear river. A dispatch boat brought orders to proceed to Beaufort, North

Carolina. The *Yazoo* put out to sea again. Next morning they landed at Morehead City, marched a mile up the railroad and took cars for Newbern. Here they arrived late in the evening, March 14. The Thirteenth proceeded on board a small boat at midnight, as a guard of commissary stores. On the fifteenth they steamed slowly up the Neuse river. Thursday, March 16, they remained in one spot all day. Friday, they steamed slowly along, and anchored at night. Saturday was a repetition of the preceding day. They tied to the bank at dark. Sunday they started at daylight and moved through the interminable cypress swamp. At noon this extraordinary journey ended, the battalion reaching Kinston. Here they met many of the Fifteenth Connecticut.

At nine and a half, next morning, they started on the return to Newbern, which they reached in *five hours*. Here they went into camp near the barracks. The ground was a drifting sand heap. March 24, eight hundred rebel prisoners arrived from Goldsborough. March 28, a large number of prisoners and refugees. March 29, seven hundred rebel prisoners came, and among them private John J. Lloyd, who had been captured at Winchester the nineteenth of September, and after various romantic adventures, had found himself there.

April 5, Captain Perkins was sent with a detail of thirty men to conduct four hundred rebel prisoners to Hart Island. The battalion remained in Newbern on provost duty giving great satisfaction to all well-disposed persons, and winning the reputation of being the handsomest and most orderly troops ever seen in Newbern. April 6, tidings came of the capture of

Richmond and Petersburgh. April 7, General Birge gave a brilliant soiree at his house in Newbern. April 8, the battalion received orders to go by rail to Morehead City, where they went into camp on the left (facing the harbor) of the railroad, and were brigaded under command of Colonel Graham, Twenty-second Iowa. April 11, news came of Lee's surrender, and the joyful event was celebrated by a great "jollification."

April 12, the writer arrived with Lieut. Gardner from rebel prisons and assumed command of the battalion.

Nothing of note occurred till May 2, when orders came to hold the command in readiness to move next morning at daylight. We remained all day and night waiting to embark. Thursday, May 4, at two P. M., we finally went on board the steamer *Neptune*. May 7, at 8 A. M. after a smooth passage from North Carolina, we disembarked at Savannah. Here we went into the buildings formerly occupied by the Fourteenth New Hampshire. Our brigade comprised the Twenty-second and Twenty-eighth Iowa, the One Hundred Thirty-first and One Hundred Fifty-ninth New York and Thirteenth Connecticut.

Our stay in Savannah was brief, lasting but four days. Orders came at two A. M., May 11, to be ready to march at eight A. M. with three days' cooked rations. At nine we marched out on the Augusta road thirteen miles and then bivouaced. When we were seven miles out, those of our New Orleans recruits, thirty or forty in number, whose term was to expire in May, were sent back to Savannah for muster out by order of General Birge. May 12, we marched sixteen miles. May 13, we marched eight miles, arriving at Sisters Ferry at nine A. M. Here we got rations that came by steamer. As evidence of the destitution of the people in this country, women and children came barefoot eight or ten miles to beg of us a little "hardtack." Fifty men of the Thirteenth were here put aboard steamer for Augusta. We left private Henry Williams, Company D, sick of small pox. He soon after died; the only man we ever lost by that disease.

For several days we continued the march, having reveille at three A. M. and starting at four. Quite a rivalry existed among the regiments in the matter of rapid marching. Two regiments, when the news came of Jeff. Davis' capture, were permitted to leave their knapsacks in order that they might sooner reach Augusta; whereupon the Thirteenth, determined not to be outdone, though heavily loaded with knapsacks, followed close on their heels and twice passed them on the road; making twenty-six miles May 16.

The people along the route looked with little favor upon the Yankee invâders as they termed us. A number of officers, at one of our halts, visited one of the fine residences and were entertained by several ladies with songs and instrumental music. One, more demonstrative than the rest, sung *Maryland, My Maryland,* with extraordinary gusto. Concluding, she turned to Dr. Clarke and said to that urbane gentlemen in a snappish way, "I spose that makes ye *mad*; don't it?" To which the Dr. retorted with provoking coolness, "O, no. We don't care what ye sing, as long as we can lick ye!" She rejoined, "We're not whipped. We're only overpowered."

"That's what we call *licked* in the North," said the Doctor.

May 19, at ten A. M. we arrived in Augusta, having marched twelve miles that morning. We went into an old Confederate shoe-factory, corner of Campbell and Ellis streets. May 21, we moved into the Confederate buildings known as the Blackie Hospital, corner of Washington and Watkins streets, on ground owned by the Orphan Asylum.

Our stay in Augusta continued till August 27. Captain Bradley was absent on Court Martial in Savannah until his resignation in August. Captain Wells had long been detached as *aide* of General Birge; Captain Perkins was Acting Inspector General on Molineux's staff. Captain Beckwith was soon detailed as ordnance officer. Surgeon Clary was Surgeon-in-chief, and in charge of the Post Hospital. Lieut. Col. Sprague, in addition to his other duties, was appointed Superintendent of Schools, and Educational Matters, and Superintendent of Public Buildings and all property appertaining to the Ordnance Department.

The battalion was assigned to provost duty which it performed to the highest satisfaction of the good people of Augusta. Their quarters became a model of neatness, and the battalion never looked finer. Hundreds of dollars were expended to procure the men white gloves and blacking. Many were the compliments we received, of which the following is a specimen:

"*Head-Quarters, Post Augusta,*
June 1, 1865.

Colonel:

The General is very much pleased with the neat and soldierly appearance of your guard this morning, and thinks it a decided criterion for the other regiments,

Respectfully yours,
HENRY LAWRENCE,
Post Adjutant.

To Col. H. B. Sprague,
Commanding Thirteenth Connecticut Vols.

On the sixth of June, 1865, the following appeared in the Augusta *Chronicle and Sentinel:*

" A stranger, who only saw the beautiful parade of the Thirteenth Battalion, Connecticut Volunteers on Friday last, or who only witnessed every morning the white gloves, the glittering arms and burnished scales of the handsome detachment which this Battalion daily sends to Head-quarters on guard duty, would hardly suppose that these men had done some of the most gallant fighting and encountered many of the severest hardships of the war for three and a half years past. Such, however, is the fact. At Irish Bend, at Winchester, at Cedar Creek, at Fisher's Hill, and in many another hard fight their colors have been riddled with shot and shell, and the earth has copiously drunk their blood. Of two thousand men who have belonged to the Thirteenth Connecticut, this little Battalion is all that remains.

" A single incident illustrates its spirit. On the fifteenth of June, 1863, after several most bloody and disastrous assaults on Port Hudson, General Banks published his famous order calling on the thirty regiments of the Union army for volunteers to form a storming column of one thousand men to lead the last desperate charge on the rebel works. Colonel Henry W. Birge, now Brevet Major General commanding defences of Savannah, immediately volunteered to lead this Forlorn Hope; and two hundred and twenty-five men and fifteen officers of his regiment, the gallant Thirteenth Connecticut, volunteered to follow him! So that this regiment alone furnished more men for this storming party than any other whole brigade. Surely, having won the honors, they have a right to wear the laurels!"

These praises were well-deserved. No troops, white or black, regulars or volunteers, ever kept their quarters, grounds, clothing, arms or accoutrements in handsomer condition than the Thirteenth at Blackie Hospital. Three bathing rooms were fitted up for the men and one for the officers. The most scrupulous cleanliness was enforced. For months Dr. Clark was not obliged to send a man to hospital.

July 18, the writer was appointed President of a board to examine Commissioned Officers with a view to their promotion or discharge.

July 21, the Thirteenth moved with the One Hundred Fifty-ninth New York to the Augusta Arsenal where they remained five weeks. July 22, the writer started for Annapolis as witness in a Court Martial, and was absent several weeks.

August 25, orders came for the battalion to move to Gainesville, Ga. August 27, the battalion proceeded to Athens, whence they marched to Gainesville, Hall County. The district of Gainesville comprised ten or a dozen counties of Northeast Georgia.

It was a position of difficulty and importance, inasmuch as it was infested with guerillas, bushwhackers and desperadoes from three States. Company A, Lieut. Gardner, was stationed at Jefferson, Jackson County; Company B, Lieut. Taylor, at Clarkesville, Habersham County; Company D, Lieut. Maddux, at Clayton, Rabun County; Companies C and E; Captains Beckwith and Sterry, at Gainesville, the battalion head-quarters. Lieut. Col. Sprague was detained at Augusta as President of a Military Commission.

About the middle of September, Lieuts. Pratt and Baldwin were detailed as members of a Court Martial at Washington, Wilkes County. Much game abounds here; and one Lieutenant is said to have displayed great enthusiasm in bagging an imaginary species of bird, known as *Yelpertrechers!* The process is as follows: After the New England mode of snaring rabbits, paths are made through the thicket, all converging to the point where the bag is. They must be hunted only by night. One person holds the bag—the post of honor! The rest of the party go away ostensibly to beat the bush and drive in the game; but really to disperse to their homes or meet at their rendezvous! How many our worthy Lieutenant would have caught had he remained all night is uncertain. But after two hours waiting, he discovered that the bag had no bottom, and not a solitary *Yelpertrecher!*

October 17, the companies received orders to concentrate at Athens, Clarke County. October 19, pursuant to new orders, A was sent to Washington, Ga.; C, to Carnesville; E, to Lexington; B and D were retained at Athens. The duties of officers at these county seats were to preserve order, approve contracts between whites and negroes, and administer the amnesty oath.

Athens is the seat of the State University. In the college buildings the Thirteenth was quartered. Drills, inspections and dress parades were held in the camps. Captain Wells, having just returned, was Provost Marshal; Lieut. Tooker, quartermaster; Lieut. Gaylord, adjutant. Sergeant Pfeiffer had charge of Cook's Armory. Sergent Santer, of the jail; Huntley, of the wood-choppers; and Beecher, of the Post Office.

November 8, Lieut. Col. Sprague arrived and assumed command of the District of Athens, which comprised the counties of Rabun, Habersham, Towns, Franklin, Banks, White, Hall, Hart, Clarke, Wilkes, Elbert, Jackson, Walton, Oglethorpe; head-quarters at Athens.

November 15, Lieut. Maddux had leave of absence. He never returned.

In the latter part of November rumors extensively prevailed of an intention among the blacks to massacre all the whites on the first of December. A negro near Watkinsville had been seen with a shot gun. Another said, "We's gwine to have our rights." Another, sixty years old, had been a servant in the Confederate army, and his master had told him he knew enough to be Captain; and so Uncle Reuben was called Major. A single-barrel pistol had been found in a black man's trunk. Mr. Phinizy of Athens, had picked up a mysterious letter containing dark hints. A secret association for mutual improvement among the colored people was known to be holding weekly meetings. Two young men came riding at a furious speed from Mistress King's plantation three miles from Athens, and reported that they had blacked their faces and had smuggled themselves into one of these secret meetings, and had heard,—well, they hadn't heard anything, but they were satisfied mischief was brewing, and they demanded a guard. Eleven negroes were dragged out of bed at Watkinsville at midnight, taken a mile off to the river bank, made to kneel on the brink, blindfolded, pistols were fired over their heads, their hands were tied, a solemn oath administered, and instant death threatened if they did not say they belonged to an armed association; and on such extorted, contradictory, and utterly vague confessions, the Sheriff of the County, and a magistrate of the (terribly) Inferior Court, had them arrested and brought before the writer. The whole country was in a state of consternation, and applications innumerable were made for guards of soldiers. And all arose out of precisely nothing. The credulity of these people was stupendous.

November 29, Lieut. Pratt was detailed for duty in the Freedmen's Bureau. December 1, Captain Wells was sent with companies A and B to Washington, Ga. December 4, the writer was appointed Commissioner of the Freedmen's Bureau for the District of Athens. The same day the battalion removed from the college buildings to the Military Academy a mile and a half distant, to give opportunity for repairs in view of the coming session.

December 6, Acting Commissary Sergeant W. H. Tucker, died from injuries received by being dashed against a tree, while on horseback three days before.

He was a brave, faithful, intelligent man. We buried him with military honors, the Episcopal service being read by Lieut. Col. Sprague.

December 23, a circus was exhibited in Athens, at which Sergeant Sperry with a guard was sent from the Thirteenth by request of the Mayor. The civil authorities soon sent back the military guard as being unnecessary, and the consequence was that the performance broke up in a "free fight."

The same day orders were received to move the battalion head-quarters to the Augusta Arsenal with Companies A and B. Company C, Lieut. Baldwin, was sent to Washington, Ga.; Company D, Captain Beckwith, was sent to Sparta, Hancock County; Company E, Captain Sterry, was left at Athens.

Christmas day was celebrated in Southern style. A great uprising of the negroes was anticipated by the feeble-minded. For abundant caution a large number of supernumerary policemen were sworn in, each of whom armed himself with a pistol and a brandy flask. Towards evening they were all drunk. The Thirteenth being on the eve of departure for Augusta, many of the soldiers were insulted and attacked on the streets. The citizens formed line of battle across the street and refused to let soldiers pass. Whereupon the latter came rushing to the Military Academy to get their muskets. Great was the alarm. Guns, pistols, knives and clubs were freely used. The venerable Dr. Hoyt, Presbyterian clergyman, a man of great worth, hastened to the writer, and begged him to use all his power to quell the riot. The mayor sent two messengers on the same errand; the first of whom was intercepted by the soldiers, beaten and sent back. The second was more successful. He brought the following communication :

Col. Sprage, Dr.

The excitement Doun Toun great. I fear there will great trouble Some of our young Men are excited and Some of yours under influence of Spirit. They have already met in combat and there wll be Serious times. I hope col You will in behalf of the law and Order Citizens protetct The Town.

You Respec.
S. C. Reese,
Mayor.

Dec. 25, 1865.

Seizing and detaining every soldier, as they came running back, the writer sent Captain Beckwith with about twenty picked men, mostly non-commissioned officers, with orders to arrest all soldiers and disorderly persons, shut up every dram shop, and notify every proprietor of places where liquor was kept, that if another glass was sold or given away the entire stock would instantly be smashed and the owner imprisoned. When the captain arrived in sight, the line of citizens broke and vanished. Perfect order reigned through the night in that literary town.

Next morning the troops left by rail.

Wednesday evening, December 27, Companies A and B arrived in Augusta. Captain Gardner was sent with A to the powder mills ; Lieut. Taylor, with B, to the arsenal. Captain Wells was detached as A. A. A. General on General King's staff.

January 3, 1866, the battalion was relieved from duty at Augusta, and ordered to garrison the District of Alatoona, Northwest Georgia, comprising about one fourth of the state, with head-quarters at Atlanta. Company B, Lieut. Taylor, was left for guard at Department Head-quarters. Lieut. Col. Sprague and Lieut. Gaylord were retained as members of a Military Commission; Captain Perkins was Provost Marshal, the duties of which office he had been discharging for several months.

Lieut. Taylor, with his company, had charge of the Augusta jail for a few weeks, and then removed to the first building occupied by the Thirteenth in Augusta, corner of Campbell and Ellis streets.

Captains Sterry and Gardner and Lieut. Baldwin arrived with E, A, and C, in Atlanta, January 10; Beckwith, with D, January 11. The soldiers were quartered in tents and in the City-Hall, and soon afterwards D and E were put into log houses. These were without floors, the ground was muddy, and the weather severe. Beckwith commanded the District; and Sterry the battalion. Little of interest occurred here. The soldiers were most uncomfortable; and despite the judicious efforts of Drs. Clary and Clark, many of them became sick.

Atlanta had been a vast wreck; a chaos of ashes, burnt walls, cinders, and the "abomination of desolation;" but it was now rapidly reviving, and the sound of the hammer and the saw was heard on every side.

In February, Lieut. Baldwin seized a rebel flag which was flying on a locomotive, as it passed through the city. The engineer and fireman were sent to Augusta, and there released under bonds by Captain Perkins, Provost Marshal. Soon after, Lieut. Baldwin was sent with

Company C to Dahlonega, to guard the U. S. Mint and other national property and preserve the peace.

In March, Lieut. Taylor with his company was sent to Atlanta.

Great discontent prevailed among the soldiers at being kept beyond the term for which they re-enlisted; they always insisting that the government had no right to detain them beyond the expiration of the war. Numerous applications by the battalion commander to secure their muster-out were unsuccessful, until April 13, 1866, when orders came for the battalion to rendezvous at Fort Pulaski for that purpose. They arrived there Friday, April 20. April 25, we were mustered out by Major Butler. April 28, we took the government boat for Savannah; where we were transferred to the ocean steamer *General Barnes*, for New York. At five o'clock P. M., April 28, we left Savannah. As we passed Fort Pulaski, we were saluted with six guns. The One hundred Seventy-sixth New York accompanied us.

Tuesday morning, May 1, we reached New York city. We were taken by government steamer to Hart Island, twenty-two miles distant. Here the enlisted men were paid on Saturday, May 5. They took the Paymaster's boat for New York City, and there dispersed. The officers were detained till Monday, May 7, when they too met for the last time, and parted.

So dissolved the last military organization from Connecticut in the service of the United States; twelve officers and one hundred and seventy-seven men only remaining of the thousands who had marched under the blue folds of our Connecticut flag.

APPENDIX.

ORIGINAL THIRTEENTH REGIMENT INFANTRY.

FIELD AND STAFF.

COLONEL.

HENRY W. BIRGE, Norwich, Nov. 9, 1861*; promoted Brig. Gen. U. S. Vols. Sept. 19, 1863.

LIEUTENANT-COLONEL.

ALEXANDER WARNER, Woodstock, April 9, 1862; resigned, July 29, 1863.

MAJOR.

RICHARD E. HOLCOMB, East Granby, Feb. 18, 1862; appointed Colonel 1st La. Vols. Aug. 16, 1862.

ADJUTANT.

WM. M. GROSVENOR, New Haven, Feb. 18, 1862; promoted Captain; disc. to rec. commission Oct. 29, 1863.

QUARTERMASTER.

JOSEPH B. BROMLEY, Norwich, Feb. 19, 1862; resigned Dec. 29, 1863.

CHAPLAIN.

CHARLES C. SALTER, New Haven, Feb. 27, 1862; resigned June 15, 1862.

SURGEON.

BENJAMIN N. COMINGS, New Britain, Feb. 18, 1862; resigned January 26, 1863.

1ST ASSISTANT SURGEON.

GEORGE CLARY, Hartford, Feb. 18, 1862; promoted Surgeon May 28, 1863.

2D ASSISTANT SURGEON.

NATHAN A. FISHER, Norwich, Feb. 4, 1862; resigned June 16, 1863.

SERGEANT MAJOR.

GEORGE W. WHITTLESEY, Norwich, Feb. 18, 1862; promoted Adjutant; resigned for disability Oct. 9, 1863.

Q. M. SERGEANT.

ANDREW T. JOHNSON, Montville, Feb. 18, 1862; promoted 2d Lieutenant Company A; killed on railroad Nov. 7, 1862.

*The first date in each case is the date of *muster*.

COMMISSARY SERGEANT.

Charles A. Tracy, Montville, Feb. 18, 1862; promoted Lieutenant 1st La. Vols. July 16, 1862.

HOSPITAL STEWARD.

William Bishop, Southington, Feb. 18, 1862; promoted Quartermaster May 1, 1864.

PRINCIPAL MUSICIAN.

Joseph Hadley, New London, Feb. 18, 1862; re-enlisted as Veteran February 8, 1864.

OFFICERS APPOINTED SINCE FIRST MUSTER.

CHAPLAIN.

Henry Upson, Berlin, June 16, 1862; resigned July 20, 1863.

2D ASSISTANT SURGEONS.

Samuel McClellan, New Haven, March 14, 1863; promoted 1st Assistant Surgeon July 9, 1863.

Lucius W. Clark, Winchester, July 9, 1863.

ORIGINAL INFANTRY COMPANY A.

CAPTAIN.

Henry L. Bidwell, Brooklyn, N. Y., Feb. 18, 1862; dishonorably discharged Aug. 25, 1862.

1ST LIEUTENANT.

John E. Woodruff, New Britain, Feb. 18, 1862; resigned June 21, 1862.

2D LIEUTENANT.

Charles H. Cornwall, New Britain, Feb. 18, 1862; promoted Captain Sept. 1, 1862.

SERGEANTS.

Richard Cowles, Farmington, Jan. 7, 1862; died Feb. 19, 1862.

Frank E. Stanley, New Britain, Dec. 22, 1861; killed at Irish Bend, La., April 14, 1863.

Hiram Griggs, Plymouth, Dec. 22, 1861; discharged April 4, 1863.

Nelson W. Steele, New Britain, Dec. 22, 1861.

Charles R. Gladden, New Britain, Dec. 22, 1861; died July 1, 1863.

CORPORALS.

Frank W. Stanley, New Britain, Dec. 30, 1861; died May, 1863, of wounds received at Irish Bend, La.

Henry H. Porter, Glastenbury, Dec. 22, 1861; discharged for disability Feb. 22, 1863.

Norman W. Warren, New Britain, Dec. 30, 1861; discharged for disability May 24, 1863.

Devereaux Jones, New Britain, Jan. 22, 1862; transferred to 1st Louisiana Regiment Aug. 17, 1862.

Walter G. Carpenter, New Britain, Dec. 30, 1861; died Nov. 17, 1862.

Newton W. Perkins, New Britain, Dec. 22, 1861; promoted 1st Lieutenant May 1, 1864.

Mortimer H. Stanley, New Britain, Dec. 22, 1861; discharged to receive commission Aug. 14, 1863.

Bernard Fagan, New Britain, Dec. 22, 1861; discharged for disability July 29, 1862.

MUSICIANS.

Charles N. Merwin, New Haven, Dec. 22, 1861; died July 5, 1863, of wounds received at Port Hudson, La.

William H. Moore, Wallingford, Feb. 27, 1862; died June, 1863.

WAGONER.

John C. North, New Britain, Jan. 7, 1862; re-enlisted as Veteran Feb. 8, 1864.

PRIVATES.

Ackley, John F., New Britain, Jan. 7, 1862.

Alger, Albert, Colchester, Dec. 22, 1861; discharged for disability May 24, 1862.

Alger, Henry, Colchester, Dec. 22, 1861; discharged for disability May 24, 1862.

Alger, William, Colchester, Dec. 22, 1861; drowned at New Orleans July 22, 1863.

Barrows, Wm. H., Farmington, Jan. 8, 1862; discharged for disability July 14, 1862.

Bassett, Milton H., New Britain, Dec. 22, 1861; discharged to enter telegraph corps, Aug. 17, 1863.

Bassett, Federick H., New Britain, Dec. 22, 1861; discharged to enter telegraph corps Aug. 17, 1863.

Benham, George B., Oxford, Dec. 22, 1851.

Billington, Dexter R., Killingly, Feb. 11, 1862; discharged to accept appointment as Hospital Steward.

Bissell, Frederick I. Glastenbury, Jan. 22, 1862; re-enlisted as Veteran Feb. 8, 1864.

Brady, Joseph P. Goshen, Dec. 22, 1861; re-enlisted as Veteran, Feb. 8, 1864.

Bronson, William C. New Britain, Dec. 30, 1861; discharged for disability May 30, 1862.

Brown, Robert, Farmington, Jan. 22, 1862; discharged for disability Dec. 31, 1863.

Carter, James W., Wethersfield, Feb. 5, 1862; discharged for disability May 24, 1863.

Clark, Linus M., Bristol, Dec. 22, 1861; re-enlisted as Veteran Feb. 8, 1864.

Connelly, Cornelius, New Britain, Jan. 8, 1862; discharged for disability Feb. 22, 1863.

Coyle, Barney, New Britain, Jan. 6, 1862.

Cunningham, Michael, Bristol, Feb. 10, 1862.

Curtiss, Joel, New Britain, Dec. 22, 1861; discharged for disability May 24, 1863.

DeWolf, Edward, Farmington, Feb. 11, 1862; died Oct. 15, 1863.

Dow, Newel, Wethersfield, Dec. 31, 1861; discharged for disability June 1, 1862.

Deming, Francis B., March 15, 1862.

Egan, Walter, New Britain, Jan. 7, 1862; re-enlisted as Veteran Feb. 8, 1864.

Ellwood, William, Newtown, Feb. 11, 1862; discharged for disability May 24, 1862.

Emmons, Nelson, Colchester, Dec. 22, 1861; discharged for disability July 5, 1863.

Fagan, Christopher C., New Britain, Jan. 6, 1862.

Fagan, John, New Britain, Jan. 6, 1862.

Gaffney, Francis J., New Britain, Dec. 30, 1861; re-enlisted as Veteran Feb. 29, 1864.

Gilbert, James, Farmington, Jan. 28, 1862; died Oct. 15, 1863.

Gilbert, Orrin C., New Britain, Jan. 6, 1862; discharged for disability May 31, 1862.

Gladden, Azariah, Farmington, Jan. 7, 1862; discharged for disability July 31, 1862.

Gladden, William H., New Britain, Dec. 22, 1861.

Haffy, James, New Britain, Dec. 31, 1861; discharged for disability May 30, 1862.

Hall, Josiah S , Bristol, Feb. 1, 1862; re-enlistod as Veteran Feb. 8, 1864.

Harlow, Edward, Wethersfield, Dec. 22, 1861; discharged for disability May 31, 1862.

Hart, Alverda S., New Britain, Dec. 22, 1861.

Hart, Henry C., Farmington, Feb. 10, 1862.

Hassan, James, New Britain, Jan. 8, 1862; died Sept. 5, 1863.

Hotchkiss, Wm. S., Farmington, Dec. 22, 1861; re-enlisted as Veteran Feb. 8, 1864.

Hurley, Thomas, New Britain, Jan. 22, 1862; died March 30, 1864.

James, Henry B., Colchester, Jan. 8, 1862; discharged for disability March 14, 1862.

Keaney, William, New Britain, Jan. 8, 1862; discharged for disability Aug. 24, 1863.

Lantry, Edward, New Britain, Dec. 30, 1861; re-enlisted as Veteran Feb. 8, 1864.

Lewis, James C., New Britain, Dec. 31, 1861; died Nov. 9, 1862.

Lloyd, John J., Farmington, Jan. 7, 1862.

Long, Julius F., East Hartford, Dec. 30, 1861; re-enlisted as Veteran Feb. 8, 1864.

Mack, Joseph S., New Britain, Dec. 30, 1861.

Maguire, John, New Britain, Dec. 31, 1861.

Martin, John, New Britain, Jan. 22, 1862; re-enlisted as Veteran Feb. 8, 1864.

Mason, David A., Killingly, Jan. 6, 1862; discharged for promotion in Corps D'Afrique Oct. 5, 1863.

Molloy, James, Berlin, Dec. 22, 1861.

Morton, Henry, New Britain, Jan. 6, 1862; re-enlisted as Veteran Feb. 8, 1864.

Northend, John, New Britain, Dec. 22, 1861; discharged for disability May 21, 1862.

Northrup, Wm. A., Milford, Dec. 22, 1861; discharged for disability July 31, 1862.

O'Brien, John, New Britain, Dec. 22, 1861; killed at Irish Bend, La., April 14, 1863.

O'Keefe, John, New Britain, Dec. 30, 1861.

Olmsted, Edgar, C. East Hartford, Dec. 30, 1861.

Oviatt, John M., Roxbury, Dec. 22, 1861.

Penfield, Loren D., New Britain, Jan. 8, 1862.

Presbrey, Edward M., Hartland, Jan. 6, 1862; discharged for disability March 27, 1863.

Pyatt, Samuel S., Farmington, Jan. 6, 1862; re-enlisted as Veteran Feb. 8, 1864.

Quigley, John, New Haven, Jan. 8, 1862; re-enlisted as Veteran Feb. 8, 1864.

Reilly, Thomas, New Britain, Dec. 30, 1861; re-enlisted as Veteran Feb. 8, 1864.

Reynolds, Patrick, Wethersfield, Jan. 22, 1862.

Riggs, Frederick J., Oxford, Dec. 22, 1861; deserted Jan 24, 1863.

Robinson, Robert, New Britain, Dec. 30, 1861; re-enlisted as Veteran Feb. 8, 1864.

Ryan, John C., Plymouth, Dec. 22, 1861; discharged for disability May 24, 1862.

Rowell, Charles R., Feb. 27, 1862.

Ralph, Curtis B., March 15, 1862; transferred to Veteran Reserve Corps May 1, 1864.

Simmons, John F., Hartland, Dec. 22, 1861.

Simmons, Lewis E., Killingly, Jan. 7, 1862; died Oct. 15, 1863.

Smith, John, New Britain, Dec. 22, 1861; re-enlisted as Veteran Feb. 29, 1864.

Stanley, Frederick N., New Britain, Dec. 31, 1861; promoted 2d Lieutenant Co. I Dec. 9, 1863.

Stoddard, Horace W., New Britain, Dec. 22, 1861; discharged for disability June 1, 1862.

Stone, Edward, Hamden, Dec. 22, 1861.

Sutliff, Friend, Plymouth, Dec. 22, 1861; re-enlisted as Veteran; died April 11, 1864.

Tubbs, John E., New Britain, Dec. 22, 1861.

Walker, William H. Hartford, Dec. 22, 1861; re-enlisted as Veteran Feb. 8, 1864.

Walker, William, Farmington, Dec. 22, 1861.

Warner, Charles E., New Britain, Feb. 10, 1862.

Weed, Edward R., Plymouth, Dec. 22, 1861; died May 27, 1863.

Willard, Edward, New Haven, Dec. 22, 1861; discharged for disability May 21, 1862.

Wolff, Francis J., New Britain, Dec. 22, 1861; re-enlisted as Veteran Feb. 8, 1864.

Woodford, Clayton, Avon, Jan. 7, 1862.

Wright, George, Plymouth, Dec. 30, 1861; discharged for disability Jan. 27, 1863.

ORIGINAL INFANTRY COMPANY B.

CAPTAIN.

Apollos Comstock, New Canaan, Feb. 18, 1862; promoted Major Nov. 5, 1863.

1ST LIEUTENANT.

William E. Bradley, New Canaan, Feb. 18, 1862; promoted Captain Sept. 1, 1863.

2D LIEUTENANT.

William C. Beecher, Southbury, Feb. 18, 1862; resigned Jan. 29, 1863.

SERGEANTS.

William G. Hawley, Newtown, Dec. 22, 1861; discharged for disability June 27, 1862.

Harvey E. Hendryx, Oxford, Dec. 22, 1861; discharged for disability Feb 28, 1863.

John J. Haight, Stamford, Dec. 22, 1861; discharged for disability June 30, 1862.

Eliakim Lockwood, Greenwich, Feb. 10, 1862; discharged for disability June 30, 1862.

George E. Fancher, Norwalk, Jan. 22, 1862; promoted 2d Lieutenant Co. D. Aug. 25, 1863.

CORPORALS.

George H. Pratt, Stamford, Jan. 11, 1862; re-enlisted as Veteran; promoted 2d Lieutenant May 1, 1864.

Henry Hitchcock, Southbury, Dec. 22, 1861; discharged for disability June 30, 1862.

Jonathan Austin, New Canaan, Feb. 18, 1862; re-enlisted as Veteran Feb. 29, 1864.
David E. Holdridge, Sherman, Dec. 22, 1861; re-enlisted as Veteran Feb. 8, 1864.
Franklin S. Twichell, Newtown, Dec. 22, 1861; re-enlisted as Veteran Feb. 8, 1864.
Edwin B. Sanford, Litchfield, Dec. 22, 1861; discharged for disability May 25, 1863.
Henry S. Conrad, Woodbury, Dec. 22, 1861; died Jan. 9, 1863.
Hurlburt C. Hayes, Torrington, Jan. 11, 1862.

MUSICIANS.

George W. Taylor, Stamford, Dec. 31, 1861.
Hiram Ruscoe, Wilton, Feb. 18, 1862; died June 26, 1863.

WAGONER.

Aaron Finnell, Greenwich, Feb. 10, 1862; discharged for disability July 5, 1862.

PRIVATES.

Ackley, Abram E., Stamford, Jan. 6, 1862; died August 9, 1863.
Avery, Aaron S., Stamford, Jan. 11, 1862; discharged Jan. 14, 1863.
Bell, Martin, Stamford, Dec. 22, 1861; re-enlisted as Veteran Feb. 8, 1864.
Benedict, Aaron, New Canaan, Dec. 22, 1861; died Nov. 28, 1862.
Bishop, Isaac W., New Haven, Feb. 1, 1862; re-enlisted as Veteran Feb. 8, 1864.
Blackman, Alfred, Norwalk, Feb. 5, 1862; discharged for disability July 5, 1862.
Blackman, Eli B., Middlebury, Feb. 1, 1862; killed at Irish Bend, La., April 14, 1863.
Blackman, Elisha S., Waterbury, Feb. 1, 1862; re-enlisted as Veteran Feb. 8, 1864.
Briscoe, Charles L., Newtown, Feb. 5, 1862; dropped from roll May 30, 1862.
Brown, John J., New Haven, Feb. 20, 1862.
Brown, John W., New Canaan, Feb. 5, 1862.
Byington, Francis C., Bridgeport, Dec. 22, 1861; deserted Jan. 25, 1863.
Casey, William E., Bridgeport, Feb. 5, 1862.
Cleaveland, Charles F., Torrington, Dec. 22, 1861; died April 8, 1862.
Conger, William E., Sherman, Dec. 22, 1861.
Dann, Eli, New Canaan, Feb. 1, 1862; discharged for disability March 5, 1862.
Davis, Charles, Southbury, Dec, 22, 1861; discharged for disability Sept. 18, 1862.
Deming, Lewins, Avon, Feb. 18, 1862; discharged for disability May 21, 1862.
Dixon, Clark, Stamford, Jan. 11, 1862; re-enlisted as Veteran Feb. 8, 1864.
Dunbar, Edward M., Torrington, Dec. 22, 1861; discharged for disability June 30, 1862.

Fairchild, Reuben A., Newtown, Feb. 18, 1862; discharged for disability July 5, 1862.

Fancher, Charles I, Norwalk, Jan. 22, 1862; discharged to join Telegraph Corps, Aug. 17, 1863.

Fancher, John F., Bridgeport, Feb. 18, 1862; discharged for disability June 27, 1862.

Farrell, John W., Newtown, Dec. 22, 1861; re-enlisted as Veteran Feb 8, 1864.

Ferris, Wm. I., Stamford, Feb. 10, 1862; died May 29, 1863.

Fleharty, William, Hamden, Feb. 10, 1862; re-enlisted as Veteran Feb. 29, 1864.

Foote, Edward A., Torrington, Jan. 11, 1862.

Gardner, Franklin, Sherman, Dec. 22, 1861 ; discharged for disability June 27, 1862.

Gardner, James, Wilton, Jan. 7, 1862; re-enlisted as Veteran Feb. 8, '64.

Gilder, Wilbur F., New Canaan, Feb. 18, 1862; discharged September 17, 1863.

Griffin, Timothy, New Haven, Feb. 10, 1862; discharged for disability Sept. 23, 1862.

Handy, Benjamin A., Canterbury, Jan. 8, 1862; " " July 7, 1862.

Hanford, William H., Wilton, Dec. 22, 1861; transferred to 2d La. Vols. Aug. 28, 1862.

Hamblin, John N., March 5, 1862; deserted.

Harting, Charles H., New Haven, Feb. 18, 1862; discharged for disability, May 21, 1862.

Hawley, Frederick E., Torrington, Dec. 22, 1861; " " Feb. 28, 1863.

Hegany, Dennis, Torrington, Dec. 22, 1861; re-enlisted as Veteran Feb. 8, 1864.

Hotchkiss, Norman, Hamden, Feb. 10, 1862.

Hotchkiss, Wooster, Derby, Feb. 10, 1862.

Hewlett, George E., Torrington, Dec. 22, 1861; transferred to 1st La. Regt. Aug. 8, 1862.

Hungerford, Martin B., Sherman, Dec. 22, 1861; died December 6, 1862.

Harris, Thomas S., Stamford, Feb. 27, 1862; discharged for disability June 30, 1862.

Hull, Edwin C., River, N. Y., March 12, 1862; discharged for disability June 30, 1862.

Jones, Banister H., Stamford, March 5, 1862; discharged for disability, May 21, 1862.

Jones, William H., New Canaan, Dec. 22, 1861; re-enlisted as Veteran Feb. 8, 1864.

Kane, John, Newtown, Jan. 6, 1862.

Keeney, Mortimer R., Bristol, Dec. 30, 1861; re-enlisted as Veteran, Feb. 8, 1864.

Keeney, Russel, Bristol, Jan. 22, 1862; discharged for disability, Sept. 23, '62.
Knapp, James R., Stamford, Feb. 10, 1862; discharged for disability March 5, 1862.
Lapman, Edward A., New Canaan, Jan. 22, 1862; discharged for disability July 29, 1862.
Lockwood, Edward C., Stamford, Dec. 22, 1861.
Lyons, George L., Waterbury, Jan. 22, 1862; discharged for disability June 27, 1862.
Mead, Benjamin L., Ridgefield, Feb. 5, 1862; re-enlisted as Veteran, Feb. 8, 1864.
Munroe, Edwin, New Canaan, Dec. 22, 1861.
Munroe, William H., New Canaan, Feb. 5, 1862; discharged for disability, July 5, 1862.
Murphey, Edward, Torrington, Feb. 20, 1862 ; died April 7, 1862.
Moore, Charles E., March 5, 1862; discharged for disability, May 13, 1863.
Nichols, Charles, New Canaan, Feb. 18, 1862; re-enlisted as Veteran Feb. 29, 1864.
Peck, Chester D., Newtown, Feb. 1, 1862; re-enlisted as Veteran, Feb. 8, 1864.
Prindle, George, Greenwich, Dec. 22, 1861; " " Feb. 8, 1864.
Ruggles, Elbert, Ridgefield, Feb. 18, 1862; " " " 29, 1864.
Ruggles, Sidney B., Ridgefield, Feb. 5, 1862, " " " 8, 1864.
Searles, George H., Stamford, Jan 6, 1862; discharged for disability June 30, 1862.
Searles, Henry C., Stamford, Feb. 18, 1862; discharged for disability, July 30, 1862.
Sarles, John E., Stamford, Jan. 6, 1862.
Seeley, William H., New Canaan, Jan. 6, 1862; discharged January 14, 1863.
Selleck, George B., Stamford, Dec. 22, 1861; died September 29, 1862.
Shephard, Harvey G., Branford, Jan. 22, 1862; discharged for disability June 15, 1862.
Sherman, George, Monroe, Feb. 1, 1862; discharged for disability July 5, 1862.
Sherman, Reuben A., Wilton, Dec. 30, 1861; discharged for disability Aug. 26, 1862.
Sherwood, Charles E., Norwalk, Feb. 5, 1862; discharged for disability Feb. 28, 1863.
Sturges, Frederick L., Ridgefield, Feb. 5, 1862; died December 12, 1863.
Sarles, Benjamin O., Stamford, Feb. 26, 1862; killed at Irish Bend, La., April 14, 1863.
Schreyer, Felix, Southbury, March 13, 1862.
Taylor, John J., Stamford, Dec. 22, 1861; died February 17, 1864.
Taylor, Roswell, Newtown, Jan. 22, 1862.
Thorne, John W., Stamford, Feb. 20, 1862; died September 6, 1863.
Thorne, Joseph, Stamford, Feb. 10, 1862; re-enlisted as veteran Feb. 29, 1864.

Tomlinson, Chas. H., New Haven, Jan. 22, 1862; killed at Irish Bend, La., April 14, 1863.

VanScoy, John A., Ridgefield, Feb. 20, 1862.

Warner, Newton J., Woodbury, Dec. 22, 1861; transferred to the Veteran reserve corps, April 30, 1864.

Weed, Francis E , New Canaan, Dec. 31, '61; re-enlisted as Veteran Feb. 8, 1864.

Weed, John P., Stamford, Dec. 31, 1861.

Wheeler, Alonzo, Bethel, Feb. 20, 1862.

Wood, Israel, New Canaan, Feb. 28, 1862; discharged for disability July 29, 1862.

Wood, Linus, New Canaan, Feb. 1, 1862; discharged for disability, July 7, 1862.

Waterbury, Henry, Darien, Feb. 27, 1862; re-enlisted as Veteran Feb. 29, 1864.

ORIGINAL INFANTRY COMPANY C.

CAPTAIN.

Charles D. Blinn, Cornwall, Feb. 18, 1862, promoted Colonel Nov. 5, 1863.

1ST LIEUTENANT.

Isaac F. Nettleton, Kent, Feb. 18, 1862; died September 26, 1862.

2D LIEUTENANT.

Charles E. Tibbetts, New Milford, Feb. 18, 1862; promoted 1st Lt. Co. A.; resign'd on disability, May 11, 1864.

SERGEANTS.

Everett S. Dunbar, Sharon, Nov. 27, 1861; promoted 2d Lt. Co. G. Sept. 1, 1863.

Charles H. Gaylord, New Milford, Dec. 17, 1861; re-enlisted as Veteran Feb. 8, 1864.

John N. Duncan, Kent, Nov. 27, 1861; discharged for disability May 13, 1863.

James T. Smith, New Hartford, Jan. 7, 1862; transferred to 1st La. Reg't. Aug. 8, 1862, as Lieutenant.

John N. Lyman, Warren, Nov. 27, 1861; re-enlisted as Vet.; promoted 2d Lt. Jan. 29, 1864.

CORPORALS.

George W. Sperry, Goshen, Nov. 27, 1861; re-enlisted as Veteran Feb. 8, 1864.

Lewis Hart, Canaan, Nov. 27, 1861; re-enlisted as Veteran Feb. 8, 1864.

Simon Potter, Kent, Nov. 27, 1861; discharged September 7, 1862.

Homer M. Welch, Kent, Nov. 27, 1861; re-enlisted as Veteran, Feb. 8, 1864.

Henry E. Merwin, Goshen, Dec 17, 1861; discharged for disability May 12, 1863.

Albert G. Williams, Canaan, Nov. 27, 1861; died November 11, 1862.

James D. Mosher, New Milford, Dec. 17, 1861; died August 6, 1863.

William H. Odell, Kent, Nov. 27, 1861; discharged February 14, 1863.

MUSICIANS.

George C. Skiff, Sharon, Nov. 27, 1861; died October 9, 1862.

Benjamin Walker, Kent, Feb. 10, 1862; discharged for disability May 31, 1862.

WAGONER.

James H. Evans, New Milford, Nov. 27, 1861, re-enlisted as Veteran, Feb. 8, 1864.

PRIVATES.

Austin, Andrew J., Kent, Dec. 17, 1861, re-enlisted as Veteran Feb. 8, '64.

Barnes, Willis, Kent, Jan. 22, 1862, " " 8, "

Beeman, William, Warren, Dec. 30, 1861, " " 8, "

Billings, Peter, Canaan, Dec. 30, 1861; " " 8, "

Brazee, Edwin, Sharon, Jan. 22, 1862; deserted August 3, 1862.

Brown, Hobby, Kent, Dec. 30, 1861; re-enlisted as Veteran Feb. 8, 1864.

Buckley, Seymour, Sharon, Nov. 27, 1861; " " 8, 1864.

Burns, Thomas, Meriden, Jan. 7, 1862; killed at Port Hudson, La., June 14, 1863.

Butler, George W., Goshen, Nov. 27, 1861; discharged for disability Mch. 11, 1863.

Brazee, George, March 11, 1862; deserted August 3, 1862.

Brockett, George, W. March 5, 1861.

Camp, Edwin T., New Milford, Nov. 27, 1861; discharged for disability Feb. 17, 1863.

Carpenter, John, Kent, Nov. 27, 1861; discharged for disability May 31, 1862.

Chaffee, Joshua B., Sharon, Nov. 27, 1861; discharged for disability Mch 4, 1862.

Clark, John, Kent, Dec. 30, 1861; died August 6, 1862.

Clemens, Lewis S., Salisbury, Nov. 27, 1861; discharged for disability Aug. 5, 1862.

Cole, Charles E., Sharon, Nov. 27, 1861; discharged for disability Feb. 25, 1862.

Cook, Alexander, Cornwall, Dec. 30, 1861.

Dauchy, Charles F., Salisbury, Nov. 27, 1861; discharged December 9 1862.

Dean, Moses, Canaan, Dec. 30, 1861; discharged for disability, Aug. 5, 1862.

DeMarchy, James M., Canaan, Dec. 30, 1861; re-enlisted as Veteran Feb. 8, 1864.

Dibble, George, Cornwall, Dec. 22, 1861.

Dingaa, James H., Kent, Jan. 22, 1862; re-enlisted as Veteran Feb. 8, 1864,

Douglass, Reuben H., Kent, Nov. 27, 1861; died September 4, 1862.

Downs, George C., Goshen, Nov. 27, 1861; died September 13, 1863.
Dunbar, Everett E., Kent, Nov. 27, 1861; re-enlisted as Veteran Feb. 8, 1864.
Erwin, George W., Canaan, Nov. 27, 1861.
Evetts, Edwin, Kent, Dec. 30, 1861; re-enlisted as Veteran Feb. 29, 1864.
Ferriss, John, New Milford, Dec. 22, 1861.
Fuller, Ethan A., Canaan, Dec. 30, 1861; re-enlisted as Veteran Feb. 8, '64.
Griffin, Chauncey, Sharon, Nov. 27, 1861; " " " 8, '64.
Green, Edmund L., Morris, Feb. 20, 1862; discharged for disability Oct. 28, 1862.
Hall, George W., Sharon, Jan. 22, 1862; re-enlisted as Veteran Feb. 8, 1864.
Hall, Homer, Kent, Nov. 27, 1861; discharged for disability March 9, 1864.
Hall, Leonidas R., New Britain, Jan. 28, 1862; transferred to 1st La. Reg't. Aug. 8, 1862, as lieutenant.
Hammond, Seneca, Kent, Nov. 27, 1861; re-enlisted as Veteran Feb. 8, '64.
Hicks, James, Goshen, Nov. 27, 1861; discharged for disability March 12, 1862.
Hotchkiss, Charles, Cornwall, Nov. 27, 1861; died March 19, 1864.
Hoxie, Joshua B., Sharon, Feb. 5, 1862.
Hutchins, John B., Kent, Nov. 27, 1861; discharged for disability May 29, 1863.
Judd, John S., Canaan, Dec. 17, 1861; discharged February 14, 1863.
Lineburg, Egbert, Amenia, N. Y., Dec. 30, 1861; re-enlisted as Veteran, Feb. 8, 1864.
Losser, Job S., Sharon, Nov. 27, 1861.
Mansfield, Norman, Salisbury, Dec. 17, 1861; discharged October 12, 1862.
Marshall, Ezra S., Kent, Nov. 27, 1861; discharged for disability Aug. 5, 1862.
Marshall, Ira, Kent, Nov. 27, 1861.
McGowan, John, Cornwall, Nov. 27, 1861; re-enlisted as veteran; died April 26, 1864.
Mitchell, Charles, Kent, Dec. 30, 1861; re-enlisted as Veteran Feb. 8, 1864.
Morris, Michael, Goshen, Dec. 30, 1861; " " " 8, 1864.
Murphy, William H., Kent, Nov. 27, 1861; " " " 8, 1864.
Nickerson, Edwin L., Cornwall, Feb. 27, 1862; killed at Irish Bend, La., April 14, 1863.
Odell, John, New Milford, Nov. 27, 1861; re-enlisted as Veteran Feb. 8, '64.
Packard, Shepard, Sharon, Nov. 27, 1861; " " " 8, '64.
Pindar, Frederick W., Kent, Nov. 27, 1861; " " " 8, '64.
Potter, Oliver, Kent, " 27, 1861; " " " 8, '64.
Pratt, Joseph H., Kent, " 27, 1861; " " " 8, '64.
Prindle, Benjamin H., Goshen, " 27, 1861; discharged October 17, 1862.
Quain, Francis, Kent, " 27, 1861; discharged for disability May 31, 1862.
Raymond, Joseph W., Danbury, Feb. 10, 1862; discharged for disability June 6, 1862.

Reynolds, William H., Kent, Nov. 27, 1861; died May 14, 1862.

Richmond, Charles, Cornwall, Nov. 27, 1861; re-enlisted as veteran Feb. 8, 1864.

Roach, John, Kent, Nov. 27, 1861; died August 18, 1862.

Roraback, James H., Cornwall, Nov. 27, 1861; re-enlisted as veteran Feb. 8, 1864.

Roraback, George, " " 27, 1861; " " " 8,'64.

Rogers, John, Sharon, Dec. 17, 1861; discharged for disability, March 10, '62.

Savage, James, Sharon, Nov. 27, 1861; re-enlisted as veteran Feb. 8, 1864.

Scott, Elias P., Kent, Nov. 27, 1861; discharged September 7, 1862.

Scott, Mortimer H., Kent, Nov. 27, 1861; re-enlisted as veteran Feb. 8, 1864.

Slover, Chester, Sharon, " 27, 1861; died February 7, 1862.

Smith, Orange, Kent, " 27, 1861.

Stowe, Vivant, " Jan. 22, 1862; discharged for disability Aug. 5, 1862.

Stuart, Frederick, Kent, Dec. 17, 1861; discharged for disability April 16, 1864.

Stuart, Herman, " Dec. 30, 1861; re-enlisted as veteran Feb. 8, '64.

Taylor, Joseph, New Milford, Dec. 17, 1861; re-enlisted as veteran Feb. 8, 1864.

Teneyck, William H., Kent, Dec. 30, 1861; discharged for disability May 13, 1863.

Thompson, Daniel, Kent, Nov. 27, 1861; re-enlisted as veteran Feb. 8, 1864.

Titus, Sylvester, Cornwall, Nov. 27, 1861; " " " 8, 1864.

Wadhams, Frank E., Goshen, Dec. 17, 1861; " " " 8, 1864.

Waldron, Frederick E., Kent, Nov. 27, 1861; died June 19, 1863, of wounds received at Port Hudson, La.

Waldron, Lockwood, Sharon, Nov. 27, 1861; discharged for disability May 31, 1862.

Wilson, Beach T., Danbury, Dec. 30, 1861; discharged for disability May 31, 1862.

Wilson, Thomas, Sharon, Nov. 27, 1861; discharged for disability Feb. 25, 1862.

Wright, Henry S., Cornwall, Dec. 30, 1861; re-enlisted as veteran Feb. 8, 1864.

Warner, Horace C., Sharon, Feb. 20, 1862; discharged for disability May 31, 1862.

Wickwire, Franklin L., March 5, 1862; died June 26, 1862.

OFFICER APPOINTED SINCE FIRST MUSTER.

1st Lieut.

Robert A. Ripley, Norwich, Dec. 31, 1862.

ORIGINAL INFANTRY COMPANY D.

CAPTAIN.

Cyrus E. Prindle, Roxbury, Feb. 20, 1862; resigned Aug. 14, 1862.

1ST LIEUTENANT.

Perry Averill, Southbury, Feb. 18, 1862; promoted Captain Co. C. Dec 9, 1863.

2D LIEUTENANT.

Joseph H. Meredith, New Haven, Feb. 18, 1862; resigned August 13, 1862

SERGEANTS.

George A. Mayne, Bridgeport, Dec. 17, 1861; transferred to 1st La. Reg't. August 8, 1862.

Lester E. Owen, New Hartford, Jan. 22, 1862; discharged for disability June 30, 1862.

Seth H. Addis, Roxbury, Jan. 7, 1862; deserted March 17, 1862.

William H. Strong, New Hartford, Jan. 7, 1862; discharged for disability Sept. 23, 1862.

Ezra M. Hull, Newtown, Dec. 17, 1861; re-enlisted as Veteran Feb. 8, '64.

CORPORALS.

John D. Hull, Roxbury, Dec. 17, 1861; discharged for disability June 30, 1862.

Timothy Whittlesey, Washington, Dec. 17; discharged to receive promotion May 21, 1863.

Eugene Ward, New York, Dec. 22, '61; discharged to receive promotion May 21, 1863.

Elias H. Dewey, New Haven, Dec. 31, 1861; transferred to Veteran Reserve Corps April 30, 1864.

Henry W. Richards, Southbury, Dec. 22, 1861; discharged for disability Sept. 23, 1862.

William Finnimore, Bridgeport, Jan. 22, 1862; re-enlisted as Veteran Feb. 8, 1864.

Lewis F. Marshall, Bridgeport, Dec. 30, 1861; discharged for disability June 30, 1862.

Charles Chapman, New Haven, Dec. 17, 1861; deserted March 17, 1862.

MUSICIANS.

Benjamin G. Loomis, New Hartford, Dec. 22, 1861; transferred to 1st La. Reg't. Aug. 8, 1862.

Andrew Holford, New Haven, Dec. 17, 1861; re-enlisted as Veteran Feb. 8, 1864.

WAGONER.

Joel Congden, Montville, Dec. 30, 1861; re-enlisted as Veteran Feb. 8, '64.

PRIVATES.

Allen, Chauncey F., Woodbury, Dec. 17, 1861; discharged for disability July 29, 1862.

Andrews, James, Norwalk, Jan 11, 1862; deserted July 10, 1862.
Andrus, Thames B., Simsbury, Dec. 22, 1861; re-enlisted as Veteran Feb. 8, 1864.
Alton, Edward, March 14, 1862.
Bishop, Henry F., Feb. 18, 1862; re-enlisted as Veteran Feb. 29, 1864.
Barbour, Henry M., New Hartford, Feb. 1, 1862; re-enlisted as Veteran Feb. 8, 1864.
Barbour, Theron, Barkhamsted, Dec. 30, 1861; discharged for disability May 24, 1862.
Bishop, Dean, Washington, Dec. 22, 1861; re-enlisted as Veteran Feb. 8, '64.
Bliss, Charles, Springfield, Mass., Dec. 22, 1861; discharged for disability, July 29, 1862.
Bottsford, John N., Bridgeport, Jan. 7, 1862; re-enlisted as Veteran Feb. 8, 1864.
Bragg, William B., New Hartford, Dec. 30, 1861; discharged Aug. 26, 1863.
Briggs, Daniel, New Milford, Dec. 22, 1861; discharged for disability May 24, 1862.
Butler, Charles, Brookfield, Jan. 22, 1862; re-enlisted as Veteran Feb 8, '64.
Butler, James, Brookfield, Jan. 22, 1862; reclaimed as deserter from 4th N. Y. Art. Feb. 21, '62.
Dillon, John, Waterbury, Jan. 28, 1862; re-enlisted as Veteran Feb. 8, '64.
Dimelow, George, Newtown, Dec. 17, 1861; re-enlisted as Veteran Feb. 8, 1864.
Doane, Edward, New Milford, Jan. 22, 1862; discharged for disability June 10, 1863.
Dolbeare, Thos. W., Montville, Jan. 22, 1862; discharged for disability Aug. 27, 1862.
Donnivan, James, New Hartford, Dec. 22, 1861; transferred to Veteran Reserve Corps April 30, 1864.
Dorain, Hugh, Enfield, Feb. 5, 1862; re-enlisted as Veteran Feb. 8, 1864.
Fiscuss, Henry, Waterbury, Dec. 22, 1862; re-enlisted as Veteran Feb. 8, 1864.
Fox, Henry F., Woodbury, Dec. 22, 1861; died November 27, 1863.
French, Ephraim L., New Hartford, Dec. 30, 1861.
Gardner, Joseph A., Montville, Dec. 30, 1861; re-enlisted as Veteran Feb. 8, 1864.
Gilmore, William, New Hartford, Dec. 22, 1861; died July 6, 1863.
Gorman, John, Hartford, Dec. 22, 1861; died August 2, 1862.
Greer, James, New Hartford, Dec. 17, 1861; discharged for disability Dec. 26, 1863.
Hayes, Alonzo, Bridgeport, Jan. 28, 1862; re-enlisted as Veteran Feb. 8, 1864.
Hayes, David, New Hartford, Dec. 22, 1861; re-enlisted as Veteran Feb. 8, 1864.
Hill, Austin H., Southbury, Dec. 22, 1861; discharged for disability May 2, 1863.

Hopkins, Roswell E., New Hartford, Jan. 7, 1862; killed in assault on Port Hudson, La., June 14, 1863.

Jennings, George F., Bridgeport, Dec. 30, 1861.

Jerome, Henry G., Montville, Dec. 30, 1861; dropped from roll, having never reported.

Johnson, John B., Feb. 18, 1862, re-enlisted as Veteran Feb. 29, 1864.

Kibbee, Seth M., New Hartford, Dec. 22, 1861; discharged for disability Aug. 27, 1862.

Kimberly, Albert A., Oxford, Dec. 30, 1861; died Dec. 6, 1863.

King, William W., Montville, Dec. 30, 1861; re-enlisted as Veteran Feb. 8, 1864.

Knapp, Charles E., Feb. 20, 1862; deserted March 17, 1862.

Lombard, Albert, Hadley, Mass., Jan. 22, 1862; deserted March 17, 1862.

Long, Henry, New Haven, Dec. 22, 1861; re-enlisted as Veteran Feb. 8, 1864.

Losaw, George, Winchester, Dec. 22, 1861; re-enlisted as Veteran Feb. 8, 1864.

Martin, Frank, New Hartford, Dec. 22, 1861; discharged May 19, 1862.

McCabe, Luke, New Hartford, Jan. 22, 1862.

McManus, Edward, New Hartford, Dec. 22, 1861; killed in assault on Port Hudson, La., June 14, 1863.

Mitchell, Joseph F., Montville, Jan. 11, 1862; re-enlisted as Veteran Feb. 8, 1864.

Munson, Charles, Newton, Dec. 22, 1861; died Aug. 29, 1863.

Northeridge, Geo. W., April 30, 1862; discharged for disability March 11, 1863.

Palmer, Frederick C., Montville, Jan. 7, 1862; re-enlisted as Veteran Feb 8, 1864.

Pellam, Wallace, Norwalk, Feb. 5, 1862; discharged for disability May 24, 1862.

Polley, Henry E., Woodbury, Dec. 22, 1861; re-enlisted as Veteran Feb. 8, 1864.

Prentice, William P., March 5, 1862.

Quinn, Matthew, New Hartford, Dec. 22, 1861.

Read, Samuel, Brookfield, Jan. 22, 1862; deserted March 17, 1862.

Reynolds, James E., Montville, Dec. 30, 1861; discharged for disability Aug. 27, 1862.

Root, Orville A., Barkhamsted, Dec. 30, 1861; discharged for disability Aug. 27, 1862.

Root, Watson R., New Hartford, Dec. 22, 1861; discharged for disability Sept. 23, 1862.

Ruby, Eli, New Milford, Dec. 22, 1861; discharged for disability March 17, 1862.

Ruby, George M., New Milford, Dec. 22, 1861; re-enlisted as Veteran Feb. 8, 1864.

Skiff, Walter, Oxford, Feb. 1, 1862; re-enlisted as Veteran Feb. 8, 1864.

Stevens, Henry M., Norwich, Jan. 11, 1862; re-enlisted as Veteran Feb. 8, 1864.
Stoddard, Horace B., Bridgeport, Dec. 17, 1861; re-enlisted as Veteran Feb. 8, 1864.
Squier, John J., Roxbury, Dec. 30, 1861; promoted 2d Lieutenant Co. F Sept. 1, 1863.
Tooker, William B., Montville, Dec. 30, 1861; re-enlisted as Veteran Feb. 8, 1864.
Tucker, Henry J., New Hartford, Dec. 30, 1861; discharged for disability Sept. 27, 1863.
Tucker, William H., Barkhamsted, Jan. 7, 1862; re-enlisted as Veteran Feb. 8, 1864.
Tyler, Martin W., New Hartford, Jan. 28, 1862; re-enlisted as Veteran Feb. 8, 1864.
Tyrrell, Stephen, Newtown, Dec. 17, 1861; re-enlisted as Veteran Feb. 8, 1864.
Taylor, Miner J., March 5, 1862; discharged for disability Aug. 27, 1862.
Vizer, Rosamond, Bridgeport, Jan. 28, 1862; re-enlisted as Veteran Feb. 8, 1864.
Welch, Patrick, New Hartford, Dec. 30, 1861; died March 7, 1862.
Welden, Edward J., New Hartford, Feb. 5, 1862; re-enlisted as Veteran Feb. 8, 1864.
Wilcox, George T., New Hartford, Dec. 22, 1861; discharged for disability June 30, 1862.
Welch, John, Feb. 10, 1862; discharged for disability May 24, 1862.

ORIGINAL INFANTRY COMPANY E.

CAPTAIN.

Eugene Tisdale, New Britain, Feb. 18, 1862; resigned April 30, 1864.

1ST LIEUTENANT.

Eugene E. Graves, Thompson, Feb. 18, 1862.

2D LIEUTENANT.

William P. Miner, Norwich, Feb. 18, 1862; promoted 1st Lieutenant Co. H Feb. 20, 1863.

SERGEANTS.

Chas. Henry Beaton, New Hartford, Dec. 22, 1861; promoted 2d Lieutenant Feb. 20, 1863.
George B. Deming, West Hartford, Dec. 22, 1861; promoted 2d Lieutenant; resigned June 26, 1863.
Stephen R. Peavy, Plainfield, Dec. 22, 1861; re-enlisted as Veteran Feb. 8, 1864.

Albert M. Cadwell, West Hartford, Dec. 22, 1861; re-enlisted as Veteran, Feb. 29, 1864.

William Blanchard, Putnam, Jan. 7, 1862; killed at Brashear City, La. June 21, 1863.

CORPORALS.

Richard Croley, New Britain, Jan. 8, 1862; re-enlisted as Veteran Feb. 8, 1864.

Chas. H. Colegrove, Norwich, Dec. 22, 1861; discharged for disability May 13, 1863.

William A. Osborn, East Windsor, Dec. 22, 1861; deserted Nov. 25, 1863.

Frank J. Underwood, Thompson, Dec. 31, 1861.

George Dennerlein, Hartford, Dec. 22, 1861; deserted March 17, 1862.

James J. Davis, Putnam, Jan. 22, 1862; discharged for disability July 29, 1862.

Charles H. Belden, New Britain, Jan. 28, 1862.

Nicholas Schue, Hartford, Feb. 27, 1862; re-enlisted as Veteran Feb. 29, 1864.

MUSICIANS.

Jas. V. Underwood, Thompson, Jan 7, 1862; died April 15, 1862.

Norman W. Beaton, New Hartford, Dec. 22, 1861; re-enlisted as Veteran Feb. 8, 1864.

Michael Hart, Dec. 30, 1861; re-enlisted as Veteran Feb. 8, 1864.

WAGONER.

Calvin B. Beebe, Montville, Jan. 7, 1862; re-enlisted as Veteran Feb. 8, 1864.

PRIVATES.

Adams, William A., Killingly, Dec. 31, 1861; re-enlisted as Veteran Feb. 8, 1864.

Albee, Henry, Thompson, Feb. 27, 1862.

Amidon, James S., Thompson, Dec. 31, 1861; dropped from roll May 23, 1862.

Amidon, Melvin A., Thompson, Dec. 31, 1861; dropped from roll May 23, 1862.

Avery, Charles C., Thompson, Feb. 11, 1862.

Bennett, Thomas B., Thompson, Jan. 22, 1862; deserted March 17, 1862.

Birge, George F., Hartford, Dec. 30, 1861; re-enlisted as Veteran Feb. 8, 1864.

Blackmar, Edm. A., Thompson, Jan. 28, 1862.

Blackmore, Francis, Putnam, Dec. 31, 1861.

Bowen, Francis C., Thompson, Jan. 22, 1862; re-enlisted as Veteran Feb. 8, 1864.

Bradley, Benjamin, Colebrook, Dec. 22, 1861; deserted Sept. 30, 1862; since died.

Barry, Robert C., March 12, 1862.

Bracken, James, jr., March 12, 1862; discharged for disability May 25, 1862.

Capen, Elbridge S., New Britain, Dec. 22, 1861; died Oc. 17, 1862.

Carey, Michael, Colebrook, Feb. 1, 1862; re-enlisted as Veteran Feb. 8, 1864.

Carroll, Thomas, Hartford, Feb. 5, 1862; died Sept. 30, 1863.

Case, Ellsworth, Barkhamsted, Feb. 27, 1862; transferred to Veteran Reserve Corps April 10, 1864.

Chase, George W., Killingly, Dec. 31, 1861.

Church, Lyman, Granby, Feb. 20, 1862; discharged for disability July 29, 1862.

Cole, James, Hartford, Dec. 22, 1861.

Connant, John, New Haven, Feb. 18, 1862.

Cruff, Sterry, Thompson, Feb. 11, 1862; discharged for disability May 20, 1862.

Daily, James W., Thompson, Feb. 26, 1862; re-enlisted as Veteran Feb. 29, 1864.

Davis, Charles A., Suffield, Feb. 20, 1862.

Davis, Horatio L., Thompson, Jan. 22, 1862; discharged for disability May 20, 1862.

Dirreen, Daniel F., Thompson, Dec. 31, 1861; discharged for disability May 20, 1862.

Doig, David, East Windsor, Dec. 22, 1861; discharged for disability May 20, 1862.

Drinkell, Urban, Hartford, Jan. 22, 1862.

Dugal, Leonard L., Naugatuck, Feb. 18, 1862; re-enlisted as Veteran Feb. 29, 1864.

Dunn, Edward P., Putnam, Feb. 1, 1862; discharged for disability May 23, 1862.

Fallon, Michael, Hartford, Dec. 22, 1861; discharged for disability May 20, 1862.

Fuller, Manchester, Plainfield, Jan. 28, 1862; discharged for disability May 25, 1862.

Gaffney, Patrick, New Britain, Jan. 28, 1862.

Gill, Henry, Killingly, Jan. 28, 1862; re-enlisted as Veteran Feb. 8, 1864.

Hall, Edwin, Killingly, Jan. 22, 1862; deserted March 17, 1862.

Harrington, James R., Thompson, Feb. 26, 1862.

Harvey, George M., Putnam, Feb. 1, 1862; re-enlisted as Veteran Feb. 8, 1864.

Hawkins, Luther C., Thompson, Feb. 26, 1862; discharged for disability Feb. 28, 1863.

Hayes, Patrick, Portland, Feb. 18, 1862.

Hoey, John, Thompson, Feb. 11, 1862.

Hogan, Martin, Wethersfield, Dec. 22, 1861; discharged for disability May 25, 1862.

Jennings, Tolman A., Thompson, Dec. 31, 1861.

Joslin, Newton, Killingly, Dec. 22, 1861; dropped from roll May 23, 1862.

Larnard, Simeon, Putnam, Jan 22, 1862; discharged for disability August 22, 1863.

Lang, Stephen, Hartford, Dec. 30, 1861.

Lauderback, Frederick, Hartford, Jan. 22, 1862; discharged for disability March 6, 1862.

McMann, Mark, New Hartford Dec. 22, 1861.

McWilliam, Henry, New Hartford, Dec. 22, 1861.

Messenger, Joel, Granby, Feb. 20, 1862; discharged for disability May 20, 1862.

Miller, Charles A., Hartford, Jan. 28, 1862; re-enlisted as Veteran Feb. 29, 1864.

Miller, Xavier, New Haven, Jan. 28, 1862; discharged for disability Feb. 28, 1863.

Mohone, John, New Hartford, Dec. 22, 1861; discharged for disability March 19, 1862.

Mollay, James, Hartford, Dec. 22, 1861; deserted August 18, 1862.

Moore, Henry, Suffield, Feb. 20, 1862; dropped from roll May 23, 1862.

Newton, Francis G., Granby, Feb. 20, 1862; discharged for disability May 12, 1863.

Oedekoven, Charles F., New Haven, Feb. 27, 1862; re-enlisted as Veteran Feb. 29, 1864.

Oedekoven, Fritz, New Haven, Dec. 30, 1861.

Parker, George, New Haven, Dec. 22, 1861; re-enlisted as Veteran Feb. 8, 1864.

Peck, Daniel R., Barrington, R. I., Jan. 28, 1862; died April 6, 1863.

Pfeiffer, Frank F. F., Thompson, Dec. 31, 1861; re-enlisted as Veteran Feb. 8, 1864.

Place, Henry, March 12, 1862.

Regan, Hugh, Putnam, Feb. 27, 1862; re-enlisted as Veteran Feb. 29, 1864.

Rice, Levi, Granby, Jan. 22, 1882.

Rice, Santa Anna, Killingly, Jan. 28, 1862; discharged for disability May 25, 1862.

Rice, William, Killingly, Jan. 28, 1862; discharged for disability May 20, 1862.

Roberts, William F., Plainfield, Dec. 22, 1861; died Dec. 28, 1863.

Rowe, James, Woodstock, Dec. 31, 1861; re-enlisted as Veteran Feb. 8, 1864.

Ryan, Edward, Hartford, Dec. 22, 1861; deserted March 17, 1862.

Schuh, Frederick, Hartford, Feb. 5, 1862; re-enlisted as Veteran Feb. 29, 1864.

Smith, James, Portland, Dec. 22, 1861; died July. 1863.

St. Clair, John, March 5, 1862; deserted Nov. 1, 1862.

Sloan, Michael, March 17, 1862.

Thornton, Thomas, Hartford, Dec. 30, 1861; deserted March 17, 1862.

Trask, John R., Putnam, Dec. 31, 1861; discharged for disability May 25, 1862.

Trask, William, Thompson, Jan. 7, 1862; discharged for disability May 25, 1862.

Twogood, Orrin, Killingly, Feb. 1, 1862.

Tyler, Fernandes H., Plainfield, Jan. 22, 1862; died Sept. 15, 1863.

Welch, John, March 5, 1862.

Welsh, Patrick, Southington, Dec. 22, 1861; discharged for disability May 25, 1862.

West, Thomas J., Thompson, Dec. 31, 1861; re-enlisted as Veteran Feb. 8, 1864.

Whitman, Elijah N., Thompson, Dec. 31, 1861; died August 8, 1863.

Wilde, Thomas, Plainfield, Jan. 7, 1862; deserted March 17, 1862.

Williams, Chas. E., New Britain, Jan. 28, 1862; deserted May 6, 1862.

Williams, Henry, Colebrook, Dec. 22, 1861; re-enlisted as Veteran Feb. 8, 1864.

Wilson, William L., Killingly, Feb. 1, 1862.

Woodruff, Lyman, Norwalk, Feb. 5, 1862.

Woodworth, John, Suffield, Feb., 1862; re-enlisted as Veteran Feb. 29, 1864.

ORIGINAL INFANTRY COMPANY F.

CAPTAIN.

James J. McCord, Norwich, Feb. 18, 1862.

1ST LIEUTENANT.

Charles J. Fuller, Hartford, Feb. 18, 1862; promoted Captain Co. D; resigned August 29, 1863.

2D LIEUTENANT.

John C. Abbot, Norwich, Feb. 20, 1862; promoted 1st Lieutenant Co. F. Sept. 1, 1863.

SERGEANTS.

Charles W. Williams, Rocky Hill, Feb. 1, 1862; discharged for disability August 26, 1862.

Chester W. Converse, Norwich, Feb. 1, 1862; discharged April 4, 1863.

William L. Webb, Rocky Hill, Jan. 22, 1862; re-enlisted as Veteran Feb. 8, 1864.

Charles A. Loomis, Norwich, Feb. 1, 1862; re-enlisted as Veteran Feb. 8, 1864.

James Torrance, Norwich, Jan. 28, 1862; killed at Port Hudson, La., May 24, 1863.

CORPORALS.

Eugene Nash, Norwich, Feb. 1, 1862; re-enlisted as Veteran Feb. 8, 1864.

George R. Case, Norwich, Jan. 22, 1862; discharged to receive commission Sept. 10, 1862.

Amos R. Ladd, Norwich, Jan. 28, 1862; discharged to receive commission.

William D. Kempton, Hartford, Jan. 7, 1862; died August 2, 1863.

John T. Reynolds, Norwich, Feb. 1, 1862; re-enlisted as Veteran Feb. 8, 1864.

George Brown, Norwich, Jan. 28, 1862.

William H. Manley, Hartford, Jan. 7, 1862; discharged for disability Nov. 27, 1862.

MUSICIANS.

Edmund Tryon, Glastenbury, Jan. 7, 1862; re-enlisted as Veteran Feb. 8, 1864.

Edwin Hazlehurst, Norwich, Jan. 28, 1862; discharged for disability May 20, 1862.

WAGONER.

Elizur B. Elmer, East Hartford, Feb. 18, 1862.

PRIVATES.

Bailey, Marvin, New Hartford, Jan. 7, 1862; discharged for disability July 29, 1862.

Barry, James, Norwich, Dec. 22, 1861; re-enlisted as Veteran Feb. 8, 1864.

Bird, Charles Maine, Jan. 7, 1862; deserted October 29, 1862.

Black, David, Norwich, Dec. 30, 1861; killed at Georgia Landing, La., Oct. 27, 1862.

Blake, George W., Norwich, Jan. 7, 1862; discharged for disability June 30, 1862.

Bogue, George F., Montville, Jan. 22, 1862; re-enlisted as Veteran Feb. 8, 1864.

Brown, David H., Norwich, Jan. 11, 1862; re-enlisted as Veteran; died May 15, 1864.

Brown, John E. Hartford, Jan. 7, 1862.

Carey, Patrick, New Haven, Feb. 1, 1862; killed at Port Hudson, La. June 14, 1863.

Carney, John, Norwich, Jan. 11, 1862; re-enlisted as Veteran Feb. 8, 1864.

Carroll, Patrick, Hartford, Jan. 8, 1862; discharged for disability May 20, 1862.

Case, James, Norwich, Dec. 30, 1861; re-enlisted as Veteran Feb. 8, 1864.

Coleman, Emilous, Hartford, Feb. 11, 1862; discharged for disability Nov. 27, 1862.

Collins, Andrew, Norwich, Jan. 7, 1862; discharged for disability May 20, 1862.

Comstock, John L., Montville, Jan. 7, 1862.

Corbet, Michael, Norwich, Dec. 22, 1861; died of wounds May 25, 1863.

Corney, Patrick, Norwich, Jan. 22, 1862.

Cosgrove, James, Hartford, Jan. 22, 1862; re-enlisted as Veteran Feb. 8, 1864.

Crocker, Byron, Norwich, Feb. 5, 1862.

Cummings, William, Norwich, Jan. 11, 1862; deserted March 17, 1862.

Douglass, Albert H., Montville, Jan. 22, 1862; discharged for disability Sept. 4, 1862.

Fowler, Hosmer, Durham, Feb. 10, 1862; dropped from roll May 22, 1862.

Fowler, Nelson, Durham, Jan 22, 1862; discharged for disability Oct. 14, 1862.

Fowler, Samuel F., Norwich, Dec. 30, 1861; re-enlisted as Veteran Feb. 8, 1864.

Gay, Jonathan P. jr., Montville, Jan. 22, 1862; discharged for disability May 14, 1863.

Gladding, Ira jr., Berlin; Feb. 5, 1862; deserted August 20, 1862.

Gorton, Nathan S., Hartford, Jan. 7, 1862.

Greene, John, Middletown, Jan. 8, 1862; died November 30, 1862.

Greenman, Rufus, Norwich, Feb. 1, 1862; discharged for disability May 13, 1863.

Hale, Edwin, Portland, Jan. 7, 1862; re-enlisted as Veteran Feb. 8, 1864.

Hickey, Patrick, Norwich, Jan. 28, 1862; deserted March 17, 1862.

Hall, George, Norwich, Dec. 22, 1861; discharged for disability May 20, 1862.

Hunt, Herschel, Glastenbury, Jan. 22, 1862; discharged for disability Nov. 27, 1862.

Hayward, John, West Springfield, Mass., Feb. 26, 1862; died March 28, 1862.

Ingham, George W., Cheshire, Nov. 27, 1861.

Jaques, David D., Norwich, Jan. 28, 1862; re-enlisted as Veteran Feb. 8, 1864.

Johnson, Abel, Norwich, Dec. 22, 1861; re-enlisted as Veteran Feb. 8, 1864.

Johnson, Marquis L., Norwich, Jan. 28, 1862; discharged for disability July 29, 1862.

Kehr, Jacob, Norwich, Jan. 28, 1862; re-enlisted as Veteran Feb. 8, 1864.

Kelley, James A., Norwich, Feb. 1, 1862.

Kellogg, Norman, Rocky Hill, Jan. 22, 1862.

Kerr, Francis, Norwich, Jan. 22, 1862; discharged for disability Nov. 23, 1863.

Laird, Daniel, Norwich, Feb. 11, 1862.

Leach, Patrick, Hartford, Jan. 28, 1862; re-enlisted as Veteran Feb. 8, 1864.

Martin, Patrick, Norwich, Jan. 22, 1862.

McLachlan, Wells, Hartford, Jan. 7, 1862; re-enlisted as Veteran; died April 20, 1864.

McKay, Daniel, New Haven, Feb. 5, 1862.

Newton, Frank L., Hartford, Feb. 5, 1862; hung June 16, 1862.

Nichol, Robert, Norwich, Dec. 30, 1861; re-enlisted as Veteran Feb. 29, 1864.

O'Niel, James, New Haven, Feb. 11, 1862; re-enlisted as Veteran Feb. 29, 1864.

Patten, Charles, Norwich, Jan. 11, 1862; re-enlisted as Veteran Feb. 8, 1864.

Phinney, Henry E., Norwich, Jan. 7, 1862.

Pierson, James, Hartford, Jan. 28, 1862; re-enlisted as Veteran Feb. 29, 1864.

Powers, Thomas, Hartford, Jan. 7, 1862; re-enlisted as Veteran Feb. 8, 1864.

Price, Orrin M., Norwich, Jan. 11, 1862; re-enlisted as Veteran Feb. 8, 1864.

Parker, John R., Hartford, Feb. 18, 1862; re-enlisted as Veteran Feb. 29, 1864.

Reynolds, James, Hartford, Jan. 28, 1862; re-enlisted as Veteran Feb. 8, 1864.

Reynolds, William, Norwich, Dec. 30, 1861.

Richmond, William L., Simsbury, Jan. 11, 1862; re-enlisted as Veteran Feb. 8, 1864.

Ryan, John, New Haven, Feb. 26, 1862; re-enlisted as Veteran Feb. 29, 1864.

Sanders, George R., Montville, Jan. 22, 1862; discharged to receive commission Sept. 24, 1863.

Sanford, Erbin K., Rocky Hill, Jan. 7, 1862; discharged for disability Feb. 22, 1863.

Shea, John, Norwich, Jan. 22, 1862; died July 18, 1863.

Shipman, John, Glastenbury, Jan. 22, 1862; discharged for disability May 14, 1863.

Shipman, William, Glastenbury, Jan. 11, 1862; re-enlisted as Veteran Feb. 8, 1864.

Smith, Augustus F.,Norwich, Jan. 11, 1862; discharged for disability May 20, 1862.

Southmayd, Joseph G., Middletown, Jan. 8, 1862; dropped from roll May 22, 1862.

Strange, William, Norwich, Jan. 28, 1862; re-enlisted as Veteran Feb. 8, 1864.

Swan, Henry, Norwich, Jan. 7, 1862; discharged for disability June 5, 1863.

Taylor, Azariah, Glastenbury, Feb. 1, 1862; discharged for disability June 7, 1863.

Tinkham, Alvis H., New Haven, Jan. 7, 1862.

Trumbull, George W., New Haven, Nov. 27, 1861; discharged for disability July 5, 1862.

Tryon, Charles E., Portland, Jan. 7, 1862; died June 28, 1863.

Vail, Patrick, Hartford, Feb. 11, 1862.

Webb, Edgar W., Rocky Hill, Feb. 1, 1862.

Whaland, William D., Hartford, Jan. 7, 1862; deserted March 17, 1862.

Witter, Charles S., Hartford, Jan. 28, 1862; discharged for disability Aug. 26, 1862.

Wood, Henry Norwich, Jan. 7, 1862; discharged for disability July 29, 1862.

Wood, John, Norwich, Jan. 7, 1862; discharged for disability June 17, 1863.

Yale, Russell, Norwich, Dec. 22, 1861; re-enlisted as Veteran Feb. 8, 1864.

ORIGINAL INFANTRY COMPANY G.

CAPTAIN.

Sylvester G. Gilbert, Hebron, Feb. 18, 1862; resigned July 16, 1862.

1ST LIEUTENANT.

Denison H. Finley, Marlborough, Feb. 18, 1862; promoted Captain July 17, 1862.

2D LIEUTENANT.

Joseph S. A. Baker, New Haven, Feb. 18, 1862; promoted 1st Lieutenant Company C. December 15, 1862.

SERGEANTS.

Samuel J. Coleman, Marlborough, Feb. 10, 1862; discharged for disability June 1, 1862.

Charles G. Burnham, Hebron, Dec. 22, 1861; discharged for disability June 1, 1862.

John A. Bartholemew, Branford, Jan. 8, 1862; discharged for disability Nov. 8, 1862.

James R. Moore, Middletown, Dec. 17, 1861; discharged for disability June 30, 1862.

Samuel L. Cook, Middletown, Dec. 17, 1861; discharged for disability July 27, 1863.

CORPORALS.

John W. Bradley, East Haddam, Jan. 22, 1862; re-enlisted as Veteran Feb. 8, 1864.

Theodore Palmer, North Branford, Jan. 28, 1862; re-enlisted as Veteran Feb. 8, 1864.

John Lincoln, Columbia, Jan. 22, 1862; re-enlisted as Veteran Feb. 8, 1864.

Frederick S. Francis, Wallingford Dec. 22, 1861; re-enlisted as Veteran Feb. 8, 1864.

Alonzo Lombard, Lebanon, Dec. 22, 1861; discharged for disability July 5, 1862.

Edwin L. Bennett, Marlborough, Dec. 17, 1861; discharged for disability June 14, 1862.

William M. Maynard, Hebron, Dec. 17, 1861; re-enlisted as Veteran Feb. 8, 1864.

Timothy Allen, Marlborough, Dec. 17, 1861; re-enlisted as Veteran Feb. 8, 1864.

MUSICIANS.

Patrick Begley, New Hartford, Dec. 22, 1861.

John Fitzgerald, New Hartford, Dec. 22, 1861; re-enlisted as Veteran Feb. 29, 1864.

WAGONER.

Jeremy T. Jordan, Lebanon, Dec. 17, 1861.

PRIVATES.

Allen, Charles, Columbia, Jan. 7, 1862; discharged Jan. 10, 1863.

Allen, Ralph, Colchester, Dec. 30, 1861; discharged for disability July 29, 1862.

Ames, Benjamin G., Hebron, Dec. 17, 1861; died January 6, 1863.

Austin, Frank, Windsor, Dec. 22, 1861.

Austin, George J., Haddam, Jan. 22, 1862; re-enlisted as Veteran Feb. 8, 1864.

Babcock, Leroy H., Old Lyme, Jan. 7, 1862; discharged for disability May 31, 1862.

Ball, James B., Marlborough, Dec. 22, 1861; transferred to 15th Regiment C. V.

Bartman, Cassius M., Lyme, Jan. 22, 1862; discharged for disability Feb. 22, 1862.

Bogue, Edmund, East Haddam, Jan. 7, 1862; died October 9, 1863.

Bogue, George, East Haddam, Jan. 7, 1862; re-enlisted as Veteran Feb. 8, 1864.

Brand, John, Bozrah, Dec. 17, 1861; re-enlisted as Veteran Feb. 8, 1864.

Burnham, David A., East Haddam, Feb. 5, 1862; discharged for disability June 1, 1862.

Brooks, Robert F., Feb. 18, 1862; discharged for disability June 14, 1862.

Bartholemew, Willis, Feb. 18, 1862; discharged for disability May 13, 1863.

Bottsford, Henry C., Feb. 10, 1862.

Chapman, Charles H., Salem, Jan. 22, 1862; transferred to Veteran Reserve Corps May 1, 1864.

Chapman, Lafayette, Marlborough, Jan. 28, 1862; re-enlisted as Veteran Feb. 8, 1864.

Clark, Charles L., East Haddam, Jan. 7, 1862; discharged for disability June 30, 1862.

Clark, John B., Middletown, Jan. 22, 1862; discharged for disability June 30, 1862.

Coleman, Josiah S., Colchester, Dec. 17, 1861; discharged for disability June 30, 1862.

Cook, Christopher, Columbia, Dec. 17, 1861; re-enlisted as Veteran Feb. 8, 1864.

Culver, Charles, Marlborough, Dec. 22, 1861; re-enlisted as Veteran Feb. 8, 1864.

Dailey, Timothy, East Haddam, Jan. 7, 1862; discharged for disability July 5, 1862.

Daniels, John F., Hebron, Dec. 17, 1861; died April 17, 1863.

Deming, Henry O., East Hartford, Dec. 17, 1861.

Dickinson, Wolcott A., Marlborough, Dec. 22, 1861; discharged for disability Oct. 16, 1862.

Donnell, George, Hamden, Feb. 1, 1862; transferred to Veteran Reserve Corps April 10, 1864.

Dorsey, John, Bristol, Jan. 11, 1862; re-enlisted as Veteran Feb. 8, 1864.

Dowd, Emery O., East Haddam, Dec. 22, 1861; discharged for disability March 10, 1862.

Dutton, Harvey, Marlborough, Jan. 28, 1862; discharged for disability May 12, 1863.

Daniels, Charles, Winchester, Feb. 18, 1862; promoted 2d Lieutenant Co. B; resigned Jan. 8, 1864.

Eldridge, Stephen, Old Lyme, Jan. 7, 1862; re-enlisted as Veteran Feb. 8, 1864.

Eldridge, John, Old Lyme, Jan. 7, 1862; deserted March 17, 1862.

Gay, James, Bozrah, Dec. 17, 1861; re-enlisted as Veteran Feb. 8, 1864.

Gay, Royal L., East Haddam, Jan. 7, 1862; discharged for disability June 30, 1862.

Gay, Moses, Bozrah, Feb. 26, 1862: died September 21, 1863.

Henderson, John, March 5, 1862.

Herman, Robert, Middletown, Feb. 10, 1862; discharged for disability May 31, 1862.

Hutchins, Charles B., Bozrah, Feb. 10, 1862; discharged to receive commission Jan. 26, 1864.

Hackette, Andrew, Hartford, Jan. 6, 1862; died April 15, 1863, of wounds received at Irish Bend, La.

Hall, Charles C., Cheshire, Dec. 22, 1861; discharged for disability July 5, 1862.

Hills, Archibald, Middletown, Dec. 30, 1861; re-enlisted as Veteran Feb. 8, 1864.

Hopkins, Albert, Branford, Dec. 22, 1861; re-enlisted as Veteran Feb. 8, 1864.

Horan, Matthew, New Hartford, Dec. 22, 1861; re-enlisted as Veteran Feb. 8, 1864.

Hudson, Charles B., Middletown, Jan. 22, 1862; discharged for disability Jan. 8, 1863.

Hurlburt, Henry A., Hermon, N. Y., Dec. 17, 1861; re-enlisted as Veteran Feb. 8, 1864.

Huxford, Francis, Marlborough, Jan. 7, 1862; re-enlisted as Veteran Feb. 8, 1864.

Hyde, James P., Colchester, Dec. 30, 1861; discharged for disability July 29, 1862.

Ingraham, Asahel, East Haddam, Feb. 5, 1862; re-enlisted as Veteran Feb. 8, 1864.

Joab, Jacob, Wallingford, Dec. 30, 1861; transferred to Veteran Reserve Corps, April 30, 1864.

Karnes, Robert, Marlborough, Jan. 22, 1862; transferred to Veteran Reserve Corps April 10, 1864.

Kerney, John, Hartford, Jan. 28, 1862; transferred to 1st Louisiana Regiment August 8, 1862.

Leonard, James, East Haddam, Jan. 22, 1862; re-enlisted as Veteran Feb. 8, 1864.

Latham, Joel E., Marlborough, Feb. 10, 1862; discharged for disability July 5, 1862.

McKnight, James, Simsbury, Feb. 18, 1862.

Martin, Datus W., March 13, 1862; discharged for disability July 5, 1862.

McGrath Walter, New Hartford, Dec. 22, 1861; re-enlisted as Veteran Feb. 8, 1864.

McKeon, John, Hartford, Dec. 30, 1861; re-enlisted as Veteran; deserted March 20, 1864.

Minor, Joseph H., Hebron, Jan. 28, 1862; discharged for disability July 5, 1862.

Moore, Daniel, New Hartford, Dec. 22, 1861; re-enlisted as Veteran Feb. 8, 1864.

Moran, Thomas, Middletown, Jan. 28, 1862; re-enlisted as Veteran Feb. 8, 1864.

Munson, Henry B., Cheshire, Dec. 22, 1861; died Dec. 27, 1862.

Nelson, Andrew, March 13, 1862.

O'Connell, Timothy, Colchester, Jan. 22, 1862; re-enlisted as Veteran Feb. 8, 1864.

Phelps, John H., East Haddam, March 5, 1862; discharged for disability May 31, 1862.

Penharlow, David D., Marlborough, Dec. 17, 1861; discharged for disability July 29, 1862.

Reynolds, Andrew J., East Haddam, Jan. 22, 1862; died Aug. 17, 1863.

Reynolds, Joseph N., East Haddam, Dec. 17, 1861; re-enlisted as Veteran Feb. 8, 1864.

Reynolds, William H., East Haddam, Jan. 7, 1862; re-enlisted as Veteran; died of wounds May 11, 1864.

Robinson, Ellis B., New Hartford, Jan. 28, 1862; re-enlisted as Veteran Feb. 8, 1864.

Robinson, Henry, Bridgeport, Dec. 22, 1861: re-enlisted as Veteran; drowned April 11, 1864.

Rodman, William C., East Haddam, Jan. 11, 1862; discharged for disability July 5, 1862.

Ryan, John, Bloomfield, Dec. 22, 1861; re-enlisted as Veteran Feb. 8, 1864.

Root, Dwight C., March 5, 1862; transferred to 2d Louisiana Volunteers Nov. 4, 1862.

Skinner, Edward, Winchester, Dec. 22, 1861; re-enlisted as Veteran Feb. 29, 1864.

Suber, Anson F., Glastenbury, Dec. 17, 1861; re-enlisted as Veteran Feb. 8, 1864.

Sidders, Charles, East Haddam, Dec. 22, 1861; re-enlisted as Veteran Feb. 8, 1864.

Sanford, Vinus M., Bethany, Feb. 18, 1862.

Tinker, Siber W., New London, Jan. 7, 1862; re-enlisted as Veteran Feb. 8, 1864.

Turner, Charles W., Hebron, Jan. 28, 1862; discharged for disability July 5, 1862.

Warner, Aaron C., Middletown, Feb. 1, 1862; died Feburuary 28, 1862.

Watrous, Frederick, Marlborough, Jan. 22, 1862.

Watrous, Hezekiah, East Haddam, Feb. 5, 1862; discharged for disability July 29, 1862.

Wheaton, John H., Lebanon, Jan. 7, 1862; discharged for disability July 5, 1862.

Wilson, David R., Marlborough, Jan. 8, 1862; discharged for disability June 14, 1862.

Wilson, Diodate G., Marlborough, Jan. 8, 1862; discharged for disability August 5, 1862.

Wilson, George H., Marlborough, Jan. 8, 1862; discharged for disability June 14, 1862.

ORIGINAL INFANTRY COMPANY H.

CAPTAIN.

Homer B. Sprague, New Haven, Feb. 18, 1862; promoted Lieutenant-Colonel November 5, 1863.

1ST LIEUTENANT.

Jonah F. Clarke, New Haven, Feb. 18, 1862; died January 27, 1863.

2D LIEUTENANT.

Julius Tobias, New Haven, Feb. 18, 1862; resigned September 5, 1862.

SERGEANTS.

Oscar F. Merrill, New Haven, Nov. 27, 1861; discharged for disability Feb. 14, 1863.

James M. Gardner, New Haven, Dec. 30, 1861; transferred to 1st Louisiana Regiment Aug. 18, 1862.

Everett C. Andrews, New Haven, Feb. 1, 1862; discharged for disability Feb. 28, 1863.

Frederick Thesing, New Haven, Nov. 27, 1861; discharged for disability May 23, 1862.

Charles H. Grosvenor, New Haven, Feb. 5, 1862; transferred to 1st Louisiana Regiment August 18, 1862.

CORPORALS.

George H. Twichell, New Haven, Jan 28, 1862.

William H. Huntley, New Haven, Jan. 28, 1862; re-enlisted as Veteran Feb. 29, 1864.

Moses Page, New Haven, Nov. 27, 1861.

Hiram Blackman, Bridgeport, Feb. 1, 1862; re-enlisted as Veteran Feb. 29, 1864.

John Meyer, New Haven, Jan. 11, 1862; re-enlisted as Veteran Feb. 29, 1864.

William Malkin, Norwalk, Dec. 22, 1861; re-enlisted as Veteran Feb. 8, 1864.

Edward Johnson, Middletown, Nov. 27, 1861; re-enlisted as Veteran Feb. 8, 1864.

William A. Patterson, New Haven, Jan. 8, 1862; re-enlisted as Veteran Feb. 8, 1864.

MUSICIANS.

George W. Evarts, New Haven, Dec. 17, 1861; re-enlisted as Veteran Feb. 8, 1864.

Calvin G. Shepherd, New Haven, Nov. 27, 1861; re enlisted as Veteran Feb. 8, 1864.

WAGONER.

Joseph W. Munson, New Haven, Feb. 10, 1862.

PRIVATES.

Adams, Charles A., Waterbury, Jan. 22, 1862; re-enlisted as Veteran Feb. 8, 1864.

Aldrich, John W., Bristol, Jan. 8, 1862; re-enlisted as Veteran Feb. 8, 1864.

Alling, George M., Hamden, Jan. 8, 1862.

Andrews, Martin L., Plymouth, Jan. 8, 1862; discharged for disability May 30, 1862.

Andrews, Philo, Plymouth, Jan. 8, 1862; re-enlisted as Veteran Feb. 8, 1864.

Aschback, Paul, New Haven, Nov. 27, 1861; discharged for disability May 23, 1862.

Aiken, Henry Norwalk, Feb. 27, 1862; discharged for disability March 17, 1862.

Bailey, Heman W., Durham, Jan. 28, 1862; re-enlisted as Veteran Feb. 8, 1864.

Bailey, William, Dec. 17, 1861; discharged for disability Feb. 10, 1862.

Blakeslee, Asahel C., Bristol, Jan. 11, 1862; re-enlisted as Veteran Feb. 8, 1864.

Blakeslee, Albert R., Bristol, Jan. 8, 1862; re-enlisted as Veteran Feb. 8, 1864.

Blakesley, James W., Bristol, Jan 8, 1862; discharged for disability Sept. 18, 1862.

Booth, Nelson H., Bethel, Feb. 1, 1862: discharged for disability July 30, 1863.

Bowen, Thomas L., New Haven, Nov. 27, 1861; died March 9, 1863.

Brennan, Thomas, Norwalk, Dec. 17, 1861; discharged for disability Aug. 26, 1862.

Brown, John, Feb. 10, 1862; re-enlisted as Veteran Feb. 29, 1864.

Black, William, Waterbury, Feb. 18, 1862; re-enlisted as Veteran Feb. 29, 1864.

Clancey, Charles, New Haven, Nov. 27, 1861; re-enlisted as Veteran Feb. 29, 1864.

Clark, Sidney A., New Haven, Nov. 27, 1861; discharged for disability Jan. 26, 1863.

Cassin, Peter, Waterbury, Feb. 20, 1862; transferred to Veteran Reserve Corps April 30, 1864.

Coleman, John, Derby, March 5, 1862; discharged for disability May 23, 1862.

Congo, Ethal, Sherman, Dec. 22, 1861; re-enlisted as Veteran Feb. 8, 1864.

Cromwell, David, South Dover, Jan. 8, 1862; re-enlisted as Veteran Feb. 8, 1864.

Dorman, Julius H., Hamden, Jan. 22, 1862; discharged for disability Oct. 10, 1862.

Drew, Albert, New Haven, Jan. 22, 1862, deserted March 17, 1862.

Dutton, Theodore, New Haven, Jan. 8, 1862; transferred to 15th Regt. C. V.

Dobson, Michael, New Haven, Feb. 18, 1862; died March 27, 1862.

Eisley, John, March 5, 1862.

Edwards, William, East Hartford, Jan. 6, 1862; discharged for disability, July 15, 1862.

Harrison, Thomas, New Haven, Jan. 6, 1862; deserted September 19, 1863.

Hart, Patrick, New Haven, Feb. 1, 1862.

Hart, Richard, New Britain, Dec. 22, 1861; re-enlisted as Veteran, Feb. 29, 1864.

Hazen, Edmund, Derby, Jan. 22, 1862 ; discharged for disability, May 23, 1862.

Hazen, George B., Derby, Jan. 28, 1862.

Hidehogg, John, Waterbury, Jan. 22, 1862; transferred to Invalid Corps March, 15, 1864.

Hodge, Augustus, Norwalk, Jan. 28, 1862; deserted March 17, 1862.

Hopkins, James, New Haven, Dec. 17, 1861; discharged for disability Sept. 22, 1862.

Houghkirk, Wm. H., New Haven, Feb. 10, 1862.

Higany, Michael, Torrington, Feb. 20, 1862; re-enlisted as Veteran Feb. 29, 1864.

Jones, Benjamin, Stamford, Jan. 8, 1862; died April 8, 1862.

Jahn, Emil, Stamford, March 13, 1862.

Keefe, Jeremiah, Stamford, March 5, 1862.

Kulverinsky, Charles, New Haven, Feb. 10; re-enlisted as Veteran Feb. 29, 1864.

Lanahann, Michael, Waterbury, Jan. 22, 1862; deserted March 17, 1862.

Leary, Patrick, Waterbury, Jan. 22, 1862; died August 21, 1863.

Lane, Henry L., Plymouth, Feb. 20, 1862; died May 5, 1863.

Latus, Albert, Bridgeport, Feb. 18, 1862; discharged for disability, Sept. 22, 1862.

Lockwood, Edward A., Stamford, Jan. 11, 1862; discharged for disability Sept. 22, 1862.

Malone, James A., Hamden, Jan. 8, 1862; re-enlisted as Veteran Feb. 8, 1864.

McDonough, Thomas, New Haven, Dec. 17, 1861; re-enlisted as Veteran Feb. 29, 1864.

McGrath, Michael, Waterbury, January 22, 1862; re-enlisted as Veteran Feb. 8, 1864.

Miesbach, William, Bridgeport, Jan. 22, 1862; discharged for disability, Aug. 26, 1862.

Mitchell, Peter, New Haven, Nov. 27, 1861; re-enlisted as Veteran Feb. 8, '64

Meissner, Louis, New Haven, Feb. 27, 1862 ; promoted 1st Lieutenant Co. D.; died of wounds April 29, 1864.

Moran, Philip, March 5, 1862; discharged for disability May 23, 1862.

Nettleton, Edgar A., Durham, Feb. 10, 1862; transferred to Invalid Corps March 15, 1864.

Nolan, James, Milford, Jan. 22, 1862; re-enlisted as Veteran Feb. 29, 1864.

Nugeon, Charles E., Colebrook, Feb. 1, 1862; re-enlisted as Veteran Feb. 8, 1864.

O'Neil, Dennis, New Haven, Dec. 22, 1861; re-enlisted as Veteran Aug. 3, 1863.

O'Connor, Martin, New Haven, Dec. 22, 1861; re-enlisted as Veteran Feb. 8, 1864.

Otto, John, New Haven, March 13, 1862.

Page, Edward A., Guilford, Jan. 11, 1862; discharged for disability May 23, 1862.

Patterson, Francis, New Haven, Jan. 8, 1862; re-enlisted as Veteran Feb. 8, 1864.

Prior, Alfred W., Norwalk, Dec. 17, 1861; discharged for disability May 30, 1862.

Quinn, John, Waterbury, Jan. 28, 1862; discharged for disability June 8, '64

Ranney, John, Waterbury, Jan. 22, 1862; re-enlisted as Veteran Feb. 8, 1864.
Riggs, Charles S., Derby, Nov. 27, 1861.
Russell, Alfred, North Branford, Jan. 22, 1862.
Roswell, Emery J., Middlebury, Feb. 18, 1862; discharged for disability September 20, 1862.
Scribner, George, Norwalk, Jan. 28, 1862; deserted March 17, 1862.
Scribner, William F., Wilton, Feb. 1, 1862; died February 23, 1862.
Shannon, James, Milford, Feb. 1, 1862; re-enlisted as Veteran, Feb. 8, '64.
Simpson, John, Clinton, Jan. 28, 1862; re-enlisted as Veteran Feb. 8, 1864.
Slade, Thomas, Feb. 10, 1862.
Smith, William H., New Haven, Nov. 27, 1861.
Strong, David S., New Haven, Jan. 22, 1862; deserted May 22, 1863.
Telford, George, Madison, Jan. 22, 1862; discharged May 23, 1862.
Vanderwater, Wm. G., New Milford, March 5, 1862.
Willey, John A., New York, Jan. 22, 1862; deserted March 17, 1862.

ORIGINAL INFANTRY COMPANY I.

CAPTAIN.

Henry L. Schleiter, New London, Feb. 18, 1862; resigned January 11, '63.

1ST LIEUTENANT.

Frank Wells, Litchfield, Feb. 19, 1862; promoted Captain, January 29, '64.

2D LIEUTENANT.

Joseph Strickland, New London, Feb. 18, 1862; promoted 1st lieutenant; killed at Port Hudson, La., June 14, 1863.

SERGEANTS.

James E. Metcalf, New London, Feb. 1, 1862; discharged for disability June 28, 1862.
Louis Beckwith, New London, Jan. 7, 1862; promoted 2d lieutenant Co. K., Jan. 27, 1863.
Wallace W. Smith, Plymouth, Jan. 11, 1862; re-enlisted as Veteran Feb. 8, 1864.
Charles C. Fisher, Litchfield, Jan. 11, 1862; discharged for disability May 20, 1862.
Samuel S. Taylor, Litchfield, Jan. 11, 1862; re-enlisted as Veteran Feb. 8, 1864.

CORPORALS.

Abner N. Sterry, New London, Jan. 8, 1862; re-enlisted as Veteran; promoted 2d lieutenant May 1, 1864.
Englebert Sauter, New London, Jan. 7, 1862; re-enlisted as Veteran Feb. 29, 1864.

Charles R. Wright, Salisbury, Jan. 11, 1862; discharged, time out Dec. 1864.

Danforth K. Beebe, New London, Jan. 7, 1862; discharged, time out Dec. 1864.

Charles Bay, Woodbury, Jan. 11, 1862; discharged, time out Dec. 1864.

Charles Thomas, Litchfield, Jan. 11, 1862; discharged for disability May 20, 1862.

Albert Martins, Bridgeport, Jan. 11, 1862; deserted March 17, 1862.

James Duff, Litchfield, Jan. 11, 1862; re-enlisted as Veteran Feb. 8, '64.

MUSICIAN.

James McAllister, New Haven, Feb. 18, 1862; deserted August 29, 1862.

WAGONER.

Albert Bunnell, Litchfield, Jan. 11, 62; re-enlisted as Veteran Feb. 8, 1864.

PRIVATES.

Adams, Henry, New Haven, Feb. 18, 1862; deserted March 17, 1862.

Albretch, William, Vernon, Jan. 11, 1862; re-enlisted as Veteran Feb. 8, 1864.

Baker, William, Litchfield, Jan. 11, 1862; died September 2, 1862.

Banker, Hubert, Litchfield, Jan. 11, 1862; discharged for disability May 19, 1862.

Banker, Philo, Litchfield, Jan. 11, 1862; re-enlisted as Veteran February 8, 1864.

Barnes, Anson E., New Haven, Feb. 1, 1862; re-enlisted as Veteran Feb 29, 1864.

Beckwith, Ira M., Waterford, Jan. 22, 1862; discharged January 31, 1863

Beebe, Elvin, New London, Jan. 7, 1862; discharged Dec. 1864.

Beizer, Frederick, New London, Jan. 7, 1862; discharged Dec. 1864.

Benedict, William, Litchfield, Jan. 11; discharged for disability May 20, 1862.

Betz, Edward, New London, Jan. 7, 1862; died November 7, 1862.

Birge, Cornelius, Litchfield, Jan 11, 1862; discharged for disability Sept. 29, 1862.

Bronson, Andrew, Litchfield, Jan. 22, 1862; deserted March 17, 1862.

Brower, George W., New Haven, Feb. 10, 1862; discharged for disability Feb. 28 1862.

Burgart, Ulrich, New Haven, Jan. 11, 1862; re-enlisted as Veteran Feb. 8, 1864.

Burke, Michael, Litchfield, Jan. 11, 1862; re-enlisted as Veteran, Feb. 1864.

Catlin, Charles, Litchfield, Jan. 11, 1862; died September 2, 1863.

Chapel, Alonzo, Litchfield, Jan. 11, 1862; died February 23, 1863.

Chappell, Charles E., New London, Jan. 28, 1862; discharged Dec. 1864.

Cogswell, Edward, Litchfield, Jan. 11, 1862.

Crandall, Anderson L., New London, Jan. 22, 1862; discharged Dec. 1864.

Curtiss, Evits H., Litchfield, Jan. 28, 1862; discharged Dec. 1864.

Daniels, John L., New London, Jan. 7, 1862; discharged for disability Oct. 2, 1863.

Daniels, Robert, New London, Jan. 7, 1862; droped from roll May 31, 1863, never reported.

Davidson, Ira A. Litchfield, Jan 11, 1862; re-enlisted as Veteran Feb. 8, 1864.

Darley, William, New Britain, Jan. 11, 1862; re-enlisted as Veteran Feb. 29, 1864.

Fisher, Edward E., Litchfield, Jan. 11, 1862; re-enlisted as Veteran, Feb. 8, 1864.

Ferris, Smith W., Feb. 20, 1862; died March 12, 1862.

Franz, Joseph, New London, Jan. 22, 1862; re-enlisted as Veteran Feb. 8, 1864.

Frink, Seth, Litchfield, Jan. 22, 1862; deserted March 17, 1862.

Geer, David H., New London, Feb. 10, 1862; discharged, Dec. 1864.

Gilbert, George C., New London, Jan. 7, 1862; discharged, Dec. 1864.

Halleck, Loren, Litchfield, Jan. 11, 1862; discharged for disability July 15, 1862.

Harris, William H., Litchfield, Jan. 11, 1862.

Harris, James, New London Jan. 28, 1862; discharged for disability Feb. 28, 1863.

Havens, George R., New London, Jan. 7, 1862.

Herbert, Patrick, Litchfield, Jan. 22, 1862; re-enlisted as Veteran Feb. 8, 1864.

Herbert, Garrett, Litchfield, Jan. 22, 1862; re-enlisted as Veteran Feb. 8, 1864.

Hines, Patrick, New London, Jan. 7, 1862; re-enlisted as Veteran Feb. 8, 1864.

Holloway, Ezra M., New London, Jan. 22, 1862; discharged for disability June 28, 1862.

Immich, Peter, New London, Feb. 1, 1862; re-enlisted as Veteran Feb. 29, 1864.

Johnson, Lewis, Litchfield, Jan. 11, 1862; discharged for disability May 30, 1862.

Kelleher, Jeremiah, Litchfield, Jan. 11, 1862; died.

Keeney, John L., New London, Jan. 22, 1862; re-enlisted as Veteran, Feb. 8, 1864.

Kinley, John M., Litchfield, Jan. 11, 1862; taken prisoner at Winchester.

Kettenbach, Max, March 14, 1862; mustered out Dec. 1864.

Lester, Ambrose E., New London, Feb. 10, 1862; mustered out Dec. 1864.

Mayo, Henry, Litchfield, Jan. 11, 1862; discharged for disability May 20, 1862.

McGee, Thomas, Litchfield, Jan. 11, 1862; re-enlisted as Veteran Feb. 8, 1864.

Monroe, Cornelius M., New London, Jan. 7, 1862.

Munger, Trueworthy, Litchfield, Jan. 11, 1862; discharged for disability May 26, 1863.

Nowbury, Clifford C., Harwinton, Jan. 11, 1862.

Niles, Calvin N., New London, Jan. 7, 1862; re-enlisted as Veteran Feb. 8, 1864.

Norris, William H., Litchfield, Jan. 11, 1862; re-enlisted as Veteran Feb. 8, 1864.

Ostrander, Charles, Litchfield, March 5, 1862; deserted March 17, 1862.

Ostrander, George, Litchfield, Jan 11, 1862; deserted March 17, 1862.

Parker, William R., Litchfield, Jan. 11, 1862; deserted March 17, 1862.

Parmalee, Cornelius, Litchfield, Jan. 11, 1862; mustered out Dec. 1864.

Peacock, Patrick, Litchfield, March 5, 1862; mustered out Dec. 1864.

Phillips, Amos S., New London, Jan. 7, 1862; dropped from roll May 31, 1862, having never reported.

Plaum, Adam, New London, Jan. 22, 1862; prisoner at Cedar Creek and died in prison.

Pond, George L., Litchfield, Jan. 11, 1862; re-enlisted as Veteran Feb. 8, 1864.

Preston, Francis W., New London, Jan. 11, 1862; mustered out Dec. 1864.

Provost, Rufus, Litchfield, Jan. 22, 1862; re-enlisted as Veteran Feb. 8, 1864.

Parsons, William S., March 10, 1862; dropped May 31, 1862; having never reported.

Read, Micah, New London, Jan. 22, 1862; discharged for disability Feb. 6, 1864.

Richmond, Edward S., Litchfield, Jan. 11, 1862; killed by explosion at Opelousas railroad, La., Nov. 7, 1862.

Roath, Leonard G., New London, Jan. 22, 1862; killed at Irish Bend, La., April 14, 1863.

Robinson, James, Goshen, Jan. 11, 1862; deserted March 17, 1862.

Rogers, Gardner B., New London, Feb. 10, 1862; died February 21, 1862.

Rogers, Julius B., New Haven, Jan. 11, 1862; discharged for disability May 30, 1862.

Root, George, Litchfield, Jan. 22, 1862; re-enlisted as Veteran Feb. 8, '64.

Shelley, Frederick J., New London, Jan. 22, 1862; mustered out Dec. '64.

Starks, George, Litchfield, Jan. 11, 1862; discharged for disability May 30, 1864.

Steine, Adam, New London, Jan. 7, 1862; died May 23, 1863.

Stillman, George B., New London, Feb. 10, 1862; mustered out Dec. 1864.

Tatem, Samuel, Jr., New London, Jan. 22, 1862; mustered out Dec. 1864.

Thomas, Edward O., Litchfield, Jan. 11, 1862; re-enlisted as Veteran Feb. 29, 1864.

Tyrell, Payne S., New Haven, Feb. 1, 1862; died Feb. 23, 1862.

Wadhams, Fred'k L., Goshen, Jan. 11, 1862; mustered out Dec. 1864.

Watrous, Samuel N., New London, Jan. 22, 1862; re-enlisted as Veteran Feb. 8, 1864.

Wakefield, William C., Litchfield, Jan. 11, 1862; discharged for disability Sept. 29, 1862.

Whiteman, Henry, New Haven, Feb. 1, 1862; re-enlisted as Veteran Feb. 8, 1864.

Winters, Cornelius, New Haven, Jan. 28, 1862; deserted March 17, 1862.

ORIGINAL INFANTRY COMPANY K.

CAPTAIN.

Alfred Mitchell, Norwich, Feb. 18, 1862; resigned March 11, 1864.

1ST LIEUTENANT.

Jared D. Thompson, New Haven, Feb. 18, 1862; resigned Feb. 20, 1863.

2D LIEUTENANT.

William F. Norman, New Haven, March 10, 1862; promoted 1st lieutenant Co. H., Jan. 27, 1863.

SERGEANTS.

William C. Gardner, Hartford, Feb. 10, 1862; promoted 1st lieutenant Co. B., Sept. 1, 1863.

John C. Kinney, Darien, Jan. 11, 1862; promoted 1st lieutenant Jan. 29, 1864.

Charles W. Merwin, New Haven, Nov. 27, 1861; discharged for disability June 27, 1863.

George G. Smith, Putnam, March 1, 1862; discharged for disability July 5, 1862.

John T. Wheeler, New Haven, Feb. 18, 1862; promoted 2d lieutenant Co. D. ; killed by explosion on Opelousas railroad Nov. 7, 1862.

CORPORALS.

Samuel B. Dunn, New Haven, Dec. 30, 1861; re-enlisted as Veteran Feb. 8, 1864.

Frank C. Bristol, Cheshire, Nov. 27, 1861; re-enlisted as Veteran Feb. 8, 1864.

Charles Morris, New Haven, Dec. 22, 1861; died June 30, 1863.

Bennett W. Pierce, Southbury, Nov. 27, 1861; re-enlisted as Veteran Feb. 29, 1864.

Charles E. Humphrey, Orange, January 11, 1862; discharged for disability March 16, 1864.

George A. Winslow, Killingly, Dec. 22, 1861; re-enlisted as Veteran Feb. 8, 1864.

Jared T. Buel, New Haven, Dec. 22, 1861; discharged for disability July 7, 1862.

Hobert E. Mansfield, Waterbury, Nov. 27, 1861.

MUSICIANS.

Thomas A. Francis, East Haddam, Feb. 10, 1862; died August, 1862.

William Riley, Monroe, Dec. 22, 1861; re-enlisted as Veteran Feb. 8, 1864.

WAGONER.

Charles E. Hitchcock, New Haven, Nov. 27, 1861.

PRIVATES.

Allen, Abner, New Haven, Nov. 27, '61; discharged for disability July 5, 1862.

Allen, Thomas, New Haven, Dec. 17, 1861; discharged for disability March 11, 1863.

Aldrich, Welcome W., Thompson, Dec. 22, 1861; discharged for disability July 5, 1862.

Andrews, John A., New Haven, Feb. 27, 1862; discharged for disability July 5, 1862.

Baldwin, Herbert C., Oxford, Nov. 27, 1861; re-enlisted as Veteran Feb. 8, 1864.

Bassett, Henry, Monroe, Nov. 27, 1861; discharged for disability March 13, 1862.

Beecher, Louis, New Haven, Dec. 17, 1861; discharged for disability May 20, 1862.

Beecher, Miles J., New Haven, Nov. 27, 1861; re-enlisted as Veteran Feb. 8, 1864.

Benedict, Chauncey, New Haven, Feb. 5, 1862; discharged for disability May 20, 1862.

Benedict, John, Litchfield, Dec. 22, 1861; discharged for disability March 2, 1863.

Benson, Benjamin E., Putnam, Dec. 22, 1861.

Benway, Thomas, Southbridge, Massachusetts, Dec. 22, 1861; discharged for disability July 5, 1862.

Brainard, Ezra, Haddam, Nov. 27, '61; re-enlisted as Veteran Feb. 8, 1864.

Caldwell, Smith P., New Milford, Nov. 27, 1861; disability Jan. 19, 1863.

Chase, Daniel, Putnam, Dec. 22, 1861; discharged for disability October, 1862.

Clancy, George, New Haven, Nov. 27, 1861.

Cojer, William J., Monroe, Nov. 27; re-enlisted as Veteran Feb. 8, '64.

Comstock, John C., Nov. 27, 1861; died February 9, 1862.

Cramm, John, Shelby, Massachusetts, Feb. 18, 1862; killed at Port Hudson, La., June 14, 1863.

Cunningham, James, Hartford, Dec. 17, 1861; reclaimed as deserter from 9th C. V [27, 1863.

Dainger, Thomas, New Haven, Jan. 7, 1862; discharged for disability, June

Dale, Robert, New Haven, Dec. 30, 1861; deserted March 17, 1862.

Daley, Charles W., Monroe, Nov. 27, 1861.

Daley, James S., Monroe, Nov. 27, 1861.

Dalton, Patrick, New Britain, Dec. 30, 1861; re-enlisted as Veteran Feb. 29, 1864.

Downes, George, Oxford, Nov. 27, 1861; died October, 1862.

Doolittle, Frank H., Nov. 27, 1861; died Dec. 25, 1861.

Eaves, Samuel, Southbury, Nov. 27, 1861.

Gall, John, Milford, Nov. 27, 1861; re-enlisted as Veteran Feb. 8, 1864.

Garvey, Thomas, New Haven, Dec. 17, 1861; discharged for disability May 20, 1862.

Gazette, Marshall, Putnam, Dec. 30, 1861; deserted March 17, 1862.

Gilbert, Charles B., New Haven, Nov. 27, 1861; transferred to Veteran Reserve Corps May 1, 1864.

Goldsmith, George, Milford, Nov. 27, 1861, died March 13, 1862.

Gordon, George, Southbury, Nov. 27, 1861; discharged for disability July 5, 1862.

Hall, Herbert K., Orange, Jan. 11, 1862; discharged for disability July 7, 1862.

Hitchcock, Frank B., New Haven, Nov. 27, 1861; re-enlisted as Veteran Feb. 8, 1864.

Hollinger, Robert, New Haven, Nov. 27, 1861; re-enlisted as Veteran Feb. 8, 1864.

Hornby, Richard, Putnam, Dec. 21, 1862; re-enlisted as Veteran Feb. 8, 1864.

Hughes, Henry M., New Haven, Nov. 27, 1861; discharged for disability July 5, 1862.

Kain, Charles F., New Haven, Nov. 27, 1861; discharged for disability July 7, 1862.

Kies, Horace A., Killingly, Dec. 22, 1861; discharged for disability July 7, 1862.

Kennady, George, New Haven, Nov. 27, 1861; discharged for disability July 5, 1862.

Larned, Edward A., Putnam, Feb. 18, 1862; died June 6, 1862.

Lee, Newell J., Putnam, Feb. 18, 1862; re-enlisted as Veteran Feb. 29, '64.

McCabe, John, New Haven, Jan. 8, 1862; re-enlisted as Veteran Feb. 8, '64.

McDermott, John, New Haven, Dec. 30, 1861, re-enlisted as Veteran Feb. 8, 1864.

McGreevy, Michael, New Haven, Feb. 1, 1862; transferred to Veteran Reserve Corps April 10, 1864.

Morris, Thomas, New Haven, Dec. 22, 1861; re-enlisted as Veteran Feb. 8, 1864.

Mahoney, Patrick, Portland, March 14, 1862.

Nisbett, Richmond, New Haven, Nov. 27, 1861; dismissed by Court-Martial July 18, 1862.

Nugent, John, New Haven, Jan. 11, 1862.

O'Donnell, Richard, New Haven, Nov. 27, 1861; re-enlisted as Veteran Feb. 8, 1864.

Pardee, Alfred B., Orange, Jan. 12, 1862; discharged for disability May 20, 1862.

Phile, Benjamin, New Haven, Dec. 17, 1861; died December, 1862.

Pushee, Gilman W., Oxford, Dec 30, 1861; discharged for disability May 20, 1862.

Raffile, Charles, New Haven, Nov. 27, 1861; discharged for disability July 5, 1862.

Riggs, Charles S., Naugatuck, Nov. 27, 1861; discharged for disability Jan. 29, 1863.

Russell, George C., Haddam, Jan. 22, 1862; re-enlisted as Veteran Feb. 8, 1864.

Ryan, William, Dec. 22, 1861; died February 17, 1862.

Scoville, Bennett, Oxford, Nov. 27, 1861; re-enlisted as Veteran Feb. 8, 1864.

Scoville, Charles, Oxford, Nov. 27, 1861; discharged for disability May 20, 1862.

Sellwood, George H., New Haven, Nov. 27, 1861; discharged for disability July 5, 1862.

Smith, John 1st., Smithtown, Jan. 7, 1862; discharged for disability July 5, 1862.

Smith, John 2d, Marlborough, Feb. 20, 1862; discharged for disability July 5, 1862.

Stanford, Bernard, New Haven, Dec. 30, 1861; re-enlisted as Veteran Feb. 8, 1864.

Stanley, Edward, New Haven, Dec. 17, 1861; re-enlisted as Veteran Feb. 29, 1864.

Stone, Horatio, North Branford, Nov. 27, 1861; discharged for disability Feb. 28, 1863.

Storer, John, New Britain, Dec. 22, 1861.

Tiernan, Bartley, New Haven, Nov. 27, 1861; re-enlisted as Veteran Feb. 8, 1864.

Tracy, John, Plymouth, Dec. 22, 1861.

Young, Ashley, Ashford, Dec. 22, 1861; discharged for disability, July 7, 1862.

RECRUITS FOR THIRTEENTH REGIMENT.

Abrams, Emile, B,* June 24, 1862; discharged November 16, 1863.

Astenhoffer, Joseph, D, May 22, 1862.

Astenhoffer, Antonio, D, May 22, 1862.

Assant, Christian, F, May 19, 1862; killed by railroad accident Nov. 7, 1862.

Arnold, John, K, June 24, 1862; discharged November 16, 1863.

Addis, Walter, K, Nov. 11, 1863; assigned deserter from 24th Reg't C. V.

Anderson, George, H, Naugatuck, Feb. 27, 1864.

Antonie, Sam. Joseph, H, May 1, 1863; colored cook.

Blakesley, Sandy, A, May 20, 1862; deserted May 10, 1864.

Bunger, Michael, A, May 24, 1862.

Bahle, Frederick, A, May 24, 1862.

---

*The *letter* after the name, indicates the Company to which the recruit was assigned.

Baer, Frederick, A, May 24, 1862; transferred to 1st Regt. La. Vols., Aug. 24, 1862.

Black, Andrew, A, May 30, 1862.

Booth, Thomas, B, May 28, 1862; deserted March 20, 1864.

Balling, George M., B, June 26, 1862.

Bergline, Theodore, B, June 26, 1862.

Buhler, Otto, B, June 30, 1862, discharged for disability Sept. 28, 1863.

Brown, James, D, May 22, 1862.

Bertz, Charles, D, May 24, 1862; killed at Cane River Ferry, La., April 23, 1864.

Bowman, Otto, E, May 20, 1862; discharged for disability May 20, 1864.

Babcock, John, E, May 21, 1862.

Baer, Abraham, E, May 21, 1862.

Brown, Jacob, E, July 24, 1862.

Black, William, F, May 19, 1862.

Bayerdoufer, Jacob, F, June 24, 1862; discharged November 16, 1863.

Burns, Edward, F, Aug. 2, 1862.

Blake, John, H, May 18, 1862.

Brown, Nathaniel, H, May 19, 1862.

Bach, Adam, H, May 21, 1862.

Berger, Dionis, I, May 21, 1862.

Brokley, Anton, I, May 21, 1862, deserted July, 1864.

Bowman, Fritz, I, May 21, 1862.

Beier, George, I, Sept. 1, 1862.

Bennett, John, K, May 19, 1862; deserted August 24, 1863.

Bieber, Peter, K, May 19, 1862.

Brady, John, K, May 19, 1862; died February 7, 1863.

Breene, Michael, K, May 19, 1862; discharged.

Busecks, Rudolph, K, May 19, 1862.

Bothe, Charles, A, June 23, 1862; discharged November 16, 1863.

Blakeslee, Norman, H, Oxford, Dec. 8, 1863; died April 26, 1864.

Brannock, Kay, A, Westport, Dec. 26, 1863.

Beckwith, Frank, Colchester, Jan. 4, 1864; Not taken up on rolls June 30, 1864.

Brown, George, B, Colchester, Jan. 4, 1864; deserted March 16, 1864.

Buckley, Daniel C., A, Norwich, Jan. 19, 1864.

Blosopolos, Kannoris, Norwich, February 1, 1864. Not taken up on rolls June 30, 1864.

Barry, Richard, K, Lebanon, Feb. 9, 1864.

Black, John, B, Lisbon, Feb. 9, 1864.

Brown, William A., B, Bethel, Feb. 20, 1864.

Bremer, David, B, Salem, Feb. 18, 1864.

Barber, William, B, Salem, Feb. 18, 1864; deserted March 20, 1864.

Brady, Thomas, B, Hampton, Feb. 18, 1864.

Brower, George, B, Windham, Feb. 18, 1864.

Brown, James, K, Groton, Feb. 25, 1864; deserted March 20, 1864.

Black, Thomas, K, Lebanon, Feb. 25, 1864; deserted March 20, 1864.
Brophy, William, K, Middletown, Feb. 25, 1864; deserted March 20, 1864.
Brennan, Edward, A, Middletown, Feb. 29, 1864; deserted March 25, '64.
Brown, William, Madison, March 2, 1864; not taken up on rolls June 30, 1864.
Brown, George, Portland, March 18, 1864, not taken up on rolls June 30, 1864.
Buel, George, East Haven, March 28, 1864, not taken up on rolls June 30, 1864.
Burns, Barney, C, Woodstock, April 1, 1864.
Coyne, Thomas, A, May 23, 1862; deserted March 25, 1864.
Campbell, John, A, July 31, 1862.
Cook, Charles, B, May 26, 1862.
Coleman, Dennis, C, May 24, 1862.
Covers, Philip, C, Sept. 12, 1862; discharged November 16, 1863.
Cravey, John, D, May 21, 1862; died December 30, 1863.
Clousink, Henry, F, May 19, 1862.
Connelly, John, F, May 19, 1862.
Cain, Patrick, H, May 19, 1862.
Crawford, William B., G, May 27, 1862.
Conner, John, G, Aug. 2, 1862; deserted October, 1862.
Cooper, Edward, G, Aug. 12, 1862.
Corbin, Edward, G, Aug. 12, 1862.
Cressolle, Octave, G, Oct. 1, 1862.
Cashin, James, H, May 18, 1862.
Connelly, John, H, May 19, 1862.
Conzelman, Jacob, H, May 19, 1862; discharged for wounds, Sept. 12, '63.
Cearck, William, I, May 18, 1862; transferred to Veteran Battalion.
Coffee, Jeremiah, I, May 21, 1862; died of wounds received at Irish Bend, Louisiana.
Clinton, Thomas, K, May 19, 1862; in confinement; drop'd from rolls.
Croul, Charles C., H, Lebanon, Feb. 25, 1864.
Carroll, Richard, Middletown, Feb. 25, 1864; not taken up on rolls June 30, 1864.
Chandler, Richard, Middletown, Feb. 29, 1864; not taken up on rolls June 30, 1864.
Collins, James, Westbrook, March 10, 1864; not taken up on rolls June 30, 1864.
Connelly, Daniel, Cromwell, March 14, 1864; not taken up on rolls June 30, 1864.
Curbey, Abram, K, Sterling, April 12, 1864.
Carroll, James, Sterling, April 19, 1864; deserted April 24, 1864.
Dias, Juan, B, June 24, 1862; discharged November 16, 1863.
Duggan, Martin, C, May 22, 1862.
Deutsch, John, D, June 24, 1862; discharged November 16, 1863.
Douglas, George, E, May 21, 1862.

Doran, Thomas, F, May 19, 1862; deserted May 20, 1863.
Daniels, John, G, June 8, 1862; dismissed August 18, 1862.
Doyle, Dennis, H, May 19, 1862.
Dillon, James, I, May 20, 1862; killed in action Sept. 19, 1864.
Duress, John, I, May 20, 1862; transferred to Veteran Battalion.
Dessens, Francis, K, May 19, 1862.
Didion, Joseph, K, May 19, 1862; deserted June 4, 1863.
Ducros, Clement, K, May 19, 1862; deserted June 4, 1863.
Duffy, Thomas, K, May 19, 1862.
Dutton, Joseph, K, Nov. 11, 1863; assigned deserter from 28th C. V.
Douglass, Robert K., Middletown, Feb. 25, 1864; not taken up on rolls June 30, 1864.
Donahue, Henry, B, Middletown, Feb. 27, 1864.
Donly, Peter H., Naugatuck, Feb. 29, 1864; not taken up on rolls June 30, 1864.
Deal, Thomas, Middletown, March 8, 1864; not taken up on rolls June 30, 1864.
Downy, Joseph, Portland, March 18, 1864; deserted April 7, 1864.
Dowser, Harry, K, Sterling, April 9, 1864.
Davis, James, Bridgeport, April 2, 1864; not taken up on rolls June 30, 1864.
Emmerick, Balthazar, B, Bridgeport, July 17, 1862.
English, Edmund, E, May 19, 1862; deserted.
Eckerle, Frederick, F, May 19, 1862.
Enland, Alexander, I, Aug, 4, 1862; died July 10, 1863.
Eisler, Joseph, K, Bridgeport, May 19, 1862.
Ellison, Edward, K, May 19, 1862.
Enright, James, H, Hartford, Feb. 19, 1864.
Edwards, Samuel, A, Portland, March 16, 1864.
Enright, James, A, Portland, March 21, 1864.
Emerson, Charles, Sterling, April 19, 1864; deserted April 24, 1864.
Fesk, Albert, B, May 26, 1862.
Fay, Michael, B, May 28, 1862.
Flannery, Thomas, B, June 26, 1862.
Fielder, Thomas, C, May 20, 1862.
Fitzpatrick, Thomas, D, May 20, 1862; died October 28, 1863.
Fitzpatrick, Phillip, D, May, 20, 1862; discharged for disability Feb. 1, 1864.
Falkling, Gotlieb, D, May 21, 1862.
Fee, John, D, May 21, 1862.
Fruin, Richard, D, May 26, 1862.
Foetish, Louis, G, June 1, 1862.
Fifer, Charles H., G, June 1, 1862, discharged for disability, July 3, 1863.
Fogerty, John, H, May 19, 1862; killed at Washington, La., April 27, 1863.
Finley, Daniel B., G, Marlborough, Aug. 19, 1862; died May 23, 1863.

Fingin, Byron, G, June 1, 1862.
Freed, John, A, July 26, 1862; died April 14, 1863.
Foster, George, Groton, Jan. 13, 1864; not taken up on rolls June 30, 1864.
Fauls, John, K, Windham, Feb. 18, 1864.
Fillow, Jesse B., H, Morris, Feb. 22, 1864.
Fisher, Charles, C, Portland, March 19, 1864.
Frazier, John, A, Branford, March 28, 1864.
Grouse, Benjamin, B, May 28, 1862; discharged for disability Oct. 10, 1863.
Gentien, Peter, B, May 21, 1862.
Gaylor, Newton, D, May 21, 1862.
Golden, James, D, May 21, 1862.
Geize, Adam, E, May 21, 1862.
Geibel, George, E, May 21, 1862.
Greer, James, E, May 21, 1862.
Gates, John, E, May 21, 1862, transferred to Perkins Cavalry July 17, 1862.
Graff, Henry, F, Aug. 1, 1862; discharged Nov. 16, 1863.
Garcia, Joseph, F, Sept. 17, 1862; killed at Cane River Ferry, La., April 23, 1864.
Gunter, Thomas L., G, June 1, 1862; killed at Cane River Ferry, La., April 23, 1864.
Graves, John, I, May 18, 1862; transferred to Veteran Battalion.
Griffin, Thomas, K, May 19, 1862; deserted August 24, 1863.
Grafton, Edward C., H, North Stonington, Feb. 10, 1864.
Gardner, Daniel, C, Salem, Feb. 18, 1864.
Green, Robert, Lebanon, Feb. 25, 1864; not taken up on rolls June 30, '64.
Gorman, William, I, Westbrook, Feb. 24, 1864; transferred to Veteran Battalion.
Gerbrick, Thomas, A, Middletown, Feb. 26, 1864; deserted March 25, '64.
Gardner, William H., C, Winchester, Feb. 22, 1864; deserted April 17, '64.
Griffing, James, Naugatuck, May 28, 1864.
Hughs, Benjamin, B, May 28, 1862.
Head, James H., B, Sept. 1, 1862; deserted March 20, 1864.
Heidrick, Casper, D, May 21, 1862.
Hettinger, Louis, D, May 21, 1862.
Heiness, Peter, D, May 21, 1862.
Hultz, John, D, Sept. 21, 1862.
Hanns, Frederick, E, May 21, 1862.
Howland, George W., E, May 26, 1862.
Hanson, Peter, F, May 19, 1862; transferred to Veteran Reserve Corps April 30, 1864.
Hawthorn, George, G, June 23, 1862.
Hamilton, Francis L., G, July 15, 1862; transferred to Veteran Reserve Corps April 30, 1864.
Hanlon, Patrick, H, May 22, 1862.
Haley, James, I, May 21, 1862; transferred to Veteran Battalion.

Hecker, Charles, I, May 20, 1862; transferred to Veteran Battalion.
Hewitt, Joseph, I, May 21, 1862; discharged for disability Aug. 5, 1863.
Holtzerland, Ferdinand, I, May 21, 1862; discharged for disability May 13, 1863.
Hosley, Peter, I, May 19, 1862; deserted July, 1864.
Howard, Daniel, K, May 19, 1862.
Hunt, John, G, June 1, 1862.
Hart, Francis J., C, Meriden, Dec. 4, 1863.
Hempstead, Charles Y., B. Hartford, Dec. 21, 1863.
Hagadon, Francis T., K, North Stonington, Feb. 13, 1864.
Hex, William, Franklin, Feb. 17, 1864; not taken up on rolls June 30, '64.
Hanson, Frederick, A, Middletown, Feb. 27, 1864.
Heime, George, Middletown, Feb. 29, 1864; not taken up on rolls June 30, 1864.
Huntley, William, Middletown, Feb. 29, 1862; not taken up on rolls June 30, 1864.
Hill, Frank, C, Middletown, March 1, 1864; deserted April 12, 1864.
Herrick, Edward, Woodstock, April 1, 1864; not taken up on rolls June 30, 1864.
Ille, Jacob, D, Woodstock, June 24, 1862; discharged Nov. 16, 1863.
Ichelberger, John, Portland, March 22, 1864.
Johnson, Robert, D, May 22, 1862.
Jordan, John, H, May 19, 1862.
Joice, John, I, May 30, 1862; discharged June 20, 1862.
Jackson, William, Naugatuck, Dec. 7, 1863; deserted December 15, 1863.
Johnson, William R., C, Groton, Feb. 12, 1864.
Jones, Charles, Windham, Feb. 17, 1864; not taken up on rolls June 30, 1864.
Johnson, Edward, Weston, March 11, 1864; not taken up on rolls June 30, 1864.
Kallahan, Francis, A, May 24, 1862.
Kinney, John, A, May 24, 1862.
Knerzer, Leonard, B, June 27, 1862; discharged November 16, 1863.
Klein, John, B, June 17, 1862; drowned June 2, 1864.
Krieg, William, K, May 18, 1862.
Kilay, Timothy, C, May 20, 1862; deserted October 24, 1862.
Kelly, James, C, May 20, 1862; deserted September 30, 1862.
Kuhlman, Jacob, D, May 20, 1862.
Kamp, Julius, D, May 21, 1862.
Koeing, Christopher, E, June 24, 1862; discharged Nov. 16, 1863.
Kostenbader, John M., F., May 22, 1862.
Kallahan, Patrick, F, June 6, 1862.
Kemple, Joseph, G, June 1, 1862; deserted August 25, 1863.
Kearney, Michael, G, August 4, 1862.
Kendrick, Samuel, G, Sept. 16, 1862; deserted August 25, 1863.

Kennedy, Patrick, H, May 19, 1862.
Keating, William, H, May 19, 1862.
Kramer, William, K, Aug. 25, 1862; deserted March 20, 1864.
Kelly, Michael, C, Lebanon, Feb. 9, 1864.
Kosehik, Gottlieb, C, Fairfield, Feb. 16, 1864.
Kimball, Alvah, C, Middletown, March 3, 1864.
Kimball, William, C, Middletown, March 8, 1864.
Kelley, John, Madison, March 10, 1864; not taken up on rolls June 30, '64.
King, Peter, Middletown, March 10, 1864; not taken up on rolls June 30, 1864.
Kelley, John, Guilford, April 28, 1864; not taken up on rolls June 30, '64.
Lynch, William, C, May 20, 1862; deserted August 3, 1862.
Leab, John, C, June 24, 1862; deserted September 10, 1862.
Leitner, Valentine, H, May 19, 1862.
Lannan, John, H, May 22, 1862.
Langley, Jacob, K, May 19, 1862; deserted March 20, 1864.
Leleitner, Albert, G, July 15, 1862.
Levvie, Isaac B., K, Canton, Nov. 20, 1863.
Lawton, James, Hamden, Feb. 4, 1864; not taken up on rolls June 30, '64.
Luddy, James, D, Lebanon, Feb. 10, 1864.
Leibelsperger, Samuel, A, Middletown, Feb. 29, 1864.
Lee, Frederick, C, Middletown, March 10, 1864.
Leonard, Thomas, A, Sterling, April 8, 1864.
Matthews, Stephen A., A, July 31, 1862; died of wounds April 29, 1864.
Mohren, John, B, May 28, 1862.
McGarigal, Terry, B, June 26, 1862.
Muilheizer, Andreas, B, June 24, 1862; discharged November 16, 1863.
McGuire, James, C, May 21, 1862; died September 6, 1863.
Maddux, John, C, May 24, 1862; promoted 2d Lieut. May 1, 1864.
Miller, William, E, May 26, 1862; died January 22, 1863.
Murphy, Michael, E, July 1, 1862.
Midsch, Conrad, F, May 19, 1862; transferred to Invalid Corps March 15, 1864.
McCormick, Thos. R., F, May 19, 1862.
Miller, Jacob, F, Sept. 15, 1862.
Mint, William, F, Aug. 3, 1862.
Mark, Frank, G, July 15, 1862.
Mason, John V., G, Sept. 16, 1862.
McDonald, Edward, I, May 19, 1862; discharged for disability Oct. 19, '63.
McCann, William, K, May 18, 1862; discharged for disability Dec. 30, '62.
Murphy, Patrick, D, Hampton, Feb. 18, 1864.
McSweeney, Edward, D, Killingworth, Feb. 24, 1864; deserted June 12, 1864.
McBride, William, B, Middletown, Feb. 27, 1864; deserted March 20, 1864.
McLellan, John, B, Naugatuck, Feb. 27, 1864.

Marion, Francis, A, March 15, 1863; colored cook.
Morgan, Richard, C, Portland, March 18, 1864; deserted June 23, 1864.
Marsh, Howard, G, Ellington, March 9, 1864.
May, Frank, I, Litchfield, June 15, 1864; colored cook, transferred to Veteran Battalion.
Nelson, Henry, A, May 23, 1862.
Newhouse, Moses, G, Aug. 12, 1862.
Nerherin, Joseph, I, Aug. 5, 1862; discharged for disability Feb. 7, 1863.
Nops, Benedict, I; died February 23, 1863.
Nelson, Philip, K, Middletown, Feb. 25, 1864.
Opl, Francis A., B; June 24, 1862; discharged November 16, 1863.
O'Brien, Cornelius, D, Danbury, Feb. 20, 1864.
Peterson, Solon, B, May 26, 1862.
Pinsard, Victor, B, Aug. 2, 1862; deserted September 1, 1863.
Poush, Frederick, D, May 21, 1862.
Pope, Andrew I., E, May 21, 1862; transferred to Perkins Cavalry, July 17, 1862.
Pfeiffer, George, F, May 20, 1862.
Perrett, Andrew, F, May 20, 1862.
Perault, Joseph A, F, Sept. 9, 1862.
Pendergrast, John, G, Sept. 8, 1862.
Pflaummer, Edward, K, May 18, 1862; deserted November 10, 1863.
Payne, Clarence D, K, Stonington, Jan. 9, 1864; deserted April 22, 1864.
Parker, Henry, E, Bethany, March 22, 1864.
Pierce, Charles, K, Sterling, April 12, 1864.
Quinn, Hugh, G, July 15, 1862; discharged for disability Feb. 28, 1863.
Rausch, Nicholas, A, July 31, 1862.
Robertson, Morant, J., B; Sept. 6, 1862.
Roderiggs, Bernard, D, May 21, 1862.
Roby, George N., E, May 20, 1862; deserted February 17, 1863.
Reihle, John, E, May 20, 1862.
Rutledge, Calvin W., E, May 21, 1862.
Reagan, Andrew, E, July 24, 1862.
Rowen, Charles, G, June 1, 1862.
Reamey, Charles, G, June 1, 1862; deserted January 1, 1864.
Remy, Philip A., I, June 30, 1862; transferred to Veteran Battalion.
Rehm, Michael, I, June 24, 1862; discharged Nov. 16, 1863.
Reltrath, Henry, I, May 20, 1862; taken prisoner August, 1864.
Rivers, Charles, K, May 19, 1862; deserted August 20, 1862.
Ryan, William, A, Middletown, March 5, 1864; deserted March 20, 1864.
Ryan, Philip, Westbrook, March 10, 1864; not taken up on rolls June 30, 1864.
Read, William, Westbrook, March 10, 1864; not taken up on rolls June 30, 1864.
Remington, James, C, Middletown, March 10, 1864.

Rice, James, Middletown, March 10, 1864; not taken up on rolls June 30, 1864.
Smith, Patrick, A, May 30, 1862; deserted January 17, 1864.
Schmitt, Louis, B, June 26, 1862.
Schweikert, Philip, B, June 26, 1862.
Shaffer, John, B, July 23, 1862.
Smith, James, B, Sept. 1, 1862.
Shandua, John, D, May 21, 1862.
Schliemann, Andrew, D, June 24, 1862; discharged November 16, 1863.
Schnell, John, E, May 20, 1862; deserted December 1, 1863.
Sheer, Martin, G, June 1, 1862.
Suarman, John, G, June 1, 1862.
Smith, Patrick, G, Aug. 5, 1862.
Sharden, Martin, J., G, Aug. 20, 1862; died July 24, 1863.
Schlosser, Antoine, G, July 21, 1862.
Smith, Henry, H, May 19, 1862.
Sanders, Bernhart, H, May 19, 1862.
Smith, Daniel, H, May 19, 1862.
Secelle, Theodore, F, May 19, 1862; drowned August 23, 1863.
Schultz, Frederick, H, May 20, 1862.
Senvas, Bernhart, I, May 21, 1862; deserted July, 1864.
Smith, Edward, I, May 18, 1862; transferred to Veteran Battalion.
Smith, John, I, May 21, 1862; deserted October 1, 1862.
Sprower, Hyronimus, I, May 20, 1862; discharged to receive commission.
Sanders, Hermann, K, May 19, 1862.
Shambley, William C., K, May 19, 1862; deserted March 23, 1864.
Soukerp, Wensel, K, May 19, 1862.
Steifen, John, K, May 18, 1862.
Smith, William, K, Ledyard, Jan. 9, 1864.
Stannard, Asa B., C, Nov. 11, 1863; assigned deserter from 24th C. V.
Stocking, Samuel, C, Nov. 11, 1863; assigned deserter from 25th C. V.
Smith, Frank, K, Montville, Feb. 6, 1864; deserted March 20, 1864.
Still, George W., Franklin, Feb. 17, 1864; not taken up on rolls June 30, 1864.
Steward, Thomas, A, Salem, Feb. 26, 1864; deserted March 25, 1864.
Stafford, Thomas, Naugatuck, Feb. 29, 1864; not taken up on rolls June 30, 1864.
Sullivan, Henry, B, Middletown, Feb. 29, 1864; deserted March 20, 1864.
Stealer, Charles, Middletown, March 10, 1864; not taken up on rolls June 30, 1864.
Silvey, John, Bethany, March 22, 1864; not taken up on rolls June 30, '64.
Smith, James, Woodstock, April 1, 1864; not taken up on rolls June 30, 1864.
Thompson, James, K, Groton, Jan. 13, 1864; deserted March 20, 1864.
Thompson, George, I, Middletown, Feb. 24, 1864; deserted December, '64.

Thompson,George J. Middletown, Feb. 29, 1864; not taken up on rolls June 30, 1864.
Trodon, Adam, Middletown, March 10, 1864; deserted May 25, 1864.
Thomson, John, Portland, March 17, 1864; deserted June 9, 1864.
Ulrich, Peter, D, June 24, 1862; discharged November 16, 1863.
Urbaine, Charles, E, May 21, 1862.
Ufford, Daniel, K, Nov. 11, 1863; assigned deserter from 23d C. V.
Underhill, William, K, East Lyme, Feb. 2, 1864.
Verdella, Leopold, C, Oct. 23, 1862; deserted September 15, 1863.
Vogel, Joseph, E, May 20, 1862.
Vogel, August, F, May 19, 1862.
Vogt, John, I, May 26, 1862; discharged for disability March 11, 1863.
VonderDann, Henry, K, Hamden, Feb. 3, 1864.
Vrooman, Byron, Woodstock, April 1, 1864; not taken up on rolls June 30, 1864.
Wright, William, A, Aug. 24, 1862
Williams, George, C, May 22, 1862; deserted September 30, 1862.
Williams, John, C, May 30, 1862.
Walters, Louis, D, May 21, 1862.
Welch, Thomas, D, May 21, 1862; discharged for disability March 27, '63.
Wilson, August, E, May 20, 1862.
White, Edward, E, May 21, 1862.
Warner, John, E, May 23, 1862.
Wagner, Albert L., E, May 21, 1862.
Walter, John, H, May 19, 1862.
Welch, Henry, H, May 19, 1862; died November 25, 1863.
Westenburger, John, H, May 18, 1862.
Wolff, Louis, H, May 19, 1862.
Wagner, Charles, I, May 21, 1862; deserted July, 1864.
Wagner, Charles F., I, Aug. 4, 1862; transferred to Veteran Battalion.
Wirt, Michael, A, Aug. 26, 1862.
Westhus, Bernhardt, K, May 21, 1862; died October 3, 1863.
Wilson, Charles F., K, Marlborough, Dec. 26, 1863.
Weed, William A., Ridgefield, Jan. 5, '64; not taken up on rolls, June 30, '64.
Wheelock, John E, Stonington, Jan. 9, 1864; discharged to receive commission, Feb. 24, 1864.
Wood, John, Colchester. Jan. 4, 1864; deserted March 25, 1864.
Wanzel, James M. C, Nov. 11, 1863; assigned deserter from 23d C. V.
Williams, John, New Haven, Feb. 11, 1864; deserted.
Watson, John, A, Middletown, Feb. 24, 1864; deserted March 25, 1864.
White, Thomas, Naugatuck Feb. 25, 1864; not taken up on rolls June 30, 1864.
Williamson, James, D, Middletown, Feb. 27, 1864; died May 14, 1864.
Wood, George, Winchester, Feb. 22, 1864; not taken up on rolls June 30, 1864.

Wright, Isaac, A, Portland, March 16, 1864.

Willson, John, Portland, March 16, 1864; not taken up on rolls June 30 1864.

Wray, William, A., Wolcott, March 22, 1864.

Willand, Nathaniel H., K, East Haven, March 24, 1864.

Whaland, Thomas, Chester, April 5, 1864; not taken up on rolls June 30 1864.

Wheeler, Henry, Sterling, April 19, 1864; deserted April 24, 1864.

Wells, Ephraim, B, New Haven, June 28, 1864; colored cook.

Young, Marcus, G, July 15, 1862; deserted October 30, 1862.

Zahn, Bernhart, H, May 19, 1862.

Zamphiropolos, Michael, K, Norwich, Feb. 1, 1864.

RECRUITS FOR THIRTEENTH REGT. CONNECTICUT VOLS.

FROM JULY 1ST TO DEC. 29TH 1864.

John Buckley,
Charles A. Bowen,.
Edmund C. Bingham,
Michael C. Burke,
Rowland C. Brown,
Elam Barber,
Daniel G. Carpenter,
Thomas O. Callaghan,
Edward Casey,
Emil Chawoin,
Eugene Davidson,
Ernst Dallye,
James Donelly,
Peter Dechamp,
George Elmer,
John Fisher,
Bernard Fagan,
George Francis,
Henry P. Gangloff,
Thomas S. Gaynor,
Joseph Goodblood,
Joseph Hackney,
Henry Harper,
William R. Hayes,
Michael Hefferman,
Thomas Holmes,
Thomas Hart,
Peter McGregor,
John McNeil,
William Montgomery,
James McLaughlin,
James L Mason,
Thomas Mead,
Joseph Monahan,
John H. Norman,
Horace Newton,
Andrew Pawlik,
Michael Penrgrast,
Charles Rhodes,
John Ryan,
Alexander Robert,
August Rossel,
James Sirley,
John Smith,
Frank T. Spencer,
James Snyder,
William Slino,
Patrick Sullivan,
Thomas Stritch,
William Schmidt,
August Simon,
Thomas Smith,
Louis Tanfer,
James W. Turner,

Andrew Hutton,
Daniel Hoctor,
Peter Kelly,
William Kinsilla,
John Kellcher.
Merritt Lyman,
John Laffey,
Arthur Launay,
Louis Louis,
Francis Meney,
John Mooney,
Alexander Theobald,
William H. Woodworth,
James H. Woodworth,
Andrew Walter,

Joseph D. Whitney,
George Weaver,
John Wilson,
Thomas Wiseman,
James A. Willis,
John Sullivan.

LIST OF KILLED AND WOUNDED AT GEORGIA LANDING,

OCTOBER 27, 1862.

John Vogt, Co. I, private, badly wounded.
Diones Berger, I, private, slightly.
J. Coffee, I, private, slightly.
E. McDonald, I, private, slightly.
J. Duff, I, private, slightly.
John Farrell, B, private, flesh wound.
Byron Crocker, F, private, slightly.
Charles Patten, F, slightly.
Jacob Miller, F, private, slightly.
David Black, F, private, killed.
Ellis B. Robinson, G, private, slightly.
Walter Skiff, D, private, slightly.
William Prentiss, D, private, in the neck.
Co. K., none.
Co. H., none.
Edward Blackmore, E, corporal, slightly in leg.

BATTLE OF IRISH BEND.

LIST OF CASUALTIES IN THIRTEENTH CONNECTICUT VOLUNTEERS ON THE 14TH OF APRIL, 1863.

Officers.

Captain H. B. Sprague, Co. H., wounded slightly in the hand and arm.

Captain Charles J. Fuller, Co. D., wounded slightly in leg by spent ball.

Lieut. Joseph Strickland, wounded slightly in arm.

Lieut. John C. Kinney, wounded slightly in leg.

Enlisted Men.

First Sergeant Frank E. Stanley, A, killed.

Private John O'Brien, A, killed.

Sergeant Frank W. Stanley, A, wounded in leg by minnie ball near the knee joint, afterward died of the wound.

Private Thomas Hurley, A, wounded in the arm.

Private Thomas Coyne, A, wounded in the thigh.

Private John Smith, A, wounded in the forehead.

Private John Freed, A, wounded in lung, afterward died.

Private Charles Tomlinson, B, killed.

Private Eli B. Blackman, B, killed.

Private Benjamin O. Sarles, B, killed.

Private Benjamin Grouse, B, wounded in leg by piece of shell, thigh amputated.

Corporal Edwin Nickerson, C, killed.

Private Ira Marshal, C, wounded seriously in shoulder.

Private George Ewin, C, wounded through the lung.

Private Leopold Verdella, C, wounded in the leg slightly

Corporal George Sperry, C, wounded in the hip.

Corporal Walter Skiff, D, wounded in leg slightly.

Private H. J. Tucker, D, wounded in the hip.

Private John Shandaa, D, wounded in the mouth, fracturing lower jaw badly.

Private Hugh Doran, D, wounded in leg.

Private John B. Johnson, D, wounded in shoulder.

Private James Greer, E, wounded in leg.

Corporal George Brown, F, wounded in leg.

Corporal George W. Ingham, F, wounded in abdomen severely.

Private Conrad Midsch, Co. F, wounded in leg severely.

Private William Black, F, wounded in foot slightly.

Private Orrin M. Price, F, wounded in foot.

Private John Karney, F, wounded in hip.

Private Andrew Hackett, G, wounded in scrotum, afterward died.

Private John Suarman, G, wounded in arm.

Private Maurice Newhouse, G, wounded in cheek.

Corporal Jacob Joale, G, wounded in hand.

Private Anthony Schlosser, G, wounded in hand.

1st Sergeant Alfred Russell, H, wounded in the neck severely.

Sergeant Nathaniel Brown, H, wounded slightly.

Corporal Nelson Booth, H, wounded in leg severely.

Private David Cromwell, H, wounded in arm.

Private Michael Higancy, H, wounded in shoulder.

Private J. Couzelman, H, wounded in leg severely.

Private V. Leitner, H, wounded in shoulder.

Private Michael McGrath, H, wounded in head.

Private Thomas Slade, H, wounded in leg.
Private W. G. Vanderwater, H, wounded in hand.
Private L. Wolf, H, wounded in head, slightly.
Corporal Leonard G. Roth, I, killed.
Private Jeremiah Coffee, I, wounded in side, afterward died of wound.
Private Charles Hecker, I, wounded in leg.
Private William Serk, I, wounded in hand.
Private John McDermot, K, wounded in leg.
Private Venzel Soukup, K, wounded in arm severely.

Number of officers wounded, 4.
Number of enlisted men wounded, 43.
Number of enlisted men killed, 7.

The following is a list of officers engaged in action at Irish Bend, La., April 14, 1863.

FIELD AND STAFF OFFICERS.

George W. Whittlesey, Adjutant.
George Clary, Assistant Surgeon.
Henry Upson, Chaplain.

COMMANDING OFFICERS OF COMPANIES.

Charles D. Blinn,	Captain	Company	C.
Eugene Tisdale,	"	"	E.
James J. McCord,	"	"	F.
Homer B. Sprague,	"	"	H.
William M. Grosvenor,	"	"	I.
William E. Bradley,	1st Lieutenant	Company	B.
Perry Averill,	"	"	D.
Charles E. Tibbetts,	"	"	A.
Joseph S. A. Baker,	"	"	G.
William F. Norman,	"	"	K.

OTHER LINE OFFICERS.

Frank Wells,	1st Lieutenant	Company	I.
Joseph Strickland,	"	"	F.
Robert A. Ripley,	"	"	C.
John C. Kinney,	2d Lieutenant	Company	A.
Louis Beckwith,	"	"	B.
Newton W. Perkins,	"	"	C.
Charles H. Beaton,	"	"	E.
George B. Deming,	"	"	H.
Louis Meisner,	"	"	I.
Charles Daniels,	"	"	K.

ASSAULT ON PORT HUDSON, JUNE 14, 1863.

HEAD-QUARTERS, 13TH CONN. VOLS.
BEFORE PORT HUDSON, June 14th, 1863.

GENERAL:

I have the honor to report the action taken by the 13th Connecticut Volunteers, in the engagement of the 14th inst., before Port Hudson, as follows :

As per order, we moved from our position in rear of Duryea's Battery, at half-past two A. M., to the Jackson Road, and rested near the bridge on the right of said road, (going toward Port Hudson,) in rear of the rifle pits, where the remaining regiments of the brigade joined us. At daylight we were ordered forward and moved to the plateau beyond the rifle pits, and rested on left of the road in rear of 1st Brigade. At seven A. M. we were ordered to support the 1st Brigade, as they moved on the enemy's works. The 13th held the right of our brigade, and following by the flank along the ravine close in rear of the 1st, the regiment filed into line, the right forming under cover of a ridge of ground about one hundred yards from the enemy's works. As there was not room enough to form the whole regiment in line there, I ordered Lieutenant Gardner, Acting Adjutant, to take the five left companies, pass through a ravine, and form in line under cover of another ridge on the left of the ravine, and nearly parallel with the right. Soon after, Lieutenant Gardner was wounded, as also Captain Grosvenor, Company I, still the left moved steadily to the position referred to. At this point, Colonel Holcomb, commanding 1st Brigade, fell while leading his command to the charge, and his right gave way. I ordered my right to advance to their support, which they did under a heavy fire from the enemy's works. Lieutenant Strickland, commanding Company F, fell here, killed instantly, still they maintained the position nobly. At this time, I ordered the regiment to file around the left of this position, and move forward through a ravine to a height which overlooked the enemy's works and not more than twenty or thirty yards from them. As this was the nearest point I could reach without a direct assault of the enemy's works which we had no instructions to do, I concluded to maintain that position and await orders. A regular detail of sharpshooters were kept at work on the brow of the height till sunset, when a strong picket was ordered to occupy it, which we did till about ten P. M., when we were relieved and ordered to our old position which we left on the morning of the action. We lost twenty-two killed and wounded, which I have reported with name, rank and company in full.

Very respectfully,
Your obedient servant,
CAPTAIN A. COMSTOCK,
Commanding 13th C. V.

To
HORACE J. MORSE,
Adjutant-General State of Connecticut.

A List of Casualties in 13th C. V. before Port Hudson, June 14, 1863.

KILLED—*Company C*—Private Thomas Burns.
Company D—Corporal Edward McManus.
Company F—1st Lieutenant, Joseph Strickland.
Private Patrick Carey.

WOUNDED—*Company A*—Drummer, Charles Merwin—afterwards died.
Company B—Private, John P. Weed.
Company C—Privates, Frederick Waldron,—since died.
James H. Dingae.
Company D—Privates, Roswell E. Hopkins.
Peter Hiness.
Dean Bishop.
James Golden.
Joseph Astenhoffer.
Company E—Private, August Wilson.
Company F—2d Lieutenant, William C. Gardner.
Company G—Private, George Donell.
Company H—Private, Edgar A. Nettleton.
Company I—Captain, William M. Grosvenor.
Corporal, Frederick J. Shelley.
Company K—Privates, Bennett Scovill.
Richard Hornby.
John P. Cramm.

RECAPITULATION.

KILLED,	Commissioned Officer,	1
	Enlisted Men,	3
WOUNDED,	Commissioned Officers,	2
	Enlisted Men,	16
	Total,	22

GEO. W. WHITTLESEY,
Adjutant 13th Conn. Vols.

HEAD-QUARTERS, 13TH CONN. VOLS.,
MORGANZIA, LA., May 23rd, 1864.

SIR:

I have the honor to transmit herewith a List of Killed and Wounded in the 13th Regiment Conn. Vols., at Cane River Ferry, April 23rd, 1864.

I am, Sir, very respectfully,
Your obd't servant,
C. D. BLINN,
Col. Comd'g.

HORACE J. MORSE,
Adjutant-General State of Connecticut.

LIST OF KILLED AND WOUNDED IN THE 13TH CONN. VOLS. AT CANE RIVER FERRY, APRIL 23RD, 1864.

KILLED—*Company D*—Private, Charles Britz.

KILLED.—*Company F*—Private, Joseph Garcia.
Company G—Private, Thomas L. Gunter.

WOUNDED—*Company A*—Privates, Stephen A. Matthews, mortally.
Julius F. Long, slightly.
Company B—Sergeant, Francis C. Weed, slightly.
Company D—1st Lieutenant Louis Meissner, mortally.
Privates, Dean Bishop, slightly.
Henry M. Stevens, slightly.
Company E—Privates, Nicholas Schue, slightly.
Mark McMann, "
William A. Adams, "
Company F—Privates, Frederick Eckle, slightly.
Patrick Martin "
Company G—Sergeant, William Reynolds, mortally.
Corporal, Frederick Francis, severely.
Company H—Private John Meyers, slightly.
Company I—Sergeant, Francis Preston, severely.
Corporals, Fritz Bowman, slightly.
Cornelius Monroe, "
Privates, James Dillon, "
George Pond, "
Edward Fisher, "
Company K—Private, Richard O'Donnell, severely.

RECAPITULATION.

KILLED,	Enlisted Men, - - - - - -	3
WOUNDED,	Commissioned Officers, - - - - -	1
	Enlisted Men, - - - - - -	20
	Total, - - - -	24

C. D. BLINN,
Col. Commanding Regt.

HEAD-QUARTERS 13TH REGIMENT CONN. VOLS.,
IN THE FIELD, NEAR HARRISONBURG, VA., Sept. 28th, 1864.

SIR:

I have the honor to transmit herewith a list of killed, wounded and missing of my regiment in the battles of Winchester and Fisher's Hill.

I am, Sir, very respectfully,
Your ob'd't servant,
C. D. BLINN,
Col. Commanding.

To HORACE J. MORSE,
Adjutant-General, State of Connecticut,
Hartford, Conn.

,ist of Killed, Wounded, Prisoners, and Missing, 13th Conn. Vols., at the Battle of Winchester, Sept. 19th, and Battle of Fisher's Hill, Sept. 22d, 1864.

Winchester, Va., September 19th, 1864.

KILLED—*Company A*—Private, Michael West,
Company C—Private, Oliver Potter.
Company E—Private, James Coles.
Company F—Private, Daniel Laird.
Company H—Private, William Malkin.
Company I—Private, James Dillon.

WOUNDED—*Company A*—Private, F. Deming.
William Walker.
F. Meney.
Company B—Sergeant, E. Ruggles.
Privates, E. S. Blackman.
T. McGarrigal.
Company C—Corporal, J. H. Pratt.
Company D—Private, J. Dillon.
Company E—Privates, H. Parker.
G. M. Harvey.
J. Warner.
P. Hayes.
Company F—Sergeant J. T. Reynolds.
Private, James Case.
Company G—Corporals, J. Suarman.
A. Leleitner.
Private, A. Ingraham.
Company H—Sergeant, N. Brown.
Corporals, H. Bailey.
A. Blakeslee.
Privates, E. Congo.
William Keating.
Company I—Sergeant E. Sauter.
Corporals, D. H. Geer.
F. Shelley.
Privates, J. A. Davidson.
E. Cogswell.
W. W. Smith.
Company K—1st Sergeant, S. B. Dunn.
Sergeant, M. J. Beecher
Corporals, R. Hollinger.
N. J. Lee.
Privates, B. Benson.
M. Campbell.

Privates William Cojer.
J. Fauls.
H. Vander Dahn.

PRISONERS—Field and Staff—Lieut. Col. H. B. Sprague.

Company A—Privates, J. J. Lloyd.
William H. Walker.

Company B—1st Lieutenant, William C. Gardner.
1st Sergeant, F. E. Weed.
Sergeant, F. S. Twitchell.
Corporal, W. W. Jones.
Privates, J. Kane.
J. E. Sarles.

Company C—1st Sergeant, H. M. Welch.
Corporal, W. H. Murphy.
Private, W. Barnes.

Company D—Sergeant, A. Holford.
Corporal, L. Walters.
Privates, D. Bishop.
E. J. Weldon.
J. B. Andrus.

Company E—Sergeant, R. Croley.
Privates, C. Miller.
A. Geize.

Company F—Privates, P. Corney.
A. Vogel.

Company G—Privates, M. Kearney.
C. Rowen.
D. Moore.
G. Austin.
J. Brand.

Company H—Corporal, H. W. Bailey.

Company I—Privates, W. W. Smith.
F. L. Wadhams.
J. M. Kienly.

MISSING—*Company B*—Privates, T. Bradley.
J. Black—prisoner two months.
J. Thorn—absent without leave.

Company E—Private, J. Greir—wounded and in 6th Corps [Hospital.

Company G—Private, A. Schlosser—wounded.

RECAPITULATION.

KILLED,	Enlisted men, - - - - - -	6
WOUNDED,	Enlisted men, - - - - - - -	37
PRISONERS,	Commissioned officers, - - - - -	2
"	Enlisted men, - - - - - - -	29

MISSING, Enlisted men, - - - - - - 5

Total, - - - - - 79

Fisher's Hill, Va., September 22d, 1864.

WOUNDED—*Company A*—Private, K. Brennock.
Company K—Private, P. Nelson.

HEAD-QUARTERS, 13TH CONN. VOLS.,
IN THE FIELD, October 26th, 1864.

SIR:

I have the honor to transmit herewith a list of the killed, wounded and missing, of my regiment in the action of October 19th, 1864.

* * * * * * * *

I am, sir, very respectfully,
Your obedient servant,
C. D. BLINN,
Col. Commanding.

To
HORACE J. MORSE,
Adjutant-General State of Connecticut,
Hartford, Conn.

List of killed, wounded and missing of the 13th Reg't. Conn. Vols. at the battle of Cedar Creek, Oct. 19th, 1864.

KILLED—*Company G*—Private, Louis Foetish.
Company K—Sergeant, George A. Winslow, Color-Sergeant.

WOUNDED—Field and Staff—Major, Apollos Comstock.
Company A—Private, Frederick Hanson.
Company B—Corporal, Peter Gentier.
Private, Charles Nichols.
Company C—Private, Alexander Cook.
Company E—Private, Charles A. Davis.
Company G—Corporal, George Bogue.
Private, Albert Hopkins.
Company H—Corporal, William Black.
Private, Albert Blakeslee.
Company I—Corporal, Fritz Bowman.
Private, Patrick Hines.
Company K—Sergeant, Herbert C. Baldwin.
Corporals, Rudolph Busick.
George C. Russell.
Privates, William J. Cojer.
Michael Zamphiropholos.

MISSING—PRISONERS.—*Company D*—Privates, Frederick Jennings.
Stephen Tyrrell.

Company D—Bernhard Rodriggs.
Company E—Private, John Hoey.
Company F—Private, James Reynolds.
Company G—Private, Vinus M. Sanford.
Company I—Private, Adam Plaum.
Company K—Privates, Charles F. Wilson.
James Donnelly.

RECAPITULATION.

Killed, - - - - - - - -	2
Wounded, - - - - - - - -	17
Missing, - - - - - - - -	9
Total casualties, - - -	28

LIST OF FIELD AND STAFF OFFICERS.

THIRTEENTH REGIMENT CONN. VOLS.

Colonel Henry W. Birge, Norwich, Nov. 2, 1861, promoted to be Brigadier General, Sept. 19, 1863.

Colonel Charles D. Blinn, West Cornwall, Nov. 5, 1863; mustered out Jan. 6, '65; term expired.

Lieutenant-Colonel Alexander Warner, Woodstock, Nov. 5, 1861; resigned July 29, 1863.

Lieut. Col. Charles D. Blinn, West Cornwall, Oct. 5, 1863; promoted to be Colonel, Nov. 5, 1863.

Lieut. Col. Homer B. Sprague, New Haven, Nov. 5, 1863; transferred to Veteran Battalion.

Major Richard E. Holcomb, Granby, Nov. 5, 1861; appointed Colonel 1st La. Regt., August, 1862.

Major Alfred Mitchell, Norwich, May 12, 1863; declined appointment Sept. 22, 1863.

Major Homer B. Sprague, New Haven, Oct. 5, 1863; Com'd. Lieut. Col. Nov. 5, 1863; Col. 11th C. D. A., Nov. 11, 1863.

Major Apollos Comstock, New Canaan, Nov. 5, 1863; mustered out Jan. 6, 1865, term expired.

Adjutant, William M. Grosvenor, New Haven, Dec. 25, 1861; promoted to be Captain, Dec. 31, 1862.

Major George W. Whittlesey, Norwich, Dec. 31, 1862; honorably discharged Oct. 8, 1863, for disability.

Adjutant Frederick N. Stanley, New Britain, Oct. 19, 1864; mustered out (as 2d Lieut.) Jan. 6, 1865; term expired.

Chaplain, Charles C. Salter, New Haven, Feb. 5, 1862; resigned June 15, 1862.

Chaplain, Henry Upson, Berlin, June 16, 1862; resigned July 20, 1863.

Quartermaster, Joseph B. Bromley, Norwich, Nov. 12, 1861; honorably discharged Dec. 29, 1863.

Quartermaster William Bishop, Southington, May 1, 1864; mustered out Jan. 6, 1865; term expired.

Surgeon, Benjamin N. Comings, New Britain, Nov. 6, 1861; resigned Jan. 26, 1863.

Surgeon George Clary, Hartford, May 23, 1863; transferred to Veteran Battalion.

Sur. Nathan A. Fisher, Norwich, March 7, 1863; declined commission.

1st Assistant Surgeon, George Clary, Hartford, Nov. 9, 1861; promoted to be Surgeon May 23, 1863.

1st Assistant Surgeon Samuel McClellan, New Haven, July 9, 1863; mustered out Jan. 6, '65; term expired.

2d Assistant Surgeon, Nathan A. Fisher, Norwich, Feb. 4, 1862; promoted to be Surgeon, March 7, 1863.

Samuel McClellan, New Haven, March 14, 1863; promoted to be 1st Assistant Surgeon, July 9, 1863.

Lucius W. Clark, Winsted, July 9, 1863; transferred to Veteran Battalion.

FIELD AND STAFF VETERAN BATTALION THIRTEENTH CONNECTICUT VOLUNTEER INFANTRY.

Homer B. Sprague, Lieut. Col.; transferred from 13th Regt. Connecticut Vols.

George Clary, Surgeon; transferred from 13th Regt. Connecticut Volunteers.

Lucius W. Clarke, Assistant Surgeon; transferred from 13th Regt. Connecticut Volunteers.

NON-COMMISSIONED STAFF.

John L. Keeney, Sergeant-major; promoted from private Company B.

William W. King, Quartermaster Sergeant; promoted from private Co. D.

Frederick C. Palmer, Hospital Steward; promoted from Corporal Co. B.

Calvin B. Beebee, Commissary Sergeant; transferred from 13th Regt. Connecticut Vols.

DISCHARGED.

Charles H. Gaylord, Sergeant-major; promoted to 2d Lieut. January 11, 1865.

DESERTED.

Joseph Hadley, Drum-major; deserted Aug. 27, 1864, at New Haven, Ct.

COMPANY "A" VETERAN BATTALION, THIRTEENTH CONNECTICUT VOLUNTEERS.

William C. Gardner, Captain; promoted from 1st Lieut. to Captain, Dec. 22, 1865.

Isaac W. Bishop, 1st Sergeant; promoted from Sergeant to 1st Sergeant July 1, 1865.

Orrin M. Price, Sergeant; transferred from Company F, as Sergeant, Dec. 29, 1864.

George F. Bogue " " " " " " Dec. 29, 1864.

James O'Neil, " " " " " "

Clark Dickson, Sergeant; promoted from private to Sergeant, Jan. 1, '66.

George Brown, Corporal; transferred as Corporal from Company F, Dec. 29, 1864.

John Ryan, " " " "

John R. Parker, " " " "

Wm. L. Richmond, " " " "

Mortimer R. Keeney, Corporal; promoted to Corporal, July 1, 1865.

Henry Waterbury, " " " July 1, 1865.

Edmond Tryan, Musician; transferred as musician from Company F, Dec. 29, 1864.

Austin, Jonathan,	Private.			
Bissell, Frederick I.	"			
Black, William,	"			
Brown, William A.	"	Vol. recruit,	joined	Feb. 20, 1864.
Carney, John,	"			
Donohue, Henry,	"	"	"	Feb. 20, 1864.
Fleharty, William	"			
Fowler, Samuel F.	"			
Fraser, John,	"	"	"	March 28, 1864.
Gaffney, Francis J.	"			
Gardner, James,	"			
Hanson, Frederick,	"	"	"	Feb. 27, 1864.
Hale, Edwin,	"			
Heganny, Derwin,	"			
Hall, Isaiah,	"			
Johnson, Abel,	"			
Jaquays, David D.	"			
Kelly, Peter,	"	"	"	Aug. 30, 1864.
Kinney, John,	"			
Kehr, Jacob,	"			
Lennard, Thomas,	"	"	"	April 8, 1864.
Leibensperger, Samuel,	"	"	"	Feb. 29, 1864.
Minney, Francis,	"	"	"	April 16, 1864.

Maguire, John,	Private, Volunteer recruit, joined Jan. 30, 1865.
Nichols, Charles,	"
Patten, Charles,	"
Peck, Chester D.	"
Perritt, Andrew,	"
Powers, Thomas,	"
Prindle, George,	"
Quigley, John,	"
Robinson, Robert,	"
Ruggles, Sidney, B.	"
Rigley, Thomas,	"
Shipman, William,	"
Smith, John,	"
Sullivan, Henry,	" " " Feb. 27, 1864.
Marion, Francis,	colored under cook.

DISCHARGED.

William E. Bradley, Captain; discharged by resignation Aug. 14, 1865.

Dunbar, Everett E., Sergeant; discharged to accept commission as 2nd Lieutenant, April 25, 1865.

Reynolds, John F., Sergeant; discharged May 1st, 1865, by Special Order, No. 1, Head-Quarters, Department of the East.

Ruggles, Elbert L., Sergeant; discharged May 6, 1865, for disability.

Weed, Francis E., Sergeant; discharged August 12, 1865, by order of War Department.

Mohran, John, Corporal; discharged June 26, 1865, expiration of term of service.

Gentier, Peter, Corporal; discharged Aug. 12, 1865.

North, John C., Wagoner; discharged October 27, 1865, by order of War Department.

Balling, George W., Private; discharged Aug. 12, 1865; expiration of term of service.

Blackman, Elisha S., Private; discharged July 20, 1865, for disability at Knights Hospital, New Haven, Conn.

Campbell, John, Private; discharged Aug. 16, 1865; expiration of term of service.

Case, James, Private; discharged July 3, 1865, for disability.

Connelly, John, " discharged Aug. 26, 1864, for disability.

Emmerick, Balthazar, Private; discharged Aug. 12, 1865, expiration of term of service.

Fay, Michael, Private; discharged Aug. 12, 1865; expiration of term of service.

Fest, Albert, Private; discharged Aug. 12, 1865; expiration of term of service.

Gangloff, Henry, Private; discharged June 31, 1865, for disability.

Hempstead, Charles Y., Private; discharged Sept. 13, 1865, by order of War Department.

Jones, William W., Private; disch'd May 12, 1865; by order of War Dept.

Kallahan, Patrick, Private; discharged June 26, 1865; expiration of term of service.

Kallahan, Francis, Private; discharged June 26, 1865; expiration of term of service.

McGarrigal, Terry, Private; discharged Aug. 2, 1865; expiration of term of service.

Miller, Jacob, Private; discharged July 18, 1865; expiration of term of service.

Nelson, Henry, " discharged May 1, 1865; expiration of term of service.

Peterson, John, " discharged June 26, 1865; expiration of term of service.

Robertson, Morunt J., Private; discharged June 26, 1865. ex. term of ser-[vice.

Rouche, Nicholas, Private; discharged for disability, August 16, 1865, by order of War Department.

Ryan, William, Private; discharged June 23, 1865, by Special order Headquarters Dept. of the East.

Schmidt, Louis, Private; discharged May 12, 1865; expiration of term of service.

Smith, James, Private; discharged July 18, 1865, by Special Order, Head-Quarters Department of the South.

Sailes, John E., discharged July 18, 1865; expiration of term of service.

Webb, William L., Private; discharged Aug. 12, 1865; by order of War Department.

Wolff, Francis J., Private; discharged for disability Aug. 12, 1865; by order of War Department.

TRANSFERRED.

George H. Pratt, 2d Lieutenant; transferred to Company C, January 8, 1865.

William B. Tooker, 2d Lieutenant; transferred to Company D, Aug. 2, 1865.

Benjamin L. Mead, Corporal; transferred to Company D, Dec. 31, 1864.

Bergline, Theodore, Private; transferred to Company D, Dec. 31, 1864.

Clark, Louis M., Private; " " Feb. 13, 1865.

Fisher, John, " " " Dec. 31, 1864.

Flannery, Thomas, Private; " " Dec. 31, 1864.

Pyatt, Samuel S., " " " Dec. 31, 1864.

Reynolds, James, " " B, Dec. 31, 1864.

Schwikart, Philip, " " B, Dec. 31, 1864.

Schaffer, John, " " D, Dec. 31, 1864.

Stranger, Irwin A., Private; transferred to Company D, Dec. 31, 1864.

Ephraim, Wells, colored cook; transferred to Company D, Dec. 31, '64.

DIED.

Twitchell, Franklin S., Sergeant; died Dec. 19, 1864, while prisoner of war at Salisbury, N. C.

Cosgrove, James, Private; died Sept. 1, 1865, at Jefferson, Jackson Co., Georgia.

Vogel, August, Private; died while prisoner of war, Salisbury, N. C.

DESERTED.

Brennick, Kennedy,	Private;	deserted	July 28, 1865, at Augusta, Ga.
Black, John,	"	deserted	July 28, 1865, "
Lantry, Edwin,	"	"	July 5, 1865, "
McLaughlin, James,	"	"	Dec. 6, 1864; Relay House, Md.
Thorne, Joseph,	"	"	Aug. 26, 1865, Augusta, Ga.
Walker, William H.,	"	"	Aug. 28, 1865, Athens, Ga.
Wright, Isaac,	"	"	July 27, 1865, Augusta, Ga.
Wright, William,	"	"	Feb. 9, 1864, Thibodeaux, La.
Yale, Russell,	"	"	Oct. 6, 1865, Jefferson, Ga.

COMPANY "B" VETERAN BATTALION THIRTEENTH CONNECTICUT VOLS.

Frank Wells, Captain; promoted from 1st Lieutenant to Captain, March 17, 1864.

Samuel S. Taylor, 2d Lieutenant; promoted from Sergeant Company B, to 2d Lieutenant Co. B, Jan. 11, 1865.

Garrett Herbert, 1st Sergeant; promoted from Sergeant to 1st Sergeant Jan. 1, 1865.

Englebert Sauter, Sergeant; Sergeant at Original Organization of Battalion.

Edward Thomas, Sergeant; promoted from Corporal Aug. 1, 1865.

Henry F. Bishop " " to Sergeant Nov. 24, 1866.

Hugh Dorain, " " from Corporal Nov. 1, 1865, to Sergeant, Dec. 13, 1865.

Michael Burke, Corporal; promoted to Corporal Nov. 24, 1865.

Ulrich Burghart " " " Nov. 25, 1865.

Henry M. Whiteman, Corporal; promoted to Corporal Nov. 24, 1865.

Edward E. Fisher, " " " Dec. 13, 1865.

Albrich, William,	Private.	
Barbour, Henry M.,	"	
Barnes, Anson E.,	"	
Botsford, John N.	"	
Davidson, Eugene,	"	Vol. recruit, joined Sept. 7, 1864.

Dillon, John,	Private.	
Fisher, John,	"	Vol. recruit, joined Aug. 16, 1864.
Gardner, Joseph A.,	"	
Gorman, William,	"	Vol. recruit, joined Feb. 26, 1864.
Hayes, Alonzo,	"	
Herbert, Patrick,	"	
Immich, Peter,.	"	
Johnson, John B.,	"	
Long, Henry,	"	
Losaw, George,	"	
McGee, Thomas,	"	
O'Brien, Cornelius,	"	Vol. recruit, joined Feb. 20, 1864.
Polley, Henry E.,	"	
Remy, Philip A.,	"	
Reltrath, Henry,	"	
Reynolds, James,	"	
Root, George,	"	
Smith, William,	"	Vol. recruit, joined Jan. 9, 1864.
Skiff, Walter,	"	
Stevens, Henry M.,	"	
Stoddard, Horace B,	"	
Tyler, Martin W.,	"	
Underhill, William,	"	Vol. recruit, joined Feb. 2, 1864.

Frank May, colored under cook.

Abner M. Sterry, 2d Lieutenant; promoted to 1st Lieutenant and transferred to Company D, Jan. 7, 1865.

John C. Kinney, 1st Lieutenant; resignation accepted by General Order War Department, Jan. 7, 1865.

William B. Tooker, 1st Sergeant; promoted from 1st Sergeant Co. B to 2d Lieutenant Co. A, Jan. 11, 1865.

John Duress, Sergeant; discharged June 26, 1865, by expiration of term of service.

Fritz Bowman, Corporal; discharged June 26, 1865, by expiration of term of service.

Louis Walters, Corporal; discharged May 26, 1865, by expiration of term of service.

George W. Everts, Musician: discharged Aug. 2, 1865, for disability.

Albert Bunnell, Wagoner; discharged Dec. 19, 1865, by General Order, War Department.

DISCHARGED.

Atzenhoffer, Antonio, rivate; discharged June 26, 1865, by expiration of term of service.

Birger, Dennis, Private; discharged June 26, 1865, by expiration of term of service.

Brown, James, Private; discharged June 26, 1865, by expiration of term of service.

Cearck, William, " discharged June 26, 1865, by expiration of term of service.

Davidson, Ira A., " discharged Aug. 12, 1865, by General Order, War Department.

Duffy, Thomas, " discharged Aug. 24, 1865, by expiration of term of service.

Ellison, Edward. " discharged June 26, 1865, by expiration of term of service.

Falklink, Gotlieb, " discharged June 26, 1865, by expiration of term of service.

Fruin, Richard, " discharged June 26, 1865, by expiration of term of service.

Finnemore, William, Private; discharged Aug. 12, 1865, by General Order, War Department.

Gaylor, Mortimer, " discharged June 26, 1865, by expiration of term of service.

Greaves, John, " discharged June 17, 1865, by expiration of term of service.

Hines, Patrick, " discharged Aug. 12, 1865, by General Order, War Department.

Holford, Andrew, " discharged Aug. 12, 1865, by General Order, War Department.

Heiness, Peter, " discharged June 26, 1965, by expiration of term of service.

Heeker, Charles, " discharged June 26, 1865, by expiration of term of service.

Heedricks, Casper, " discharged June 26, 1865, by expiration of term of service.

Hettinger, Louis, " discharged June 26, 1865, by expiration of term of service.

Kuhlman, Henry, " discharged June 26, 1865, by expiration of term of service.

Monahan, Joseph, " discharged Oct. 9, 1865, by expiration of term of service,

Mitchell, Joseph T, " discharged Aug. 11, 1865, for disability.

Provost, Rufus, " discharged Oct. 11, 1865, by General Order War Department.

Pond, George J, " discharged July 19, 1865, for disability.

Pouch, Frederick, " discharged June 26, 1865, by expiration of term of service.

Rodrigues, Bernard, " discharged Aug, 12, 1865, by General Order War Department.

Schwikart, Philip, " discharged May 25, 1865, by expiration of term of service.

Simon, Auguste, Private, discharged Aug. 21, 1865, by General Order War Department.

Smith, Edward, " discharged June 26, 1865, by expiration of term of service.

Smith, Wallace W., " discharged September 7, 1865, by General Order, War Department.

Snyder, James, " discharged Nov. 3, 1865, by General Order War Department.

Tyrrell, Stephen, " discharged Sept. 15, 1865, by General Order No. 1, Head-Quarters, Department of the East.

Wagnor, Charles, " discharged May 18, 1865, by expiration of term of service.

TRANSFERRED.

Frederick Palmer, Corporal; transferred by promotion to Hospital Steward, Jan. 7, 1865.

William H. Norris, Corporal; transferred to Veteran Reserve Corps, June 30, 1865.

Joel Congdon, Private, transferred to Co. "C," S. O., No. 3, Headquarters 13th C. V., Jan. 3, 1865.

Robert Johnson, Private; Vol. recruit, transferred to Department N.W. Dec. 27, 1864.

John L. Keeney, Private; transferred by promotion to Sergeant-major, Jan. 1, 1865.

DIED.

William H. Tucker, Sergeant; died at Athens, Ga., Dec. 6, 1865.

Andrews, Thomas B., Private; died Nov. 7, 1864, while prisoner of war in Salisbury, N. C.

Banker, Philo, Private; died May 6, 1865, at New Milford, Connecticut.

Bishop, Dean, Private; died December 21, 1864; while prisoner of war Salisbury, N. C.

Plaum, Adam, Private; died December 5, 1864, while prisoner of war, Salisbury, N. C.

Riley, William, Private; died June 8, 1865, at New Haven, Connecticut.

Vogel, August, Private; died Feb. 14, 1865, while prisoner of war, Salisbury, N. C.

Weldon, Edward J., Private; died Nov. 24, 1864, while prisoner of war, Salisbury, N. C.

DESERTED.

Butler, Charles, Private; deserted Sept. 27, 1865, at Clarksville, Ga.

Fiscus, Henry, Private; deserted March 1, 1866, at Augusta, Ga.

Hoctor, Daniel, Private; deserted March 27, 1865, at Newbern, N. C.

Harper, Henry, Private; deserted Jan. 11, 1865, Camp Russell, Va.

Meade, Thomas, Private; deserted Aug. 22, 1865, Augusta, Ga.
Thompson, George, Private; deserted Dec. 14, 1864, Camp Russell, Va.
Wiseman, Thomas, Private; deserted Aug. 22, 1865, Augusta, Ga.

COMPANY "C" VETERAN BATTALION, THIRTEENTH CONN. VOLUNTEERS.

Newton W. Perkins, Captain; transferred from Co. D, 13th C. V. to Co. C 13th Batt.

George H. Pratt, 1st Lieutenant; promoted from 2d Lieutenant to 1st Lieut. Jan. 8, 1865, transferred from A to C.

Miles J. Beecher, 1st Sergeant; Vet. Vol., promoted to 1st Sergeant, Jan. 11, 1865.

Bennett, W. Pierce, Sergeant; " " Sergeant, Oct. 19, 1864.

Frank C. Bristol, Sergeant; " " to Sergeant from Corporal, July 11, 1865.

Frank F. Phiffer, Sergeant; " " to Sergeant from Corporal, Aug. 23, 1865, transferred from E to C.

Frank B. Hitchcock, Sergeant; Vet. Vol. promoted to Corporal Aug. 23, 1865, to Sergeant March 1, 1866.

George C. Russell, Corporal; Vet. Vol. Corporal at organization of Battalion, absent since March 3, 1866.

John Gall, Corporal; Vet. Vol. Corporal at organization of Battalion.

Philip Neilson, Corporal; " " " "

Bernard Fagan, Corporal; Vol. recruit promoted to Corporal, Feb. 1, 1864, absent without leave since March 24, 1866.

Isaac B. Levvie, Corporal; Vol. recruit promoted to Corporal March 1, '66.

Richard Hornby, Corporal; Vet. Vol. promoted to Corporal March 1, '66.

Joseph Congden, Wagoner; Vet. Vol. transferred from D to C.

Barry, Richard,	Private;	Vol. recruit.
Brainard Ezra,	"	Vet. Vol.
Sutton, Patrick,	"	"
Hagadon, Thomas P.	"	Vol. recruit.
Laddy, James,	"	" transferred from H to C.
McCabe, John,	"	Vet. Vol.
McGrath, Michael,	"	" transferred from H to C.
Montgomery Wm.	"	Substitute recruit.
Norman, John H.,	"	Vol. recruit.
O'Callahan, Thos.,	"	Sub. recruit.
Pierce, Charles,	"	Vol. recruit.
Ryan, John,	"	Sub. recruit.
Stanly, Edward,	"	Vet. Vol.
Sullivan, John,	"	Sub. recruit.
Vandertam, Henry,	"	Vol. recruit.

Walter, John, Private; Vet. Vol.; transferred from H to C, absent sick in Hospital.

Wells, Ephraim, under-cook; transferred from A to C.

DISCHARGED.

John W. Maddux, 2d Lieutenant; dishonorably dismissed for absence without leave since Dec. 1865.

Everett E. Dunbar, 2d Lieutenant; resigned Aug. 16, 1865.

Herbert Baldwin, 1st Sergeant; Vet. Vol. discharged Jan. 11, 1865, mustered as 2d Lieutenant, Jan 11, 1865, assigned to E.

Newell J. Lee, Sergeant; Vet. Vol. discharged May 22, 1865, for disability.

Nathaniel Brown, Sergeant; Vet. Vol.; discharged Feb. 10, 1865, for disability caused by wounds.

Herman Sanders, Sergeant; Vol. recruit discharged June 26, 1865, by expiration of term of service.

Robert Hollinger, Corporal; Vet. Vol. discharged June 27, 1865; for disability caused by wounds.

Samuel G. Carpenter, Corporal; Sub. recruit discharged Aug. 12, 1865, by telegraph order War Department, A. G. O.

Barber, Elam, Private; drafted, received discharge Aug. 12, 1865, telegraph order War Department, A. G. O.

Bowen, Charles A., Private; Sub. recruit, received discharge Aug. 12, '65.

Brown, Roland C., " drafted, received discharge Aug. 12, 1865.

Burke, Michael, " Sub. recruit, received discharge Aug. 12, 1865.

Campbell, Michael, " discharged June 20, 1865, by expiration of term of service.

Coper, William J., " Vet. Vol. discharged June 27, 1865.

Crarel, Charles C., " Vol. recruit, discharged Aug. 20, 1865, transferred from H to C.

Dallege, Earnest, Private; Sub. recruit, discharged Aug. 12, 1865, by telegraph order, War Department, A. G. O.

Doyle, Dennis, Private; Vol. recruit, discharged June 26, 1865, Hartford, Conn., by expiration of term of service.

Donnelly, James, Private; Sub. recruit, discharged Aug. 12, 1865, by telegraph order, War Department, A. G. O.

Elemer, George, Private; Sub. recruit, discharged Aug. 12, 1865, telegraph order, War Department, A. G. O.

Finlis, John, Private: Vol. recruit, discharged Jan. 6, 1865, for disability.

Gorman, Thomas L., Private; Sub. recruit, discharged Aug. 12, 1865, by telegraph order, War Department, A. G. O.

Hays, William B., Private; drafted recruit, discharged Jan. 5, 1865, by order Major General Grover, in the field.

Hafferman, Michael, Private; Sub. recruit, discharged May 30, 1865, for disability.

Holmes, Thomas, Private; Sub. recruit, discharged Aug, 12, 1865, by telegraph order, War Department, A. G. O.

Kanseller, William, Private; Sub. recruit, discharged Aug. 12, 1865, by telegraph order, War Department, A. G. O.

King, William, Private; Vol. recruit, discharged June 26, 1865, by expiration of term of service.

Newton, Horace, Private; Sub " discharged Aug. 12, 1865, by telegraph order, War Department, A. G. O.

O'Donnell, Richard, Private, Vet. Vol. discharged June 5, 1865, for disability.

O'Donnell, Michael, Private; Vol. recruit, discharged March 6, 1865.

Paulick, Andrew, Sub. recruit, discharged Aug. 12, 1865, by telegraph order, War Department, A. G. O.

Payne, Clarence D., Private; Vol. recruit, discharged Sept. 21, 1865; by telegraph order, War Department, concerning prisoners.

Pendergrast, Michael, Private; Sub. recruit, discharged Aug. 12, 1865, by telegraph order, War Department.

Rhodes, Philip, Private; Sub. recruit, discharged Aug. 12, 1865.

Russell, Auguste, Private; Sub. recruit, discharged June 26, 1865, by expiration of term of service.

Ryan, William, Private; Sub. recruit, discharged Jan. 26, 1865, by expiration of term of service.

Strett, Thomas, Private; Sub. recruit, discharged Aug. 12, 1865, by telegraph order, War Department, A. G. O.

Sullivan, Patrick, Private; Sub. recruit, discharged Aug. 12, 1865, by telegraph order, War Department, A. G. O.

Stephen, John, Private; Vol. recruit, discharged June 26, 1865, by expiration of term of service.

Sine, William, Private; Sub. recruit, discharged May 27, 1865, for disability.

Sinkup, Neuzel, Private; Vol. recruit, discharged March 9, 1865, for disability.

Woatler, Andrew, Private; Sub. recruit, discharged Nov. 25, 1865, by expiration of term of service.

Wirternberger, John, Private; Vol. recruit, discharged June 26, 1865, by expiration of term of service.

Whitney, Joseph, Private; Sub. recruit, discharged Aug. 12, 1865, by telegraph order, War Department, A. G. O.

Wilson, Charles F., Private; Vol. recruit, discharged Aug. 12, 1865, by telegraph order, War Department, A. G. O.

TRANSFERRED.

Dinzer, Harris, Private; Vol. recruit, transferred to V. R. C. June 26, 1864.

Zanphuropolis, Michael, Private; Vol. recruit, transferred to V. R. C. April 23, 1865.

DIED.

DeChamps, Peter, Private; Sub. recruit, died March 14, 1865, Savannah, Ga.

DESERTED.

Rudolph, Burick, Corporal; Vol. recruit; deserted Jan. 11, 1865, Baltimore, Maryland.

Anderson, George, Private; Sub. recruit, deserted Jan. 28, 1865, Baltimore, Maryland, transferred from H to C.

Buck, Adam, Private; Vol. recruit, deserted Nov. 24, New Orleans, La., transferred from H to C.

Behi, Charles, Private; Sub. recruit, discharged Aug. 20, 1865, recruiting depot.

Campbell, Alexander, Private; Sub. recruit, deserted Aug. 26, 1865, recruiting depot.

Coisery, Edward, Private; Sub. recruit, deserted Jan 11, 1865, Baltimore, Maryland.

Hildt, Charles, Private; Sub. recruit, Aug. 6, 1865, recruiting depot.

Hutton, Andrew, Private; Sub. recruit, deserted Jan. 11, 1865, Baltimore, Maryland.

Johnson, William B., Private; Vol. recruit, deserted from confinement at Fort Jefferson, transferred from H. to C.

Kallahen, John, Private; Sub. recruit, deserted Jan. 11, 1865, Baltimore, Maryland.

Louis, Louis, Private; Sub. recruit, deserted Aug. 8, 1865, Baltimore, Md.

Murdy, Henry, Private; Vol. recruit, deserted April 16, 1866, Dahlonega, Georgia.

Murphy, Patrick, Private; Sub. recruit, deserted from confinement at Port Jefferson, transferred from H. to C.

Miller, Fritz, Private; Sub. recruit, deserted from recruiting depot, Aug. 6, 1865.

Nolan, James, Private; Vet. Vol., deserted Jan. 8, 1865, at Baltimore, transferred from H to C.

Roberts, Alexander, Private; Sub. recruit, April 16, 1866.

Seville, Bennett, Private; Vet. Vol., deserted July 30, 1865, at Augusta, Georgia

Turner, James W., Private; Sub. recruit, deserted Jan. 11, 1865, at Baltimore, Md.

Theobold, Alexander, Private; Sub. recruit, deserted April 16, 1866, at Dahlonega.

Willard, Nathaniel, Private; Vol. recruit, deserted July 30, 1865, at Augusta, Ga.

Taufer Willis, Private; Sub. recruit, deserted July 30, 1865, at Augusta, Georgia.

Willis, James A., Private; Sub. recruit, deserted July 30, 1865, at Augusta, Ga.

COMPANY "D" VETERAN BATTALION THIRTEENTH CONN. VOLUNTEERS.

Louis Beckwith, Captain; assigned to command Company.

William B. Tooker, 1st. Lieutenant; promoted from 2d Lieutenant Co. A. to 1st Lieutenant Co. D, June 20, 1865.

Charles H. Gaylord, 2d Lieutenant; promoted from Sergeant-major to 2d Lieutenant, Jan. 2, 1865.

Francis Huxford, 1st Sergeant.

Theodore Palmer, Sergeant.

Leonard L. Dougal, "

John Lincoln, Jr., "

Thomas J. West, "

John Suarman, Corporal.

Anson Sulzer, "

Edward Skinner, "

Charles Culver, " promoted to Corporal Sept. 29, 1865.

Howard T. Marsh, " " " " Sept. 29, 1865, vol. recruit, March 9, 1864.

Walter McGrath, Corporal, " " " " "

Frederick Schul, " " " " Jan. 23, 1866.

John Fitzgerald, musician.

Norman W. Beaton, "

Francis C. Bowen, wagoner.

Austin, George J.,	Private.	
Brand, John,	"	
Birge, George F.,	"	
Cadwell, Albert M.,	"	
Carey, Michael,	"	
Dunton, Charles,	"	Vol. recruit, Jan. 23, 1865.
Dorsey, John,	"	
Eichelberger, John,	"	Vol. recruit, March 22, 1864.
Francis, Fredericks	"	Reduced from Sergeant Jan 23, 1865.
Gill, Henry,	"	
Hart, Thomas,	"	Vol. recruit, Dec. 16, 1864.
Hackney, Joseph N.,	"	Vol. recruit, Aug. 17, 1864.
Harvey, George M.,	"	
Hurlburt, Henry A.,	"	
Ingraham, Asahel,	"	
Jennings, George,	"	Vol. recruit, June 30, 1865.
Moore, Daniel,	"	
Moran, Thomas,	"	
Parker, Henry,	"	Vol. recruit, March 22, 1864.
Pyatt, Samuel,	"	
Regan, Hugh,	"	

Rowe, James, Private.
Reynolds, Joseph N. "
Ryan, John, "
Sloan, Michael, " Vol. recruit, Jan. 30, 1865.
Weaver, George, " " Dec. 7, 1864.
Woodworth, John, "
Woodworth, James H., " Vol. recruit, Aug. 10, 1864.
Woodworth, William H., " " " "

DISCHARGED.

Adams, William A., Private; discharged by order of W. D., May 4, '65.
Bergline, Theodore, " Vol. recruit, June 26, 1865, by expiration term of service.
Baer, Abraham, " " " May 21, 1865, by expiration term of service.
Brown, Jacob, " " " May 16, 1865, by expiration term of service.
Bogue, George, " " " May 4, 1865, by order W.D.
Bradley, John W., " " " June, 1865, by order Dept. of the South.
Cooper, Edward, " " " Aug. 12, 1865, on Surgeon's Certificate.
Croley, Richard, " " " May 4, 1865, by order War Department.
Crawford, William B., " " " May 28, 1865, by expiration term of service.
Cerasolle, Octave, " " " Nov. 9, 1865, by expiration term of service.
Clark, Linus M., " " " June 17, 1865, by order Headquarters, Department of the South.
Douglass, George, " " " Expiration term of service.
Eldridge, Stephen, " " " " " "
Fingan, Byron, " " " " " "
Flanney, Thomas, " " " May 15, 1865, by order War Department.
Geibel, George, " " " Expiration term of service.
Greer, James, " " " " " "
Hanns, Frederick, " " " " " "
Howland, George W., " " " " " "
Hopkins, Albert, " " " Dec. 20, 1865, by order War Department.
Reamey, Michael, " " " May 15, 1865, by order War Department.
Lelitener, Albert, " " " June 20, 1865, Surgeon's certificate.

Mark, Frank, Private; discharged June 15, 1865, by order War Department.
Maynard, William M. " " Feb. 13, 1865, by Surgeon's certificate.
Mason, John N., " " May 15, 1865, by order of War Department.
Murphy, Michael, " " May 15, 1865, by order of War Department.
Newhouse, Morris, " " May 15, 1865, by order of War Department.
Parker, George, " " on Surgeon's certificate, Nov. 5, 1864.
Peavey, Stephen R., " " June 17, 1865, by order of Department of the South.
Pendergrast, John, " " May 15, 1865, by order of War Department.
Regan, Andrew, " " Expiration term of service.
Phule, John, " " " " "
Rowen, Charles, " " " " "
Schaffer, John, " " July 31, 1865, by Surgeon's certificate.
Schue, Nicholas, " " Aug. 15, 1865, " "
Sheer, Martin, " " Expiration term of service.
Schlosser, Antoine, " " Order War Department, May 15, 1865.
Smith, Patrick, " " Order of War Department, May 15, 1865.
Urbaine, Charles, " " Expiration term of service.
Wagner, Albert L., " " " " "
White, Edward, " " " " "
Wilson, August, " " " " "

TRANSFERRED.

Abner N. Sterry, 1st Lieutenant; promoted to Captain and transferred to Co. E, April 23, 1865.
Mead, Benjamin L, Private; transferred to V. R. C.
Strange, William, " transferred to V. R. C. by order of Provost Marshal General, Jan. 9, 1865.

DIED.

Cook, Christopher, Private; died, date unknown.
Geize, Adam, " died in prison, Salisbury, N. C., Jan 1, 1865.
Miller, Charles A. " died at Annapolis, Md., March 22, 1865.
O'Connell, Timothy, " died at Augusta, Ga., July 23, 1865.
William Henry, " died at Sister's Ferry, Ga., May 23, 1865.

DESERTED.

Chapman, Lafayette, Private; deserted Jan. 10, 1865, at Baltimore, Md.
Francis, George, " " " "
Smith, Thomas, " " June, 1865, Augusta, Ga.
Tinker, Sebra W., " " Aug. 27, 1865. "

COMPANY "E" VETERAN BATTALION THIRTEENTH CONN. VOLUNTEERS.

Abner N. Sterry, Captain; promoted to Captain April 23, 1865.
Herbert C. Baldwin, 2d Lieutenant; promoted from 1st Sergeant Co. C to 2d Lieutenant Co. E, Jan. 11, 1865.
William H. Huntly, 1st Sergeant, Veteran Volunteer.
Charles A. Adams, " " "
George Sperry, " " "
Joseph Taylor, " " "
William H. Murphy, Corporal.
Francis Patterson, "
Daniel Goodwin, " Vol. recruit, Feb. 18, 1864.
Hobby, Brown, "
Michael Hunt, musician.
James H. Evans, wagoner.
Bailey, Heman W., Private.
Blakeslee, Asahel C., "
Brune, John, "
Clancey, Charles, "
Ango, Ethel, "
DeMarche, James, "
Fellow, Jessie B. "
Fuller, Ethan A. "
Hammond, Seneca, "
Hunt, Richard, "
Higgany, Michael, "
Kimball, Alvah, " Vol. recruit, March 3, 1864.
Kulverinski, Charles, "
McDonough, Thomas, "
Meyer, John, " Never reported to the company.
Mitchell, Peter, "
O'Connor, Martin, "
O'Dell, John, "

Patterson, William A., Private.
Ranney, John, "
Richmond, Charles, "
Rorabach, George, "
Savage, James, "
Schmidt, William, " Sub. recruit, Aug. 5, 1864.
Simpson, John, "
Shurler, Frank T. " Sub. recruit, Sept. 8, 1864.
Stuart, Harman, "
Smith, John, " Sub. recruit, Sept. 14, 1864, in confinement at Milledgeville, Ga., by sentence of G. C. M.
Thompson, Daniel, "
Titus, Sylvester, "
Wadham, Frank E., "

DISCHARGED.

William Brennan, Corporal; discharged Nov. 20, 1865, for disability at Athens, Ga.
John Blake, " " June 26, 1865, by expiration term of service.
John Lannan, musician, " June 26, 1865, by expiration term of service.
John W. Aldrich, Private; discharged Aug. 12, 1865, Savannah, Ga.
Edward Bingham, " Vet. Vol. discharged May 4, 1865, by telegraph order War Department, A. G. O.
Niram, Blackman, Private; discharged Aug. 11, 1865, for disability.
Albert R. Blakeslee, " " July 18, 1865, for disability.
Patrick, Cain, " Vol. recruit, discharged June 26, 1865, by expiration term of service.
James Cashen, Private; Vol. recruit, discharged June 26, 1865, by expiration of term of service.
Martin Duggan, Private; Vol. recruit, discharged June 26, 1865, by expiration term of service.
Thomas Fielder, Private; Vol. recruit, discharged June 26, 1865, by expiration term of service.
Patrick Hanlon, Private; Vol. recruit, discharged June 26, 1865, by expiration term of service.
Edward Johnson, Private; discharged May 4, 1865, by telegraph order, W. Department A. G. O.
John Jordon, Private; Vol. recruit, discharged June 26, 1865, by expiration term of service.
William Keating, Private; Vol. recruit, discharged June 26, 1865, by expiration term of service.
James L. Mason, Private; Sub. recruit, discharged Aug. 12, 1865, by expiration term of service.

Peter G. McGregor, Private; Sub. recruit, discharged Aug. 12, 1865, by expiration term of service.

John McNeil, Private; Sub. recruit, discharged Aug. 12, 1865, by expiration term of service.

John Mooney, Private; Sub. recruit, discharged May 4, 1865, by telegraph order.

Sheppard, Jackson, Private; Vol. recruit, discharged May 9, 1865, for disability.

Bernard Sanders, Private; Vol. recruit, discharged June 26, 1865, by expiration term of service.

Frederick Schultz, Private; Vol. recruit, discharged June 26, 1865, by expiration term of service.

Henry Smith, Private; Vol. recruit, discharged Jan. 30, 1865, for disability.

James Surly, Private; Sub. recruit, August 12, 1865, by expiration of term of service.

David VanBusrick, Private; Vol. recruit, discharged Aug. 12, 1865, by expiration term of service.

John Williams, Private; Vol. recruit, discharged June 26, 1865, by expiration term of service.

Henry L. Wright, Private; Vol. recruit, discharged Aug. 2, 1865, for disability.

TRANSFERRED.

Everett E. Dawson, 1st Sergeant; transferred to Co. A.

George W. Everett, musician; transferred to Co. B.

DIED.

Philo Andrews,	Private;	died Dec. 23, 1864, Winchester, Va.
Willis Barnes,	"	died Dec. 31, 1864, Salisbury, N.C., in enemy's hands.
Francis J. Hunt,	"	died Jan. 13, 1865, DeCamp General Hospital, New York.
Merritt Lyman,	"	died July 20, 1865, Post Hospital, Savannah.
Joseph H. Pratt,	"	died April 13, 1866, Atlanta, Ga.
Homer M. Welch,	"	died Dec. 27, 1864, prisoner, Salisbury, N. C.

PROMOTED.

John W. Maddux, 1st Lieutenant; promoted from 2d Lieutenant Co. C. Dismissed the service by Special Order No. 170, War Department, A.G. O., April 13, 1866, for absence without leave.

DESERTERS.

Peter Billings,	Private;	deserted	Feb. 19, 1866, Atlanta, Ga.
William Black,	"	"	July 27, 1865, Augusta, Ga.
Symond Buckley,	"	"	Aug. 26, 1864, New Haven, Conn.

Emile Chauvin,	Private;	deserted	Oct. 10, 1865, Gainsville, Ga.
Edwin Everett,	"	"	Aug. 26, 1864, New Haven, Conn.
Chancey Griffin,	"	"	Aug. 26, 1864, New Haven, Conn.
Joseph Goodblood,	"	"	Oct. 10, 1865, Gainsville, Ga.
William Kimball,	"	"	Oct. 29, 1864, New Haven, Conn.
Gotlieb, Kenich,	"	"	Feb. 19, 1866, Atlanta, Ga.
Arthur Lannun,	"	"	Oct. 10, 1865, Gainsville, Ga.
Egbert Sweburgh,	"	"	Aug. 26, 1864, New Haven, Conn.
Charles E. Margum,	"	"	Oct. 10, 1865, Gainsville, Ga.
Frederick W. Pinder,	Private;	deserted	Aug. 26, 1864, New Haven Ct.
James Remmington,	"	"	July 10, 1864, New Orleans, La.
James H. Rorabach,	"	"	Feb. 19, 1866, Atlanta, Ga.
Calvin G. Sheppard,	"	"	Feb. 19, 1866, Atlanta, Ga.
John Wilson,	"	"	Jan. 5, 1865, Harper's Ferry, Va.

THE SLAVE GIRL CAROLINE.*

In the last part of May, 1862, Chaplain Salter, 13th C.V., came to the writer and earnestly besought him to save the slave girl Caroline from being restored to her master. His sympathies were much enlisted in behalf of the girl, who appeared to have been cruelly treated, and who had fled to us for freedom. Caroline was accordingly appointed a laundress of Co. H, and being thus in government employ, was considered tolerably safe from the slave hunters.

It was not long before several men in pursuit of the runaway came to the writer, and at the same time an order was presented to him through intermediate commanders, of which the following is a copy:

New Custom House,
New Orleans, May 30, 1863.

Colonel:

The General directs that you send for Captain Sprague, Co. H, 13th Regt. Connecticut Volunteers, and inform him that the negress "Caroline," that he now has in his service is the property of a poor man whose wife is sick in bed, and needs this negress for a nurse. He directs further that an appeal be made to Capt. Sprague's humanity that he may drive her out, so that she may return to her master, Mr. Benedict.

Yours, &c.,
G. Weitzel,
Lt. U. S. Eng.

Col. N. A. M. Dudley, 30th Mass.

* See page 59.

The writer replied to these gentlemen, one of whom was Mr. Benedict, the master of the girl, that he was not willing to deliver her up; and that he would give his reasons in writing. He accordingly wrote out and sent to Mr. Benedict the original of the following letter:

NEW CUSTOM HOUSE,
New Orleans, May 31, 1862.

Mr. Benedict—Claimant of the slave girl " Caroline:"

SIR:

I have the honor to inform you that, agreeably to my promise, I have investigated the case of the slave girl "Caroline."

The order of the General was, "that Capt. Sprague be sent for and informed that the negress Caroline is the property of a poor man, whose wife is sick in bed, and needs this negress for a nurse." The General "further directs that an appeal be made to Capt. Sprague's humanity that he may drive her (Caroline) out, so that she may return to her master, Mr. Benedict."

Now, Mr. Benedict, if I understand the recent enactment of my government, which has been made one of the Articles of War, forbidding military officers to deliver fugitive slaves to their masters, on penalty of being cashiered, I have no right to return, or *aid* in returning, Caroline to you, either directly or indirectly.

"*Property*" is out of the question. It is immaterial, in the eye of the law, whether a white man pretends to own a black, or a black pretends to own a white. I must not deliver Caroline to you: neither should I deliver you to Caroline.

This United States law makes no exception in the case of "*poor*" masters. No; not even if the "poor man's wife is sick in bed, and needs the negress as a nurse."

Nor does this United States law, which we have sworn to obey, make any exception on grounds of "*humanity;*" possi bly because it might be difficult to decide between counter appeals to the officer's humanity in such cases. For instance, this girl appeals to my humanity to save her from you, and you appeal to my humanity to "drive her out;"—she a young and helpless girl, innocent of any crime, pleading with me to save her from hopeless and perpetual slavery; and you "a *poor* man, with a sick wife," and in need of this girl's unpaid toil, and the money which you might coin out of her body and soul, if you could only keep her degraded and enslaved, or sell her for labor or breeding or lust!

You see the law decides the case for me; making it a serious offense to aid or abet in delivering Caroline to you, and coinciding with that earlier and higher law recorded in Holy Writ, Deuteronomy xxiii, 15: "Thou shalt *not* deliver unto his master the servant which is escaped from his master unto thee." Both statutes I recommend for your perusal.

HOMER B. SPRAGUE,
Capt. Co. H, 13th Regt.
Conn. Vols.

Mr. Benedict, upon receipt of the above document, of course started off to lay it before General Butler. Accordingly, the writer had the honor of being summoned into that officer's presence on the second of June; when the following conversation occurred:

Gen.—"Are you Captain Sprague?"

S.—"I am."

Gen.—"How many servants have you?"

S.—"One."

Gen.—"What is her name?"

S.—"*His* name is Wendell Phillips, *alias* Alexander.

Gen.—"Have you not a female servant?"

S.—"Not here."

Gen.—"Have you not a colored girl in your employ named Caroline?"

S.—"I have a company laundress of that name. I understand, General, what you are driving at. She is regularly employed as laundress and is very much needed by us. Besides, she is an intelligent, smart girl, anxious for her freedom, and she has been cruelly treated by her mistress."

Gen.—"I don't look at this matter in a humanitarian light at all. I look at it simply as a military question. Now, sir, you say in this note to Mr. Benedict that the law of Congress, one of the Articles of War, forbids you to deliver fugitive slaves to their masters. There are the Army Regulations [pointing to a blue-covered book]. I require you, sir, at your peril, to point out that law."

S.—General, this book was published last August [1861]; but this law was passed this spring. Of course it's not there."

Then followed a long discussion, in which the general did most of the talking, adducing a great many considerations to show that it would be best to give up the slave to her master. The captain vehemently insisted that it would be a violation of his conscience and of the law of Congress to comply; and finally the general requested him to procure a statement of the facts from Chaplain Salter, and a copy of the law of Congress. The captain consented, and the interview terminated pleasantly.

Next day the writer sent to the General the following communication:

New Custom House,

New Orleans, June 3, 1862.

General:

Agreeably to your request, I send inclosed the statement of the chaplain of our Regiment in reference to the slave "Caroline." I also take the liberty of inclosing a copy, clipped from the New York Evening Post, of the proceedings of Congress, April 1, 1862, in which the fact of the passage and approval of the anti-slave-delivery enactment, as one of the Articles of War, is distinctly recognized. In one of the New York papers, published during the latter part of last March, I saw the enactment in full; and I doubt not it was given in all the leading journals of the North. Many of my fellow officers rejoiced with me at the time in the belief that slave-hunting by military men was forever ended.

Soon after leaving you yesterday, I received a visit from the girl's mistress, whose "sickness in bed" appears to have been of very brief duration! She told me Caroline was twenty years old at the time she bought her, some months ago, and was so described in the bill of sale. She also said Caroline was a very excellent washer and ironer. Said they paid twelve hundred dollars for her, which was almost half of their property.

Now, General, we very much need the services of these laundresses. Many of our soldiers are debilitated by this climate, and it is a most welcome relief to have this work transferred to more skillful hands; besides contributing greatly to increased cleanliness, comfort and health. If one is to be taken from us, why not another, and another, and all?

The objection which you made to their (or Caroline's) retention, on the ground of the difficulty of preventing improper intercourse between our soldiers and these women, is entirely obviated by the working of the wise plan you yourself suggested and directed us to adopt, in our interview, May 27th; by which these women are almost completely isolated from the world. Their seclusion is unbroken by any male person, except momentarily for the transmission of laundry articles or rations. Whatever may have been their habits at home—obliged to submit of course to their masters' lusts, as you told us in that interview—they are necessarily virtuous in their conduct *here*, and are likely to continue so while in this service.

I regret exceedingly that this vexatious question has been added to your innumerable cares; but I have the satisfaction of believing that when I was regimental officer of the day last week, no slave-hunter disturbed you; unless he smuggled himself within our lines by false pretenses, or exhibited a written order of admission from some proper authority. My answer to their importunities (and they came by scores) was, that if they had all along been loyal, the United States government would, in my opinion, by and by make compensation for the loss; otherwise, not; and they must wait in patience.

Pardon me, General, for occupying so much of your precious time. No man entertains a higher respect for you than I, or more cordially approves of your general military policy; and I have always been accustomed to express my admiration in regard to you and it in terms little short of enthusiasm, and to consider myself truly fortunate in having the privilege to serve under you. But that would be the saddest day of my life, when my strongest convictions of right and duty should be violated by a superior officer commanding me to deliver virtually a fugitive slave to his or her pretended owner. I beg you, General, to save yourself from further annoyance in such matters, and to spare my own feelings by dismissing this application of the master and mistress of "Caroline;" and allow me to subscribe myself ever as now, with the highest respect,

Your obedient servant,

HOMER B. SPRAGUE,

Capt. Co. H, 13th Regt. Conn. Vols.

This was accompanied with the following statement of facts by Chaplain Salter:

"On Monday, May 26th, a lady came into the Custom House with her son, to look for a fugitive from her service. I overheard the following conversation between the lady and the girl that had fled from her.

Lady.—General Butler has permitted me to come and see if you are here. I want you, Carrie, to come home with me. I have always been kind to you—have given you a nice bed—have let you visit on Sundays. It is ungrateful in you to leave me. You will be separated from your mother if you stay.

Girl.—You have treated me badly. You have beaten my mother over her head with a pan. I would rather stay and be free than see my mother again. I will not trust going back. You know you will be cruel to me. You can't take me from *here*.

The lady then told the girl that she promised to be kind, and added, with tears, 'you know I cannot afford to lose you.'

The girl replied.—I know you cannot, but I'll not go back. There was nothing insolent in the girl's language. Her words and manner indicated that she resolutely preferred her present condition, and supposed that once within our lines she was in no danger of being returned.

After the lady went, the girl stated that since the entrance of the Yankees into the city she had suffered much bad treatment. That having failed to raise a batch of bread, she was threatened with twenty-five lashes by her master. These lashes she escaped, she said, by running away.

I heard the lady testify that Caroline was twenty years of age ; was a good washer and ironer.

C. C. SALTER,

Chaplain 13th Conn. Vols."

On the back of the foregoing statement Gen. Butler wrote :

" Upon this statement let Caroline be retained as a Laundress. B. F. BUTLER."

GENERAL INDEX.

FINIS.

www.ingramcontent.com/pod-product-compliance
Lightning Source LLC
LaVergne TN
LVHW021251110826
845151LV00002BA/382
* 9 7 8 1 4 2 5 5 3 8 6 8 2 *